Lickety-Split Meals

FOR HEALTH CONSCIOUS
PEOPLE ON THE GO!

3 Books in 1

Recipes, Grocery Guide, Health & Fitness Tips

by Nutrition Expert
ZONYA FOCO, RD

ZHI Publishing

Lickety-Split Meals

Handy Conversions

3 tsp	=	1 T
2 T	=	$\frac{1}{8}$ cup
4 T	=	$\frac{1}{4}$ cup
5$\frac{1}{3}$ T	=	$\frac{1}{3}$ cup
8 T	=	$\frac{1}{2}$ cup
16 T	=	1 cup
1 cup	=	8 ozs
1 pint	=	2 cups
1 quart	=	4 cups
1 gallon	=	4 quarts

1 cup of shredded cheese	=	4 ozs
1 skinless, boneless, chicken breast half	=	4 ozs.

Abbreviations

T	=	Tablespoon
tsp	=	teaspoon
oz	=	ounce
lb	=	pound
g	=	gram
ml	=	milliliter
l	=	liter
bxs	=	boxes

Hello Canada!

1 oz	=	28 g
1 lb = 16 oz	=	453 g
1 T	=	15 ml or g
1 cup	=	237 ml or g
1 quart	=	.946 liter = 946 ml

Nutrition analysis of recipes

Recipes were computer analyzed using *Nutritionist IV* software.

When two ingredient choices are given, the first one is used for the analysis.

Optional items are included unless otherwise noted.

<1 means "less than one".

© Copyright

Direct reproduction requests in writing to:

ZHI Publishing
P.O. Box 275
Walled Lake, Michigan 48390-0275
Fax: (248) 960-8157
Email: zonya@tir.com

To order additional copies, see order form in the back or call:

ZHI Publishing **toll free** at:
1-(888) 884-LEAN

ISBN 1-890926-00-0

 Printed on recycled paper.

This book is intended as a reference to healthy eating and exercise. It is not intended as a substitute for any treatment prescribed by your doctor. It is recommended that everyone receives a checkup from a medical doctor and inquires specifically about nutrition and exercise recommendations. If you suspect that you have a medical problem, by all means, see your doctor.

The food and exercise tips discussed here are designed to help individuals in general live a more healthy, active life.

Lickety-Split Meals

Dedication

Dedicated to —

**All families and individuals seeking healthy meals
and regular exercise, despite limited time.**

May this book help you, once and for all

Make your good intentions come true!

Tip

an•gel (ān′jəl)

n. 1. One of the immortal beings attendant upon God. 2. A kind and lovable person.

Acknowledgements

While I've had the idea for this book since I was 16 years old, it would still be just that, an idea, if it weren't for so many talented, encouraging and sharing "angels" along the way.

My parents, **Grace & Don Edwards.** Among everything, I thank you for both my fine formal and informal educations. Without your love, emotional & financial support, I would have never acquired the expertise for this passion, which truly fulfills me.

My past colleagues at NutriCare of St. Joseph Mercy Health System, whom over nine years helped me "apply the book knowledge" to successful weight and cholesterol control. I'm indebted to you for practical application of lifestyle change for client counseling, and for helping me with my own weight control issues. My thanks to: **Toni DeMilde, RD; Lynne DeMoore, MS, RD; Diana Dyer, MS, RD, CNSD; Arlene Erickson, MS, RD; Dennis Gordon, RD, CDE, M. Ed; Jennie Hahn, RD; Lori Hunt, RD; Ann Jones, MS, RD; Cheryl Simon-Bell, RD;** and **Linn Storch, MS, RD.**

All the delightful clients, (you know who you are), whom over ten years I've had the privilege to work with, and therefore learn from, about the obstacles to weight loss. From you, I've learned what is needed to make "good intentions come true", and exactly what was needed to make this book work.

Janine Konkel, whom enthusiastically responded to my "thinking out loud" by volunteering to initially create the unique recipe design and typeset the first 80 recipes. Your talent, patience and support getting me over this first hurdle was immeasurable. Thank you Janine!

Dan Gauthier, who patiently typeset the remaining recipes, working well into the night, helping me with tough decisions along the way.

Lickety-Split Meals

Acknowledgements

And of course my graphic designer, (I call her *Princess*) **Vicki Grucz.** Her design surpasses the beautiful and efficient layout I dreamed of. If you have any graphic design needs, give my princess a call at (248) 446-0304.

And then there's the recipe contributors and testers: **Connie & Rich Bloom, Mini Burgess, Tom & Jean Cellantani, Barbara Christenson, Suzy Crossley, Gloria Edwards, Grace Edwards, Jo Edwards, Barb Filler, Trista Foco, Karen Hettel, Lori Hunt, Jay Johnson, Deb Norbotten, Karen Pender, Virginia Pender, Diane Petersen, Lori Poi, Stacy Rafalko, Eric & Ann Tooley, and Elizabeth Wagner.** Yes Barbara, you won the award for testing the most!

And then there are the editors, to whom I owe so much, **Barbara Christenson, Pat Materka, Diane Petersen,** and **Becky Walden.**

Holly Noble, RD, for her professional advice and fine work on the computerized nutrition analysis. Great job Holly!

Fine photographer **Murray Goldenberg** for capturing a front cover photo I'm proud of. (This is not an easy job!) If you have a photo challenge for Murray, give him a call at (248) 350-2420 in Southfield, Michigan.

Professional mentors who've helped me in so many ways, **Carol Brickenden, Barbara Christenson, Cynthia D'mour, Sheila Feigelson, PhD, Lou Anne Flanagan** and **Rob Pasick, PhD.**

My brothers **Cliff** and **Mark Edwards,** who helped teach me the value of fitness at an early age.

Caroline Smoyer, who has never stopped being the best friend in the whole wide world. I love our annual goal-writing sessions. (Hey, this year, I finally get to check this goal off!)

Scott Foco, who forever encourages me in my work. For those of you who know him, you know what a very, very lucky wife I am.

Diane Petersen, who completely rescued me. It's hard to say which of your talents helped most; editor, counselor, encourager, decision maker, recipe tester, or successful homemaker and mother of three. But together, they've made everything in this book "work". Thank you Diane, for all your dedication, talents and hard work!

Last but not least, **all the people who pre-ordered my book.** I know you waited patiently and I hope that it is everything and more than you expected.

Lickety-Split Meals

Table of Contents

Table of Contents

Table of Contents

Table of Contents

Table of Contents

Introduction

Lickety-Split Meals:
How the seed was planted

Life Lessons 101

I will never forget the summer I was 16 years old. I was working 40 hours a week at one of the nearby tourist attractions for $1.85 per hour. Every dime I made went to support my new (to me) pride and joy, Datsun 280z. I was thoroughly enjoying the independence and steps toward adulthood.

Like most 16-year-olds, Mom and Dad still saw to it that I had house chores to do. "In addition to working 40 hours a week?" I moaned.

"Welcome to adulthood," they said.

One night while I was begrudgingly doing the dishes, Mom offered a deal that I could not believe.

"You want to get out of doing dishes?" she asked.

"Well yeah," I muttered.

"Since you have your own car now, why don't you get the groceries and make the meals?" Hungry for more grown-up independence, I liked the sound of this.

Introduction

"I'll make arrangements at the bank and the IGA store so you can sign my checks," Mom explained. "You can buy however many groceries you think we need, no limits. Plan the meals, cook them, and I'll do the dishes."

"You'll do the dishes?" Well this idea sounded really good to me. Cooking definitely was more fun than doing dishes. Then her deal got even better.

"I'll also pay you for it," she said.

"Pay me?" I'd been trying to get them to pay me for doing chores for some time.

"Yes, how does $40 a week sound?"

I did not need to think about this one! I knew it took me 25 hours to bring home that much money from my other job. Had Mom lost her mind? I knew I'd better jump on this before she came to her senses. I made her shake on it, right then and there.

The first week

Fortunately, Mom agreed to help me my first week. We glanced through her Betty Crocker cookbook and her trusty recipe box. I already knew how to make 5 dinners, we decided. We agreed that for my first week I could make those 5 dinners, and we would have soup and sandwiches for the other 2 nights. No need to learn new meals the first week. "Why is she being so nice?" I wondered.

Then it was off to the grocery store. She quickly taught me her "no list" method of shopping. You walk up and down the aisles, glancing at everything. If you think we might need it, buy it. And always include a 4-pack of toilet paper. "That's all you need to know," she said.

I was trained and ready. This was going to be a piece of cake. 40 dollars a week, and no dishes. I couldn't wait!

The first week of grocery shopping, I arrived home with $120 worth of groceries. Mom would have only spent $80. Did she say anything? No. She did not want to discourage me. She knew better than to throw in the economics lesson, just yet. That could come later.

Introduction

Needless to say, a lot of food spoiled, (yes I overbought). Again, no criticism from Mom and Dad. One night while making dinner, I discovered that the can of tomatoes I had was 14 ounces and the recipe called for 28 ounces. The store was 15 minutes away. That's OK, I loved to drive my car. It's a good thing Mom never said that dinner *had* to be *on time*.

The second week

I managed to spend less this week, (only $75), but my cooking got worse. All new recipes! I really struggled getting a whole meal on the table at the same time. **Why is it, that after slaving through a recipe, I would read, "serve with hot cooked noodles and a tossed salad?" So when**

***were* you supposed to boil those *darn* noodles and make that tossed salad?**

I turned to books for help. Isn't there a book out there that instructs people on how to put an entire meal on the table? The only one I found was too gourmet and definitely over my head. I wanted simple everyday meals that my family would eat. I wanted recipes that were fast and easy-to-follow. I also needed a list of groceries to buy. **Do I have to make that list each week? Mom never did!**

And thus, the seed for Lickety-Split Meals was planted. After 6 years of college, 9 years of marriage, and hundreds of ideas from clients, the seed has blossomed. The fast, easy to follow recipes, including how

to get whole meal on the table, with the complete grocery list**, are all right here!**

And then I got to thinking…what about all the helpful tips I've collected from clients along the way? All the simple nuggets of wisdom to help win the battle with weight and cholesterol and finding time to exercise…**they too, are included for you.** You will appreciate these inspiring tips about nutrition, exercise, time management, and positive living, sprinkled page by page throughout the book.

It is my sincerest wish for this book to help you, once and for all, make your good intentions come true!

Zonya

Introduction

Why *Lickety-Split Meals* is Unique

Categorized EXACTLY to your time demands

With your demanding schedule, how much time do you have? 1 minute, 5 minutes, 15 minutes or 30 minutes? Or, would you like to put something in the oven, exercise, and then eat? Is it pasta, stir-fry or pizza tonight? Or is it breakfast time? Simply flip to the section that fits your needs.

Easy to read layout for recipes

Just glance at a recipe and you'll see how easy it is to get an entire meal on the table. Great for Busy Moms, Mr. Moms and just plain Frazzled Mom's! Excellent for high school students, college students and newlyweds.

All recipes are health conscious

The recipes are designed for today's health-minded family. It seems everyone wants to have more energy, ward off aging and raise healthy children with positive eating habits. In addition to these goals, this book is helpful for people trying to:

- ♥ Lose weight
- ♥ Lower cholesterol
- ♥ Control diabetes
- ♥ Reduce risk of cancer
- ♥ Increase energy level
- ♥ Perform well in sports
- ♥ Slow the aging process

With so many important health recommendations making headlines in the news these days, you will be assured to know that these recipes are designed to be:

- ♥ Low in fat
- ♥ Low in saturated fat
- ♥ Low in cholesterol
- ♥ Low in calories
- ♥ High in fiber

Introduction

- ♥ Moderately low in sugar content
- ♥ Moderately low in sodium content
- ♥ High in phytochemicals (anti-cancer and anti-aging compounds)
- ♥ In accordance with the *preferred* American Institute for Cancer Research recommendations for eating 9-11 fruits and vegetables per day.

Complete nutrition facts for each recipe

Are you trying to lose weight?

If so, you'll be glad to know that these recipes and menus are devised to be conducive for weight loss. You'll find the total fat, percent of calories from fat, fiber and calories to be of help in your efforts.

Be sure to follow the suggested serving sizes, for both the entrée and the accompaniments. If you are **not** trying to lose weight, simply take larger servings and/or enjoy extra bread with the meal.

Are you a *Weight Watcher*® or person with diabetes?

If so, then you will enjoy the included "Exchange Values." This tells you exactly how each recipe fits into your meal plan. This information is made available just for you, in addition to the nutrition facts information. (Note: the fat listed here refers to the number of fat servings from the fat group, and not the grams of fat for the recipe. See just below this for the actual fat grams). Information about the

total grams of carbohydrate and sugars is also included for those persons with diabetes, who are choosing to control their blood sugar by "counting carbohydrates."

Do you need to lower your cholesterol?

Then you are in luck! These low-fat and high fiber recipes and tips will help you to do exactly that. For your information, total fat, saturated fat, percent of calories from fat and cholesterol are provided for you. For more information about lowering your blood cholesterol, see my tips on pages 179.

Regardless if you have health concerns or not, as long as you would like to eat smart in as little time as possible, **then *Lickety-Split Meals* is for you!**

Introduction

Complete grocery list so you can make *any* recipe in the book

Shop from the *Lickety-Split Meals* grocery list, and you'll ALWAYS have EVERYTHING you need. Check the items you run out of, and your next week's list will always be ready.

How to get the complete meal on the table

No more slaving over a recipe only to discover, "serve with hot cooked noodles and a tossed salad." You will be instructed when to boil water, when to add the noodles, and when to make the salad, so everything is hot and ready when it's time to eat. When a helper is required to meet the time frame, simply look to the starbursts for what jobs to delegate.

Recipes eliminate any unnecessary steps

Long gone are the days of boiling the noodles first when making Lasagna and Tuna Noodle Casserole. No more mixing things in separate bowls. You save time both in preparation and clean up!

Tastes Great!

Lickety-Split Meals features tried and true family favorites. The menus are colorful, flavorful and well balanced. You will find that for nearly all the menus, there is either a serving of fruit or a dessert suggested. By ending your meal with a hint of sweetness, you will feel completely satisfied, therefore ending any tendency to "roam" the kitchen all night!

The *Lickety-Split* Weekly Menu Solution

"What's for Dinner?"

Ask any frazzled Mom how it feels when the troops ask that question, and she's wondering the same thing! May I suggest adopting my weekly menu solution? This means designating a "specific menu" to each night of the week. The recipes change, but the base menu stays the same. This allows plenty of variety, while saving hours of planning time. Take a look at the weekly menu solution and simply adjust the nights to meet your needs.

Monday	Tuesday	Wednesday	Thursday	Friday	Saturday	Sunday

Slow-Cooking Night

Is it softball night? Run past the dreaded Monday night dinner hassle and slide into home base with dinner waiting for you. You can even load the slow-cooker on Sunday night. Soup, stew, stroganoff, or fajitas, just flip through the chapter and make your selection.

15-Minute Meal Night

How's a stuffed baked potato sound? Nacho's or *Turkey Joes? Crispy Chicken Dijon?* Haven't decided? Better turn to the 5-minute section, you just lost 10 minutes!

Pasta Night

Do you feel like spaghetti, cork-screws, penne or angel hair? Red or white sauce? How about *Southwest Chili* or *Oriental Noodles* for a change? You'll never get tired of having pasta once a week!

Oven Exercise Eat Night

Didn't get in your morning workout? No Problem! Pick from enchiladas, chicken and rice, *Spanish Red Beans and Rice,* meatloaf or *Tuna Noodle Casserole.* The tasty oven meals cook while you exercise!

Pizza Night

No doubt, the family's favorite by far! Thanks to ready-made pizza crusts, making pizza at home is fast and easy. Pick from a delicious variety, which are all health smart.

Stir-Fry Night

Maybe you'll throw in some chicken, maybe beef, and always over rice. No time to clean and chop? No problem. Just follow my tips and use frozen vegetables.

30-Minute Meal Night

Put a nice Sunday meal on the table in just 30 minutes. Vegetarian, chicken, beef or fish, it's up to you!

Lickety-Split Meals

Introduction

Getting Started with *Lickety-Split Meals*

Speedisize Your Kitchen

Are you really ready to take this system to the max, and **save yourself up to 4 hours each week?** Then say *YES,* to investing the time you need to get your kitchen speedisized! Minutes spent now will save you hours in the future! (And how are you going to spend those 4 extra hours a week? Exercising, of course!)

Some people will have no problem at all turning out one of my 15-minute meals in 15 minutes. Others will swear it takes 40. The magic is in a properly equipped and organized kitchen!

1. Clean and organize your cupboards and cabinets.

Still looking for that can of tomatoes? Let me help. Group together canned fruits, vegetables, meats, tomato products, etc. Label your shelves, so that everyone putting groceries away can easily place items on their proper shelf. Hey, there's your tomatoes!

2. Clean and organize your refrigerator and freezer.

Say goodbye to wasting minutes searching for a green pepper on every shelf and in every drawer. Designate specific areas for your common items and don't forget a special shelf for leftovers. You will now be able to find things in seconds flat. Now, put on some gloves and tackle your freezer.

3. Inspect your spice rack.

How old are they? Did you get those as a wedding present? If so, and you've celebrated 3 or more anniversaries, then it's time to *spice* up your life. Throw those old spices out! But hang on to the containers. With your *Lickety-Split* spice list in hand, head out to your local bulk food store, health food store or coop, where you can purchase spices *by the ounce*. (The staff will show you how). You can purchase as little as 1 tablespoon, if that's all you want to try. Once you're back at home, it's time to alphabetize!

4. Utensil Drawer

You're only a spoon away from your completely speedisized kitchen! Now it's time to untangle that jammed utensil drawer. It should only take 2 seconds to grab just the right spatula, measuring

Introduction

spoon, measuring cup, or ladle, all without skewering yourself! (Unrecommendable acupuncture). But, *HANG* in there! If you have the wall space, hang your frequently used utensils *including your strainer.* You won't believe how much time this will save you!

Getting Equipped

To achieve the *Lickety-Split* time requirements, you will need the following:

- Microwave
- Food processor
- Electric can opener
- Slow-cooker or *Crock-Pot*® (see page 160 for buying suggestions)

- Silverstone® or T-Fal® coated cooking pans (cook with minimal fat and quick clean-up)
- Silverstone® or T-Fal® coated wok
- Plastic spatula and serving spoons (appropriate for nonstick cookware)
- Sharp knifes (And I do mean sharp!)
- Sharp vegetable peeler (yes, there is such a thing)
- Hot air popcorn popper (optional, but recommended)

Recommended ingredients that pass the test of time, taste and health

Crushed garlic in a jar

If you want to make things *Lickety-Split,* you won't have time to peel and crush fresh garlic cloves. Thus, welcome to the convenience of minced garlic in a jar. (Look in the produce section). Garlic powder can also be quickly and conveniently substituted as well. Here's the conversion:

1 garlic clove = $\frac{1}{2}$ tsp. of crushed garlic = $\frac{1}{4}$ of a tsp of garlic powder

Introduction

Fresh ground pepper

I highly recommend using a fresh pepper mill. If you have one, you know why! If you don't, simply substitute "10 grinds of fresh ground pepper" with "10 dashes of pepper." And go shopping, ehh?

Light cream cheese

I find that many people do not like the taste of fat-free cream cheese but love the taste of light cream cheese. To keep everything tasty and shopping simple, all recipes call for light cream cheese. I have carefully calculated and used the amounts that still allow the overall recipe to meet recommended guidelines.

Light sour cream

My personal experience and that of my clients, is that some recipes taste fine using fat-free sour cream, while others do not. I therefore suggest buying light, (instead of fat-free) and have analyzed the recipes accordingly. If you prefer to use fat-free, please do.

Parmesan cheese

Parmesan cheese *is* high in fat; however, the amounts called for do not add unreasonable amounts of fat. I therefore suggest using regular Parmesan cheese and have calculated the recipes accordingly. If you would like to use fat-free instead, please do. (I personally have had great results mixing regular and fat-free 50-50).

Miracle Whip® Light

While I'm aware that fat-free mayonnaise is available, I've found that for taste, many people prefer *Miracle Whip*® Light, and is therefore, what I call for throughout the book. You are welcome to substitute fat-free if you wish, and you will save a few more fat grams if you do.

Non-fat plain yogurt

This is a cooking and baking gem that I call for quite a bit. Yogurt is a nutrition dynamo, loaded with calcium, potassium, protein and other great things. It works great on baked potatoes, in a cream sauce, or in baking. Quite often I will have you mix it 50-50 with *Miracle Whip*® Light, to keep calories and fat grams down, while

Introduction

simultaneously adding valuable nutrients. You can easily transform plain yogurt into any other flavors you desire. For instance:

Vanilla = to 1 cup of plain yogurt
add 1 tsp vanilla and 1¹/₂ T of sugar

Lemon = to 1 cup of plain yogurt
add ¹/₂ tsp of lemon extract
and 1¹/₂ T of sugar

Fruited = to 1 cup of plain yogurt add
2 to 3 T of jam or preserves
(use the flavor of your choice)

Spaghetti Sauce

The goal is to find a sauce that is 5 or less grams of fat and 800 mg or less of sodium *per cup*. I have recommended *Healthy Choice*® in my recipes simply because it meets these recommendations, and is readily available. However, there are more sauces that meet and even exceed this criteria and I encourage you to shop around for the sauces you like best. Refer to page 30 for selection suggestions.

Margarine

Margarine goes through a process called hydrogenation (which makes it thick and spreadable). This process creates "trans-fatty acids" which are now believed to be almost as artery-clogging as the saturated fat in butter. Instead of margarine, opt for small amounts of oil. Yes, oil. In almost every recipe, I've managed to use a moderate amount of oil instead of margarine. Do buy a small tub of light margarine, (store it in the back of your refrigerator), and use it sparingly. (For more information about breaking the margarine habit, and whether or not butter is better, see my tip on page 184.)

Canola oil, olive oil, sesame oil

There are many different types of vegetable oils on the market. In regard to the best ratio of monounsaturated fat (the good fat), to saturated fat (the bad fat), the winners are canola oil and olive oil. I tend to use the canola in baked goods, and the olive in tomato base dishes. If you prefer to stock just one oil, make it canola. It's the most versatile and can be substituted for the others. The sesame oil lends incredible flavor to oriental flavored dishes, i.e. stir-fries. You'll only need a small bottle of this and I promise, it's worth getting. Note: You will be using only small amounts of each oil.

Introduction

Lickety-Split Meals

Oil vs. Pam cooking spray

You may be surprised to see that I call for 1 tablespoon of oil quite often in sautéing, while some nutritionists recommend using a cooking spray exclusively. 1 tablespoon of oil is perfectly acceptable for serving 4 people, if there is minimal other fat contributed. If you find that you need more oil because of sticking, buy a new nonstick pan!

Oat bran

Uncooked oat bran (similar to a dry flour) is located in the cooked cereal section in a "cream of wheat" type box. You can also buy it by the pound in the bulk food section. It's a great way to add the cholesterol lowering soluble fiber to baked goods, etc.

Whole-wheat pastry flour

This flour is very nutritious because it is a "whole grain" flour, yet is very light and cakey in texture, similar to that of white flour. It can be used in equal amounts to replace white flour in any "non-yeast" recipe. (For more information about this flour, see my tip on page 187.)

It is considered specialty flour and may be found among special brands like *Arrowhead Mills*® or *Bob's Red Mill*®. If not, request it from your grocer. I happen to buy it in bulk quantities at natural food stores or co-ops. Until you find it, you can substitute:

For each cup of whole-wheat pastry flour:

$^1/_2$ cup all-purpose and
$^1/_2$ cup whole-wheat flour
(what you do find easily in the store)

or

(as a last resort)
use 1 cup of all-purpose flour

Nuts

Nuts have many wonderful trace minerals along with fiber and the "good" kinds of fat. And as long as nuts are consumed in moderation, they are a fine addition to a healthy diet. (Eating by the handfuls is not moderation! However, it is perfectly acceptable to use $^1/_2$ cup of nuts in a recipe that serves 6.)

Introduction

Cheese (mix fat-free with reduced-fat for great tasting low fat cheese!)

The ideal is to use fat-free cheese. But what about the taste? There are good tasting low-fat cheeses available, but they run 6-7 grams of fat per ounce, which is TOO MUCH. So, when it comes to shredded cheese, why not mix fat-free with the reduced-fat, for a great compromise? I recommend *Reduced-Fat 2% Milk by Kraft®* and I mix it 50-50 with the fat-free cheese by *Healthy Choice®* or *Kraft®*. I do this with both shredded cheddar and mozzarella cheeses. This produces a wonderful, tasty and normal melting cheese for only 3 grams of fat per ounce. This is the "reduced-fat shredded cheddar and mozzarella cheeses" I am referring to in all recipes. If you prefer to use the fat-free exclusively, please do!

Grocery List

The shopping problem

You've just decided what to make only to discover, "Oh darn, I'm out of that!" You think, "Ok, I'll make this other recipe". Guess what, you're missing something for that recipe too, and so it goes for three more tries. Didn't you just get groceries four days ago? Umm, yeah, the results of "no list" shopping.

The *"old"* way

I'm sure you've heard what the *"old"* way is. "Plan out all your menus for the week and write out a complete grocery list of everything you'll need." I don't know about you, but this is just not my cup of tea! Who has the motivation, *each and every* week for such a tedious and time consuming job!?!

Your new, *Lickety-Split* shopping solution

Shop once using the *Lickety-Split* list to "get stocked." This is a *complete* list and you will now have *everything* you need to cook a one or two week's menu from this book. Here's how it works:

1. A "par-stock" column, which is the number I suggest you keep on hand.

2. A "re-stock" column, for check-marking the number you need. (Permission to copy list is granted, however see note below about the convenient *reusable* guide available).

3. The items you will need only occasionally are noted in the "For use in…" column. This allows you to quickly decide whether or not to purchase that item.

4. Hang the *Lickety-Split* list where it can be seen by everyone in the family. As soon as an item is used up, put a checkmark on the list. (Make this a family habit)!

When it's time to go shopping, your list is already made! All neatly typed and organized according to store sections, with brand name recommendations. Even Dad won't mind picking up the groceries once in a while! *Now this is living!*

Reusable Pocket-Size Guide!

- **Checkbook size with laminated pages, complete with erasable pen for repeated use!**
- **Magnets hold it to the refrigerator all week!**
- **It clips to your grocery cart!**

The Reusable Pocket-Size Guide makes your *"Lickety-Split"* list writing and shopping easier than ever!

Available by calling toll-free at
1-888-884-LEAN
This is how to live!

How to calculate your "Family FRUIT Quota" for 1 WEEK

Decide if your goal is 1, 2, 3 or 4 pieces per person each day. Keep in mind that the American Institute for Cancer Research says that 2 servings is the minimum and MORE is better!

Yes, canned fruit in it's own juice, applesauce and dried fruit can be substituted! (See page 175 to find out why juice is not recommended as one of your minimum servings.)

# in family		1	2	3	4	5	6
pieces per person per day	1	7	14	21	28	35	42
	2	14	28	42	56	70	84
	3	21	42	63	84	105	126
	4	28	56	84	112	140	168

I see your eyes popping out!!! I know this seems like WAY too much, but the facts are the FACTS!

Tips: If you have a large family, to prevent spoilage, buy ¹/₂ now and shop for the rest mid-week.
- Buy some bananas green and some yellow, for "just in time" bananas all week.
- Likewise, buy your peaches pears and kiwis, some hard, some soft.
- Store ripe, ready to eat fruit in the refrigerator and the rest at room temperature.
- A fruit bowl on your kitchen counter helps everyone remember to snack on fruit!

What about the cost?

To generate "fruit" money, spend LESS in other departments:

1. Refrain from buying soda pop and beer. It's amazing how much more affordable water is!

2. Instead of buying products like instant scalloped potatoes and Rice-a-Roni®, stick with the less expensive versions: raw potatoes and rice.

3. Serve smaller portions of meat and serve more vegetarian meals like beans and rice or pasta. Examples include: *Veggie Sghetti, 3-Bean Chili,* meatless stir-fry and bean burritos.

Presto! Money to fuel your new stepped up fruit habit!

What equals a fruit or vegetable serving?

1	Small apple, pear, orange, nectarine, kiwi etc.
2	plums
4	apricots
1 cup	berries or melon
15	grapes
2 T	raisins
4	dried apricots
¹/₂ cup	applesauce (unsweetened)
¹/₂ cup	canned fruit (own juice, drained)
¹/₂ cup	cooked vegetables
1 cup	raw vegetables
6	baby carrots

Grocery List

Restock	Par Stock	Item and size	For use in ...

Restock	Par Stock	Item and size	For use in ...

Fresh Fruits

(Choose from seasonal selections. Adjust the amount your family needs using the chart above. The par-stock numbers below are a guide for 2 people for one week.)

Restock	Par Stock	Item and size	For use in ...
_____	8	Bananas	**Breakfasts & Snacking** *Banana Bread/Cake/Muffins* *Banana Pancakes* *Summer Fresh Fruit Pie*
_____	8	Oranges	**Breakfasts & Snacking**
_____	8	Apples	**Snacking** *Scrumptious Swiss Oats ...* *Crunchy Apple Salad*
_____	1	Grapes (bunch)	**Snacking** *Ambrosia Breakfast Rice* *Almond Chicken Salad*
_____	1	Cantaloupe	**Breakfasts & Snacking**
_____	0-1	Strawberries (qt)	**Breakfasts & Snacking** *Scrumptious Swiss Oats ...* *Summer Fresh Fruit Pie*
_____	0-1	Blueberries (pt)	**Breakfasts & Snacking** *Scrumptious Swiss Oats ...* *Summer Fresh Fruit Pie*

Restock	Par Stock	Item and size	For use in ...
_____	0-1	Raspberries (pt)	**Breakfasts & Snacking** *Scrumptious Swiss Oats ...* *Summer Fresh Fruit Pie*
_____	0-8	Nectarines	**Breakfasts & Snacking** *Summer Fresh Fruit Pie*
_____	0-8	Peaches	**Breakfasts & Snacking** *Summer Fresh Fruit Pie*
_____	4-8	Pears	**Breakfasts & Snacking**
_____	4-6	Grapefruit	**Breakfasts & Snacking**
_____	4	Kiwi	**Breakfasts & Snacking** *Scrumptious Swiss Oats ...*
_____	1-2	Lemon	**Flavoring ice water** **Recipes with fish** *Pasta Slaw* *Lentil Spinach Soup* *Curried Chickpeas ...* *Broiled Orange Roughy* *Tzatziki*
_____	optional	Pineapple	**Snacking** *Marinated Sesame Chicken ...*

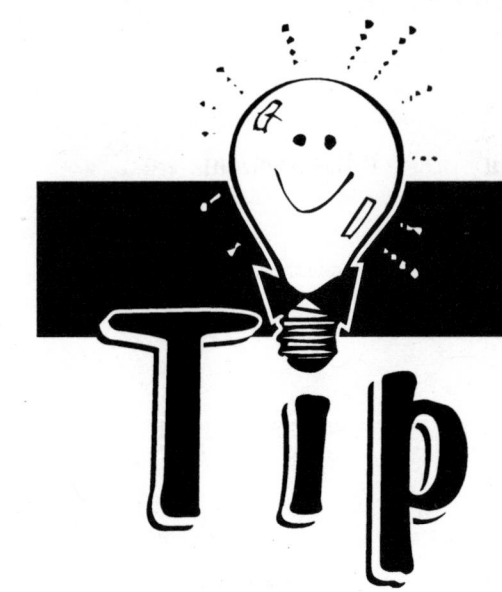

How to get your "Family Veggie Quota" for 1 WEEK

Do this math:

___# of people in your family x 3 servings per day (minimum) x 7 days a week = ____

For a family of 4 x 7 days, that equals **84 servings!**

Here's an example to fuel your family for 1 week. **Adjust** according to your preferences:

Produce	Servings
2 bundles of fresh broccoli	16
$1/2$ head of fresh cauliflower	5
(buy one head and serve $1/2$ this week and $1/2$ the next)	
2 lbs. baby carrots	12
1 bag (10 oz. each) salad greens	4
2 cucumbers	4
5 tomatoes	5
6 green/red peppers	12
8 med. potatoes	8
2 large sweet potatoes	4
2 cans of vegetable soup, corn or beets	4
2 bags (1 lb. each) <u>frozen veggies</u>	<u>10</u>
Total	**84 servings per week!!!**

Tips

1. If your cart doesn't look anything like this, increase gradually!

2. If you have a large family, to prevent spoilage, buy $1/2$ now and shop for the rest mid-week.

3. Instruct the whole family to help think "vegetables" for snacks.

4. Use your fresh produce early in the week and use frozen or canned later in the week.

5. Double the "token spoonful" of vegetables you may have grown up with.

6. Consider single serving cans of *V-8*® juice for lunches and snacks.

7. Try vegetable soup and a weekly stir-fry to help meet your weekly quota.

Grocery List

Restock	Par Stock	Item and size	For use in ...

Fresh Veggies

Each week purchase as needed to have on hand:

Restock	Par Stock	Item and size	For use in ...
_____	1	Potatoes (bag) regular or redskin	Baked Potatoes *Oven Fries* *Potato Salad*
_____	4+	Sweet potatoes or yams Don't forget these!	Baked Sweet Potatoes *Gypsy Soup*
_____	1	Onions (bag)	Used regularly
_____	optional	Green onions (bunch)	Salads *South of the Border Roll-ups* *Herbed Salmon Spread* *Oklahoma Bean Dip* *7-Layer Bean Dip* *Beanito Bean Dip and Burritos* *Great Northern Tuna Salad ...* *Chicken Dijon Stuffed ...* *Gingered Black Beans ...* *Oriental Noodle Toss ...*
_____	1+	Broccoli 2 heads are better than 1!	Used regularly
_____	1+	Cauliflower (heads)	Used regularly

Restock	Par Stock	Item and size	For use in ...
_____	1+	Baby carrots (Lg. bag)	Used regularly
_____	1	Celery (bunch)	Snacking Salads *Miracle Soup* *Potato Salad*
_____	3+	Green peppers	Used regularly
_____	1+	Red pepper	Used regularly
_____	1+	Yellow pepper	Used regularly
_____	4+	Tomatoes	Used regularly
_____	1+	Cucumbers	Snacking Salad *Tzatziki*
_____	1+	Lettuce (dark greens) If desired, pre-bagged, ready to eat	Instant tossed salads
_____	optional	Shredded carrots (bag)	*Carrot Cake* *Carrot Raisin Salad*
_____	0-2	Shredded cabbage (bags)	*Miracle Soup* *Pasta Slaw*

Tofu Buying Tips

You will find tofu in the produce section of your grocery store. Here's a summary of your options:

Fresh, packed in a small tub of water, must be refrigerated (usually a 7-10 day shelf life).

Vacuum packaged, does not require refrigeration, and offers the luxury of a 6 or more month shelf life (looks like juice boxes).

Low-fat tofu, available in the vacuum packaged varieties (Nori Nu brand).

Soft, firm, extra firm and silken refers to the texture and will have a huge effect on your recipe.

My recommendations:

The vacuum packaged is definitely the most convenient, but I've found even the "firm" variety is more "silken" and does not provide the meaty texture my recipes need. I therefore buy fresh tofu. The brand names available in the Detroit area are: *China Rose®, Soyplant®* or *Panda®*.
Tip: Changing the water every day will extend the freshness of the product a week or two past the stamped date.

While you might assume low-fat is the best choice, I've only found it available in the "silken" variety, which does not provide the meaty texture my recipes seek. Don't worry, regular tofu has only a small amount of soybean oil (healthy) and when balanced against the rest of the meal (potatoes, corn, bread, etc.) it calculates to a healthy percent of calories from fat. Because of this natural soybean oil, I use a nonstick spray with tofu recipes rather than the oil I usually call for with dishes using chicken breast and ground turkey meat.

See page 83 for information about what tofu is and it's benefits.

Grocery List

Restock	Par Stock	Item and size	For use in ...

Fresh Veggies (continued)

Each week choose 2 or 3 for variety:

Restock	Par Stock	Item and size	For use in ...
_____	0-1	Green beans	*Crispy Chicken Dijon* *Hungarian Chicken Paprikash*
_____	0-1	Asparagus (bunch) Buy frozen if you prefer	*Salmon Patties* *Chicken Dijon Stuffed ...* *Creamy Chicken Dijon*
_____	0-4	Zucchini (sm)	*Ratatouille* *Chicken Cacciatore* *Veggie Sghetti* *Southwest Chicken Pizza* *Easy Pepper Steak Stir-Fry*
_____	0-2	Yellow crooked-neck squash (sm)	*Ratatouille*
_____	0-20	Mushrooms	*Ratatouille* *Marinated Sesame Chicken ...*
_____	0-1	Eggplant (med)	*Ratatouille*
_____	0-1	Butternut squash (2)	*Cinnamon Butternut Squash*
_____	optional	Alfalfa sprouts	*Salads* *Mediterranean Lavash ...*
_____	0-20	Cherry tomatoes	*Marinated Sesame Chicken ...*

Miscellaneous Produce

Restock	Par Stock	Item and size	For use in ...
_____	1	Garlic, minced in a jar or head of fresh cloves	Basic supply
_____	1	Gingerroot, minced in a jar or a 4" fresh root	Basic supply
_____	optional	Parsley (bunch) Will keep for 3 weeks in fridge	*Curried Chickpeas ...*
_____	optional	Cilantro (bunch) Will keep for 3 weeks in fridge	*Tofu Fiesta* *7 Layer Bean Dip*
_____	0-2	Tofu, firm (see buying tips above)	*Scrambled Tofu* *Tofu Bites* *Tofu Fiesta* *Fajitas* *Sweet & Sour Stir-Fry* *Eggless Salad Sandwiches*
_____	0-2	Tofu, soft (6 oz)	*Creamy Tomato Soup*
_____	0-1	Fresh salsa	*Snacking* *Black Bean & Corn Salad*
_____	0-2	Cranberries Fresh are available in the fall. Buy several and freeze to have on hand.	*Cranberry Salad*

Buying everything on this list is going to cost me a fortune!

True, you will be writing out a big check and going home with a car full of groceries on your first "stock-up" trip. But this is "bringing the grocery store to you" so you will *always* have what you need. How much is that worth to you? To *always* have what you need. (Listen to the sound of that word again!) And you're not really spending more, you're just spending it earlier. And think, with all the time you'll be saving by not making extra trips to the store mid-week, and making your own pizza instead of having it delivered, you will recover that up front investment in **no time at all**!

What is hummus and tabouli?

For information see page 81.

Grocery List

Restock	Par Stock	Item and size	For use in …

Miscellaneous Produce (continued)

Restock	Par Stock	Item and size	For use in …
_____	0-1	**Tabouli**	*Mediterranean Lavash Roll-ups*
_____	0-1	**Pumpkin (medium)** A special Autumn treat!	*Jack in the Pumpkin*
_____	0-1	**Hummus** I recommend the roasted red pepper or hummus with spinach	Snacking *Mediterranean Lavash Roll-ups* *1 Minute Mini-Meals*

Dried Fruit

Restock	Par Stock	Item and size	For use in …
_____	1	**Raisins (box)**	**Cereal** **Baking** **Snacking**
_____	0-1	**Dried cherries (tub)**	*Broccoli & Dried Cherry Salad* *Scrumptious Swiss Oats …*
_____	optional	**Craisins (tub)** (dried cranberries)	**Salad toppings** *Scrumptious Swiss Oats …*
_____	0-1	**Apricots (box)**	**Snacking** **Office pick-me-up** *Scrumptious Swiss Oats …*

Dried Beans and Grains

Restock	Par Stock	Item and size	For use in …
_____	1	**Lentils, dried (16 oz)**	*Lentil Spinach Soup* *Baked Lentils & Rice*
_____	1	**Black beans, dried (16 oz)**	*Mexican Black Beans*
_____	1	**Garbanzo beans, dried (16 oz)**	*Gyspy Soup*
_____	1	**Split peas, dried (16 oz)**	*Split Pea Soup*
_____	2	**Instant whole-grain brown rice,** *Minute*®	**Numerous quick meals**
_____	1	**Brown rice** I highly recommend the flavor Basmati	*Baked Lentils and Rice* *Jack in the Pumpkin*
_____	optional	**Wild rice**	*Jack in the Pumpkin*
_____	1	**Barley, quick-cooking**	*Beef Barley Soup*

Try to buy whole-wheat pasta whenever possible.

If you do not find whole-wheat pasta in the pasta section, try the natural or health food section, or better yet, a finer food store like Whole Foods Market. Remember, the nutritional benefit is worth the extra effort!

A brand of pasta I highly recommend, is *Eden®*. They make high quality whole-wheat pasta, including an ingenious alternative, 50-50 pasta, which is made with $1/2$ whole-wheat and $1/2$ sifted flour. This is a great way for kids (or anyone) to "warm up" slowly to whole-wheat pasta.

Shopping Tip

Whenever I'm in Ann Arbor, I'm sure to shop at Whole Foods Market. They carry ALL the pasta, beans, tabouli, hummus, whole-wheat pastry flour, fresh produce and deli items that I absolutely love!

Storage Tip

I store my pasta in clear decorative jars on top of my cupboards. This saves me space INSIDE my cupboards and reminds me to cook pasta weekly.

Grocery List

Restock	Par Stock	Item and size	For use in ...

Pasta

The following is a recommended selection of pasta shapes to keep on hand:

Restock	Par Stock	Item and size
_____	2	**Spaghetti (16 oz)**
_____	1	**Angel hair (16 oz)**
_____	1	**Corkscrews (16 oz)**
_____	1	**Macaroni (16 oz)**
_____	1	**Shells, medium (16 oz)**
_____	1	**Penne (16 oz)**
_____	1	**Lasagna Noodles (16 oz)** Buy 2 to make a double batch
_____	1	**Egg noodles, wide(16 oz)** *No-Yolks®* are preferred

Restock	Par Stock	Item and size	For use in ...

Soups

Restock	Par Stock	Item and size	For use in ...
_____	optional	**Chicken bouillon granules, low-sodium (sm)**	**Basic supply**
_____	optional	**Beef bouillon granules, low-sodium (sm)**	**Basic supply**
_____	4	**Chicken Broth,** *Swanson Natural Goodness* **100% fat-free,** $1/3$ **less sodium (14.5 oz)**	**Basic supply**
_____	2	**Beef Broth (14.5 oz)** reduced-sodium, if available	**Basic supply**
_____	2	**Cream of mushroom soup,** *Campbell's® Healthy Request®* **(10.5 oz)**	*Tuna Noodle Salad* *Beef Stroganoff*
_____	1	**Cream of chicken soup,** *Campbell's® Healthy Request®* **(10.5 oz)**	*Creamy Chicken Enchiladas*
_____	1	**Dry vegetable soup mix,** *Knorr®* **or** *Mrs. Grass®* **(pkg)**	*Spinach Dip* *Miracle Soup*

Do you know about Eden® beans?

I highly recommend them! These are absolutely delicious, supreme quality, low sodium and organic beans. They come both plain and flavored and taste great straight from the can. (Perfect for a 1-minute mini-meal right out of your briefcase)! They are available in 15 oz. cans or in single serving 8 oz. "pull-top" cans.

This is THE marriage of convenience, health and taste that we've all been waiting for!

My favorites:

- *Eden® Black Beans with Ginger and Lemon* (8 oz. pull-tops for mini-meals & two 15 oz. size for the *Gingered Black Beans and Squash,* page 93)

- *Eden® Spicy Pintos* (8 oz. pull-tops)

- *Eden® Lentil with Sweet Onion and Bay Leaf* (8 oz. pull-tops)

- *Eden® Baked Beans, with Sorghum & Mustard* (8 oz. pull-tops & 15 oz. size)

- *Eden® Chili Beans* (8 oz. pull-tops and 2 of the 15 oz. size for the *Chili Cornbread Pie* [page 125])

- *Eden® Garbanzo Beans* (8 oz. pull-tops, perfect for topping a salad)

Find these at finer food stores like:
Whole Foods Market
(See display ad in the back.)

You can also order by calling:
Whole Foods at 1-800-780-FOOD
or
Eden Foods at 1-888-424-EDEN

Grocery List

Canned Fruits

Restock	Par Stock	Item and size	For use in ...
_____	2	Peaches, lite (16 oz)	Serve with meals
_____	2	Pears, lite (16 oz)	Serve with meals
_____	1	Apricots, lite (16 oz)	Serve with meals
_____	1	Fruit cocktail, lite (16 oz)	Serve with meals
_____	1	Mandarin oranges (15 oz)	*Ambrosia Breakfast Rice* *Almond Chicken Salad*
_____	6	Pineapple tidbits, unsweetened (8 oz)	*Crunchy Apple Salad* *Sunshine Raisin Salad* *Cranberry Salad* *Ambrosia Breakfast Rice*
_____	1	Pineapple crushed, unsweetened (8 oz)	*Carrot Cake*
_____	2	Applesauce, unsweetened (large jar)	Numerous desserts Serve with meals
_____	1	Cranberry sauce, jellied (16 oz)	*Cranberry Pork Roast*

Canned Vegetables and Beans

Restock	Par Stock	Item and size	For use in ...
_____	2	Corn (16 oz)	*Black Bean & Corn Salad*
_____	1	Wax Beans (15 oz)	*5-Bean Salad*
_____	1	Green Beans (15 oz)	*5-Bean Salad*
_____	1	Butter Beans (15 oz)	*5-Bean Salad*
_____	1	Pumpkin (29 oz)	*Pumpkin Surprise Pie* *Pumpkin Oatbran Bread ...*
_____	4	Mushrooms, sliced (7 oz)	Numerous maindishes
_____	2	Beets, sliced (15 oz)	Serve with meals Great in salads
_____	6	Stewed tomatoes (14.5 oz)	Numerous entrée's
_____	1	Tomato sauce or puree, low-sodium (16 oz)	*Mexican LaZonya*
_____	2	Black beans (16 oz)	*Black Bean & Corn Salad* *Curried Chickpeas ...* *3 Bean Chili* *Mexican 5-Bean Soup* *Oriental Noodle Toss*

Hitting the Sauce

The following are selected samples of spaghetti sauces which meet the recommended criteria of **5 or less grams of fat and 800 mg or less of sodium** *per cup.*

Per 1 cup of sauce	Fat (g)	Sodium (mg)
*Eden® Organic, no salt added**	5	20
Colavita® (average of 4 flavors)	5	490
Classico® Spicy Red Pepper	5	540
Mama Rizzo's® (average of 4 flavors)	3	510
*Healthy Choice®** or Ragu® Light***	1	780

*This is "salt to YOUR taste." Adding up to a ¼ tsp. of salt to each cup of sauce, (500 mg of sodium) would still be within the recommended guideline for sodium.

Average for the entire line.

For Comparison		
Newman's Own®	4	1,400
Progresso® Spaghetti Sauce	9	1,240
Barilla®	8	1,130

(Thirsty yet? With either one, you just consumed around ½ to ⅔ of a tsp of salt)! (Yuk)!

Grocery List

Restock	Par Stock	Item and size	For use in ...

Canned Vegetables and Beans (continued)

Restock	Par Stock	Item and size	For use in ...
_____	2	Pinto beans (48 oz jar)	*Beanito Bean Dip* *7-Layer Bean Dip* *Burritos*
_____	1	Navy beans (15 oz)	*Mexican 5-Bean Soup*
_____	2	Great Northern beans (24 oz jar)	*Great Northern Tuna ...* *White Beans & Penne Pasta*
_____	2	Kidney Beans (15½ oz)	*3-Bean Chili* *Mexican 5-Bean Soup* *Crockpot Fajitas*
_____	2	Garbanzo beans (15½ oz)	*Curried Chickpeas ...* *Oklahoma Bean Dip*
_____	1	Black-eyed peas (15½ oz)	*Oklahoma Bean Dip*
_____	2	Chili beans (15 oz)	*Chili Cornbread Pie*
_____	2	Baked beans (15 oz) (vegetarian if possible)	*1 Minute Mini-Meals*

Canned Sauces

Restock	Par Stock	Item and size	For use in ...
_____	4	Spaghetti sauce (28 oz) *Healthy Choice®* (or see above)	**Numerous Pasta** **Numerous Pizza** **Numerous Stews**
_____	2	Sloppy Joe sauce (16 oz) *Manwich®*	*Turkey Joes*
_____	1	Cacciatore sauce (24 oz) *Chicken Tonight®*	*Chicken Cacciatore*
_____	1	Sweet and Sour (24 oz) *Chicken Tonight®*	*Sweet & Sour Chicken* *Stir-frys*

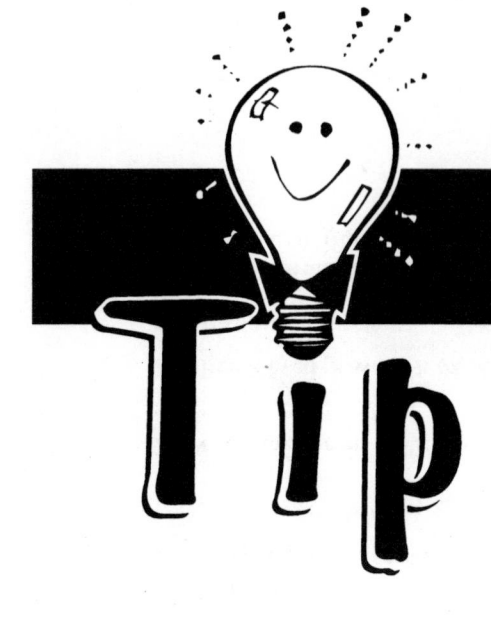

Sodium Alert!

While most of my recipes have less than 800 mg of sodium per entrée, some are higher. Eating an occasional entrée that is higher in sodium is not a problem for most people. However, for people who have been instructed to follow a "low-sodium diet," I recommend substituting sodium-free products for the reduced-sodium products whenever possible.

For added sodium-reduction:

1. Use no salt added stewed tomatoes.

2. Use no salt added spaghetti sauce (see page 30 for suggestions).

3. Use no salt added canned beans instead of the conventional brands. While rinsing and draining beans reduces sodium by about $1/3$, this can still leave a recipe too high in sodium. (Use the *Eden®* brand which has no salt added and you'll save 700-800 mg of sodium per can).

4. Use no salt added canned chicken broth. (Use *Pritikin®* or *Health Valley®* instead of the $1/3$ less sodium and you'll save about 400-700 mg of sodium per can.)

5. Buy reduced-sodium salsa. Often fresh salsa is lower in sodium than salsa in a jar. Check the label for less than 120 mg per 2 T. (Use *Gourmet Jose® Fresh Salsa* instead of *Pace® Picante* from a jar, and you'll save 280 mg per $1/4$ cup).

6. My recipes do not call for salt unless the recipe is particularly low in sodium and needs it for flavor. However, you can use a reduced-sodium salt (for instance *Morton's® Lite-Salt*) or complete salt substitute (like *No-Salt®*) or eliminate the salt I've called for altogether.

Grocery List

Photo-copy permission granted for personal shopping use only.

Canned Meats

Restock	Par Stock	Item and size	For use in ...
_____	4	Tuna, water packed (6 oz)	*Great Northern Tuna...* *Tuna Noodle Casserole*
_____	1	Tuna, water packed (6 pack of 2 oz pull-tops)	*Desk drawer lunches* *1-Minute Mini-Meal*
_____	2	Salmon, red or pink water packed (15+ oz)	*Salmon Burgers* *Herbed Salmon Spread...*
_____	4	Chicken, white meat water packed (10 oz)	*1-Minute Mini-Meals* *Simple Baked Chicken...* *Almond Chicken Salad* *Chicken Dijon Stuffed...* *Eggless Salad Sandwiches*
_____	optional	Sardines in mustard sauce (3+ oz)	*1-Minute Mini-Meals*
_____	1	Crabmeat (6 oz)	*Crab Dip*

Condiments

Restock	Par Stock	Item and size	For use in ...
_____	1	Ketchup	**Basic supply**
_____	1	Mustard, regular	**Basic supply**
_____	1	Dijon mustard *Grey Poupon®*	*Chicken Dijon Stuffed...* *Creamy Chicken Dijon* *Crispy Chicken Dijon* *Kickin' Chicken* *Potato Salad*
_____	1	Honeycup mustard or other spicy flavor of your choice	**Turkey & tuna sandwiches** *Turkey & Hot Mustard ...*
_____	1	Pimentos, chopped optional (2 oz)	*Salmon Burgers* *Oven Baked Lentils and Rice*
_____	2	Black olives, sliced (2.25 oz)	*Creamy Enchiladas* *Mexican Pizza*
_____	1	Hot pepper rings or Jalepeno rings (12 oz jar)	*Mexican Black Beans* *Hot & Spicy Pizza* *3 Bean Chili*
_____	1	Tabasco sauce	**Basic supply**

Lickety-Split Meals

Grocery List
31

Canned Meats / Condiments

What is chutney?

Chutney is the relish that traditionally accompanies Indian food, made of chopped fruits and spices like ginger, allspice, cinnamon, garlic, vinegar and hot pepper. Look for it in the specialty section of your grocery store. Trust me, it's a delicious spicy-sweet dynamo.

Miracle Whip® Light

While I'm aware that fat-free mayonnaise is available, I've found that for taste, many people prefer *Miracle Whip*® Light. Therefore, this is what I call for throughout the book. You are welcome to substitute fat-free if you wish, and you will save more fat grams if you do.

What kind of oil is best?

For the answer, see page 20.

Grocery List

Photo-copy permission granted for personal shopping use only.

Condiments (continued)

Restock	Par Stock	Item and size	For use in ...
_____	1	*Miracle Whip® Light*	**Basic supply**
_____	1	**Thousand Island dressing, light or fat-free**	**Basic supply**
_____	1	**Italian dressing lite or fat-free**	*Oklahoma Bean Dip* *Chicken & Vegetables...* *Marinated Vegetable Salad*
_____	1	*Henri's® Light TAS-TEE® Private Blend* **or any light coleslaw dressing**	*Pasta & Potato Salad*
_____	1	**Chutney, mango, pineapple or peach (8 oz) Gourmet specialty section**	*Chicken Chutney Pizza*
_____	1	**Barbecue sauce**	*Chicken & Vegetables...* *Polynesian Pizza*
_____	1	**Seafood cocktail sauce (8 oz)**	*Shrimp Pizza & Crab Dip*
_____	1	**Vinegar, Balsamic**	**Basic supply**
_____	1	**Vinegar, cider**	**Basic supply**
_____	1	**Marsala wine** cooking wine	*Chicken Marsala*

Cooking Oils

You can get by with nonstick spray and Canola oil for everything if you wish.

Restock	Par Stock	Item and size	For use in ...
_____	1	**Nonstick cooking spray**	**Basic supply**
_____	1	**Canola oil (small bottle)**	**Desserts**
_____	1	**Olive oil (small bottle)**	**Italian dishes**
_____	1	**Sesame oil (very sm)** Toasted tastes best.	**Stir-frys** **Marinade** *Oriental Noodle Toss*

Baking Supplies

Restock	Par Stock	Item and size	For use in ...
_____	1	**Sugar (5-10 lb)**	**Basic supply**
_____	1	**Brown sugar (2 lb)**	**Basic supply**
_____	1	**Powdered sugar (2 lb)**	*Carrot Cake* *Brownie Banana Split* *Chewy Multi-Grain Bars*
_____	2	**Honey (1 honey-bear and 1 re-fill jar)**	**Use on toast instead of margarine** *Breakfast in a Cookie*

What is whole-wheat pastry flour?

"Whole-wheat pastry flour" or sometimes called "whole-grain pastry flour" is very nutritious because it is a "whole grain" flour, yet is very light and cakey in texture, similar to that of white flour. It can be used in equal amounts to replace all-purpose flour in any "non-yeast" recipe. It makes wonderfully light cookies, cakes, muffins and quick breads, and the best part is; only you will know that you used "healthy" flour!

Where do you find it?

Be aware, that you will probably not find it in the standard flour section of your grocery store. It is considered specialty flour and may be found in the health food section among special brands like *Arrowhead Mills* or *Bob's Red Mill*. If you do not find it, request it from your grocer. I buy it in bulk quantities at finer food stores or co-ops. Please look for it. It really is worth the effort!

Attention Ann Arborites!

Coleman's Four Seasons on Liberty is the neatest place to stock up on whole-wheat pastry flour, the **best** produce and so much more! Grab the coupon in the back for up to $10 off and head on down there!

Grocery List

Restock	Par Stock	Item and size	For use in ...
		Baking Supplies (continued)	
_____	1	**Corn syrup (light vs dark)**	*Cinnamon Nut Buns* *Oatmeal Cookies* *Chocolate No-Bakes*
_____	1	**Pancake syrup (light)**	Basic supply
_____	optional	**Molasses**	Basic supply
_____	1	**All-purpose flour (5 lbs)**	Basic supply
_____	1	**Whole-wheat pastry flour (10 lbs)**	Basic supply (see above)
_____	1	**Cornmeal, yellow (sm. canister)**	Basic supply
_____	1	*Bisquick®,* **reduced-fat**	*Pumpkin Pie Surprise* *Applesauce Dumplings*
_____	1	**Brownie mix, reduced-fat**	*Brownie Banana Split*
_____	1	**Oatbran (1 lb. box) uncooked, similar to the way you buy** *Cream of Wheat®*	*Breakfast in a Cookie* *Ambrosia Breakfast Rice* *Pumpkin Oatbran Bread* *Oatbran Muffins*

Restock	Par Stock	Item and size	For use in ...
_____	1	**Oats, quick-cooking or old-fashioned (lg. canister)**	*Scrumptious Swiss Oats...* *Banana Oat Pancakes* *Breakfast in a Cookie* *Chocolate No-Bakes* *Oatmeal Cookies* *Chocolate Chip Cookies*
_____	optional	**Multi-grain oatmeal (sm. canister)**	*Multi-Grain Bars*
_____	1	**Non-fat dry milk (small)**	*Breakfast in a Cookie* *Chocolate No-Bakes*
_____	optional	**Non-fat dry buttermilk**	*Banana Nut Cake ...*
_____	1	**Evaporated skim milk (12 oz)**	*Pasta Primavera* *Pumpkin Surprise Pie*
_____	1	**Baking powder**	Basic supply
_____	1	**Baking soda**	Basic supply
_____	1	**Cornstarch**	Basic supply
_____	1	**Cocoa, unsweetened powder for baking**	*Chocolate No-Bakes* *Chocolate Amaretto ...*

Will I need to add on a second kitchen? This *Lickety-Split* list is HUGE!

Negatory on the second kitchen, but you will need to do some cupboard cleaning. For instance, throw out the 5 year old pudding boxes and cake decorating icing that you know it's time to toss. Bingo, a new shelf. You may even want to open up a couple of shelves in your laundry room to store extra canned items. What good is that broken flashlight anyway? Can't half of this stuff go in the garage? Bingo again. Two more new shelves. And yes, give up that junk drawer full of pens that don't write, old glasses you will never wear, and keys to what locks? I'm sure you can find another place for these precious items, like the dumpster. If the thought of this is too much to bear, simply transfer the gems to a cardboard box and place them in the basement as a safe purgatory.

And lastly, what about that drawer full of the kids' crayons, coloring books, shoe-strings, and a yo-yo? If it doesn't help you cook, get it out of there! Presto! You now have two open drawers and 3 open pantry shelves for the extra *Lickety-Split* cooking supplies you will need!

Grocery List

Restock	Par Stock	Item and size	For use in ...

Baking Supplies (continued)

Restock	Par Stock	Item and size	For use in ...
_____	1	**Tapioca, quick cooking** for thickening slow-cooker recipes	**Basic supply**
_____	2	**Vanilla pudding, instant (5.1 oz)**	*Fresh Fruit Pie* *Chocolate Chip Cookies*
_____	2	**Chocolate pudding instant (5.9 oz)**	*Chocolate-Chocolate Chip...*
_____	2	**Strawberry gelatin sugarfree (0.6 oz)**	*Fresh Fruit Pie* *Cranberry Salad*
_____	1	**Marshmallows**	**Hot chocolate** **Fat-free snack**
_____	1	**Chocolate chips** store in freezer	*Chocolate Chip Cookies*
_____	1	**Chocolate chips mini-morsels** Store in freezer.	*Chocolate Amaretto...*
_____	2	**Graham Cracker crusts regular or chocolate (9 oz. deep dish size)**	*Summer Fresh Fruit Pie*

Restock	Par Stock	Item and size	For use in ...

Peanut Butter & Nuts

(store nuts in freezer)

Restock	Par Stock	Item and size	For use in ...
_____	1	**Peanut Butter preferably natural (sm. or lg.)**	*Chocolate No-Bakes* **Snacking**
_____	1	**Chopped walnuts (8 oz)**	**Cookies** **Stir-fries** **Pancakes** *Banana Nut Cake* *Bread and Muffins*
_____	1	**Chopped pecans (8 oz)**	*Ambrosia Breakfast Rice* *Cinnamon Nut Buns* *Dried Cherry and Broccoli...*
_____	1	**Slivered almonds (8 oz)**	**Stir-frys** *Almond Chicken Salad*

Money saving tip for buying spices

If your spices are over 3 years old, empty out the jars and head to your local bulk food store, health food store or coop, where you can purchase spices *by the ounce* (the staff will show you how). You can purchase as little as 1 tablespoon, if that's all you want to try. This would cost you less than 10 cents. You buy only what you know you'll need and replenish your supply with fresh after that. No more paying $3 for a jar of spice that you'll only use a little of!

Grocery List

Restock	Par Stock	Item and size	For use in ...
		Spices and Flavorings	
_____	1	**Vanilla (lg)**	**Basic supply**
_____	1	**Lemon Extract (sm)**	**Basic supply**
_____	1	**Almond Extract (sm)**	**Basic supply**
_____	1	**Basil**	**Basic supply**
_____	1	**Cayenne pepper**	**Basic supply**
_____	1	**Chili powder (lg)**	**Basic supply**
_____	optional	**Chinese Five Spice**	**Basic supply**
_____	1	**Cinnamon (lg)**	**Basic supply**
_____	1	**Cloves**	**Basic supply**
_____	1	**Crushed red pepper flakes**	**Basic supply**
_____	optional	**Coriander**	**Basic supply**
_____	1	**Cumin, ground (lg)**	**Basic supply**
_____	optional	**Cumin Seed**	**Basic supply**
_____	1	**Curry powder**	**Basic supply**
_____	1	**Dill**	**Basic supply**
_____	1	**Garlic powder**	**Basic supply**

Restock	Par Stock	Item and size	For use in ...
_____	1	**Marjoram**	*Creamy Cauliflower Soup*
_____	1	**Dried mustard**	**Basic supply**
_____	1	**Oregano (lg)**	**Basic supply**
_____	1	**Onion flakes**	**Basic supply**
_____	1	**Paprika (Lg.)**	**Basic supply**
_____	1	**Pepper corns, whole black**	**Basic supply**
_____	1	**Poultry seasoning**	**Basic supply**
_____	1	**Pumpkin Pie Spice**	**Basic supply**
_____	1	**Rosemary**	**Basic supply**
_____	1	**Sage**	**Basic supply**
_____	1	**Salt**	**Basic supply**
_____	1	**Savory**	*Creamy Cauliflower Soup*
_____	1	**Sesame seeds**	**Basic supply**
_____	1	**Salt** (consider lite or salt sub.)	**Basic supply**
_____	1	**Thyme**	**Basic supply**
_____	1	**Mrs. Dash or Spike**	**Basic supply**
_____	1	**Taco Seasoning (pkt)**	**Basic supply**
_____	1	**Fajita Seasoning (pkt)**	**Basic supply**

Cereal Selection Tips

For healthy cereal, follow these label-reading criteria:

1. **Fat:** 2 grams of fat or less per serving. (Keep in mind that whole grains, including oats, have up to 2 grams of naturally occurring fat. The goal is to avoid cereals with "added fats").

2. **Fiber:** 4 or more grams of fiber per serving is ideal.

3. **Sugars:** Less than 10 grams of sugar. (The lower the better). Every 4 grams equals 1 teaspoon of sugar.

What is tamari?

For information, see page 134.

Iron Fortified Cereals: The good and not so good

While 100% fortification of the RDA of iron is great for people who run low in iron (like heavily menstruating women or recent blood donors), it may not be so good for others who are not low in iron. Recent concerns are based on the understanding that iron is a pro-oxidant which can be harmful in excess. Many health professionals suggest iron only be supplemented when a person is in need of it. Therefore, you may prefer to choose cereals that have been fortified with no more than 25% of iron.

PS. It's smart to use iron fortified cereals or iron supplements for 4 weeks after donating blood.

Grocery List

Photo-copy permission granted for personal shopping use only.

Restock	Par Stock	Item and size	For use in ...

Cereal

The following is a few of my favorite cereals, meeting my criteria for fat, fiber and taste.

Restock	Par Stock	Item and size	For use in ...
_____		**Wheat Germ** Tastes best toasted.	**Sprinkle on cereal Use in brownies** ***Whole-Grain Pancakes***
_____		***Grapenuts®***	**Breakfast**
_____		**Shredded Wheat with Bran**	**Breakfast**
_____		**Frosted Shredded Wheat**	**Breakfast and finger snack**
_____		***Quaker®* Oat Bran (hexagon chex in the red box)**	**Breakfast and finger snack**
_____		***Quaker®* Oat Squares**	**Breakfast and finger snack**
_____		**Corn Bran**	**Breakfast and finger snack**
_____		***Wheaties®***	**Breakfast**
_____		**Bran Flakes**	**Breakfast**

Ethnic Foods

Restock	Par Stock	Item and size	For use in ...
_____	2	**Refried Beans, fat-free (16 oz)**	**Quick burritos** ***Chicken & Bean Enchiladas***
_____	1	**Enchilada sauce** *Old El Paso®* **(10 oz)**	***Chicken & Bean Enchiladas***
_____	2	**Green chilies, chopped (4 oz)**	***Creamy Enchiladas Southwest Pizza South of the Border Roll-ups Mexican 5-Bean Soup***
_____	2	**Waterchestnuts, sliced (8 oz)**	***Spinach Dip Saucy Almond Chicken...***
_____	3	**Salsa, hot, medium or mild (16 oz)**	**Numerous entrees Snacking**
_____	1	**Soy sauce reduced-sodium (lg)**	**Numerous entrees** ***Appeteasers***
_____	optional	**Tamari sauce reduced-sodium (sm)**	***Marinated Sesame Chicken Kabobs Simple Tofu Bites***
_____	2	**Sweet n' sour sauce** *LaChoy®* **(10 oz)**	***Easiest Stir-Fry Ever***

(See page 38 for more selection suggestions!)

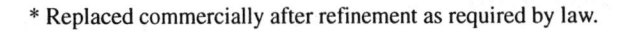

Nutrients lost when whole-wheat is refined

86%	Vitamin E	75%	Fiber
81%	Niacin*	70%	Vitamin B-6
80%	Riboflavin*	67%	Folic Acid
77%	Thiamin*	50%	Pantothenic acid

* Replaced commercially after refinement as required by law.

Now you know WHY I make all the fuss about whole-wheat flour!

Why buy Lavash?

For information, see page 80.

Grocery List

Restock	Par Stock	Item and size	For use in ...

Bread Products

Buy according to your family's needs, all breads freeze well!

Restock	Par Stock	Item and size	For use in ...
_____		**100% whole-wheat bread,** *Brownberry®, Koepplinger's®, Healthy Choice®, Roman Meal®*	
_____		**Rye or Pumpernickel bread, round loaf**	*Spinach Dip in ...*
_____		**Pita bread, whole-wheat**	**Pita sandwiches** *Pita Pizza*
_____		**Hamburger buns, whole-wheat if possible**	*Salmon Burgers*
_____		**Rolls, whole-wheat or nine-grain**	**Serve with meals**
_____		**English muffins, whole-grain if possible**	**Breakfasts**

Restock	Par Stock	Item and size	For use in ...
_____	1	**Bagels, whole-grain if possible**	**Breakfasts Snacking** *1 Minute Mini-Meals*
_____	1	**Flour tortillas, 8" (pkg of 10) fat-free, no lard**	**Option for corn tortillas** *South of the Border Roll-ups* **Burritos** *Chicken Enchiladas Crockpot® Fajitas Mexican LaZonya*
_____	1	**Corn tortillas** These freeze well.	*Mexican LaZonya*
_____	1-2	**Lavash, flat breads**	**Roll-up sandwiches Appeteasers**
_____	1-4	**Pizza crusts, ready-made** *Boboli® or Oliveri®*	**Friday night Pizza's**
_____	1-4	**Rice cakes popcorn cakes**	**Snacking** *1 Minute Mini-Meals*
_____	1	**Bread Crumbs unseasoned**	*Tantalizing Turkey Loaf Crispy Chicken Dijon*

Tips for selecting a "healthy" commercial stir-fry sauce

Comparing the labels for stir-fry sauces can be quite confusing. Sometimes the serving size is 1 T, sometimes it's ¹/₂ cup! What should be the appropriate serving size? I find ¹/₄ cup works nicely, and an 8-ounce jar serves 4 very well. In the sweet and sour type sauces, fat is not an issue but sodium is. Take a look at the following to get an idea of what's out there. I've adjusted all the portions to ¹/₄ cup. (That's 4 tablespoons).

<u>Sodium per ¹/₄ cup</u>

Chicken Tonight® Sweet & Sour Sauce .... 170 mg
LaChoy® Sweet and Sour Sauce .... 210 mg
Kraft® Sweet 'n Sour Sauce .... 250 mg
Kikkoman® Sweet & Sour Sauce.. 380 mg
LaChoy® Stir-Fry Vegetables 'n Sauce .... 410 mg
Lawry's® Stir-Fry Oriental Style Cooking Sauce.............................. 1,320 mg
Kame® Szechuan Sauce .... 1,640 mg

As you can see, some are a salt mine!

Your goal is 250 mg or less per ¹/₄ cup.

Grocery List

Restock	Par Stock	Item and size	For use in ...
		Snacks	
_____	1	**Chocolate syrup** *Hershey's®* **(squeeze bottle kind)**	**Chocolate milk** **Drizzling over fruit** *Brownie Banana Split*
_____	1	**Hot cocoa mix**	**Snacking**
_____	1-2	**Baked tortilla chips** *Tostitos®*	*Guiltless Nacho's Supreme* *7 Layer Bean Dip* *Oklahoma Bean Dip* *Crockpot® Fajitas* *Mexican Black Beans* *Mexican 5-Bean Soup*
_____	1-2	**Potato chips** **Baked Lays®**	**Snacking** **Sandwiches** **Soups**
_____	0-1	*Fig Newtons®* **regular or fat-free**	**Snacking** **Desserts** **Lunchbox treat**

Restock	Par Stock	Item and size	For use in ...
_____	0-1	**Gingersnaps**	**Snacking** **Desserts** **Frozen yogurt sandwiches** **Lunchbox treat**
_____	0-12	**Fortune cookies** (only 30 calories each, fat-free and fun)	**Stir-fry dinners**
_____	1	**Saltines, whole-wheat**	**Snacking** **Soups**
_____	1-2	*Triscuits®*, **reduced-fat**	**Snacking** **1-Minute Mini-Meals**
_____	1	**Graham crackers, low-fat**	**Snacking** **Desserts** **Frozen yogurt sandwiches**
_____	1-2	**Popcorn, microwave** *Orville Redenbacher®* *Smart Pop®* **or** *Pop Secret®* **by Request**	**Snacking** **Soups**

Should we give eggs a break?

Egg yolks certainly do have a lot of cholesterol (a full day's allowance in just 1) AND 5 grams of fat. Egg whites, on the other hand are fat and cholesterol free. The recommendation is to consume fewer than 4 egg yolks a week and fewer (or none) if you have high cholesterol.

I choose to limit egg yolks by diluting them with egg whites, as called for in these recipes. I find this convenient and economical. This provides some of the color and texture of eggs, while staying within the weekly recommendation. However, to completely omit egg yolks from your diet, replace each egg yolk with 2 whites. You can also use egg substitutes: $1/4$ cup replaces 1 egg.

Margarine or butter?

For information see page 184.

Light cream cheese and sour cream vs. fat-free

I find that many people do not like the taste of fat-free cream cheese but love the taste of light cream cheese. Likewise, while some recipes taste fine using fat-free sour cream, others do not. To keep everything tasty and shopping simple, all recipes call for light cream cheese and light sour cream. I have carefully calculated and used the amounts that still allow the overall recipe to meet the recommended guidelines. Again, you are welcome to substitute fat-free if you wish, and you will save more fat grams if you do.

Grocery List

Restock	Par Stock	Item and size	For use in ...
		Eggs & Dairy	
_____	2	**Dozen eggs (or egg substitute)**	**Various uses**
_____	1-2	**Skim or ½ % milk (gal)**	**Various uses**
_____	2	**Soy milk, optional**	**Pancakes** **Baking** **Cereals** *Scrumptious Swiss ...*
_____	1	**Margarine, light (tub)**	**Used in one recipe only:** *Chocolate No-Bakes*
_____	1	**Spray butter,** *I Can't Believe It's Not Butter®*	**Variety of uses**
_____	1	**Sour cream, light (16 oz) fat-free if you prefer**	*Creamy Chicken Enchiladas* *Chicken and Bean...* *Chicken Paprikash* *Simple Baked Chicken...* *Creamy Chicken Dijon* *Chicken Dijon Stuffed...* *Guiltless Nachos Supreme* *Beef Stroganoff* *Appeteasers* *Spinach Dip* *South of the Border Roll-ups*

Restock	Par Stock	Item and size	For use in ...
_____	1	**Cream cheese, light (8 oz) fat-free if you prefer**	*Appeteaser* *Turkey and Hot Mustard...* *South of the Border...* *Chocolate-Amaretto...* *Carrot Cake* *Brownie Banana Split* *Oatmeal Cookies*
_____	1	**Cottage cheese, light or non-fat (16 oz)**	*1-Minute Mini-Meals*
_____	1	**Ricotta cheese, light (15 oz) buy 2 for double batch**	*LaZonya*
_____	1	**String Cheese, part-skim mozzarella**	*1-Minute Mini-Meals*
_____	1	**Non-fat plain yogurt (16 oz)**	**Baking** **Mixing with** *Miracle Whip®* **Light 50-50** *Smoothies*
_____	6	**Non-fat fruited yogurts (8 oz) optional**	**Snacking** **Breakfasts** **Lunches**

How does cheese fit into a healthy diet?

I would really miss cheese if I had to give it up, wouldn't you? And thanks to so many low-fat and fat-free cheeses on the market, we don't have to!

The ideal is to use fat-free cheese. But what about taste? There are great tasting low-fat cheeses available, but they run 6-7 grams of fat per ounce, which is TOO MUCH. So, when it comes to shredded cheese, why not mix fat-free with reduced-fat for a great compromise? I recommend *2% Milk by Kraft®* and I mix it 50-50 with the fat-free cheese by *Healthy Choice®* or *Kraft®*. This produces a wonderful, tasty and normal melting cheese for only 3 grams of fat per ounce. I do this with both cheddar and mozzarella. This is the "reduced-fat shredded cheese" I am referring to in all recipes. If you prefer to use the fat-free exclusively, please do!

The next trick is to keep your portion to 1 ounce only (equal to $1/4$ cup of shredded cheese). This actually goes a long way melted across a serving of broccoli, pizza or nachos! Enjoy!

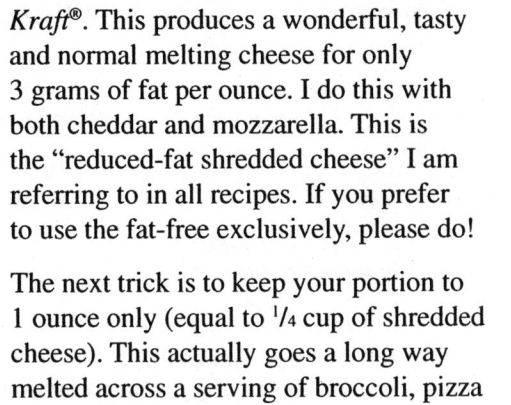

Parmesan cheese

Parmesan cheese *is* high in fat. However, the amounts called for in this book do not add unreasonable amounts of fat. I therefore suggest using regular Parmesan cheese and have calculated the recipes accordingly. If you would like to use fat-free instead, please do. (I personally have had great results mixing regular and fat-free, 50-50).

Grocery List

Restock	Par Stock	Item and size	For use in ...

Eggs & Dairy (continued)

Restock	Par Stock	Item and size	For use in ...
_____	1	Parmesan cheese, regular or fat-free	Numerous entrees
_____	1	Mozzarella, shredded, fat-free, *Kraft®* or *Healthy Choice®*	Numerous entrees
_____	1	Mozzarella, shredded part-skim	Numerous entrees
_____	2	Cheddar cheese, shredded fat-free, *Kraft®* or *Healthy Choice®*	Numerous entrees
_____	2	Cheddar cheese, sharp shredded, *2% Milk by Kraft®*	Numerous entrees

Make your own reduced fat yet still delicious cheese, by mixing the two white cheeses and two cheddar cheeses together. Do this when putting groceries away so you don't forget. Freezes well!

Convenience Meats

Restock	Par Stock	Item and size	For use in ...
_____		Smoked turkey breast slices	Sandwiches *Turkey Roll-ups with Lavash*
_____		Ham, 98% fat-free chunk or slices (1 lb.)	Pizza topping *Split Pea Soup* *Breakfast Casserole* *Scrambled Omelette*

(When putting groceries away, chop and divide ham into 8- 2 oz portions. Freeze in air-tight bags).

_____	optional	Canadian bacon	

Seafood

Restock	Par Stock	Item and size	For use in ...
_____		Orange Roughy, fresh or frozen filets (lg. bag)	*Broiled Orange Roughy*
_____		Trout, fresh (2 lbs.)	*Delicate Baked Trout*
_____		Shrimp, frozen, cooked ready to eat (12 oz bag)	*Shrimp Pizza* *Pasta Primavera*

Red meat. Where do you draw the line?

All you have to do is follow these 3 guidelines, and you can enjoy red meat up to 3 times per week!

#1 Choose lean. NOT prime rib, but tenderloin or filet mignon; NOT hamburger but ground sirloin. Whatever you do, don't worry about it costing more, because guideline #3 will offset the cost. Besides, you either pay now…or you pay later!

#2 Trim well. Trim all meats *meticulously*.

#3 Think small. Keep your portion to 4 ounces. (This looks like the size of a deck of cards). Fill the plate up with lots of vegetables and a big baked potato. Of course slicing the meat up for stir-fry or pepper steak works great. Try it!

What about pork?

See page 167 for good news about today's pork!

Grocery List

Photo-copy permission granted for personal shopping use only.

Restock	Par Stock	Item and size	For use in …

Poultry • Beef • Pork

Restock	Par Stock	Item and size	For use in …
_____		**Chicken breasts, skinless, boneless (4 lbs)** Buy individually frozen or to save on sodium buy fresh and freeze each breast half individually	*Marinated Sesame…* *Creamy Chicken Dijon* *Skillet Chicken &…* *Chicken Marsala* *Chicken Paprikash* *Southwest Chicken Pizza* *Chicken Chutney Pizza* *Saucy Almond Chicken…* *Sweet & Sour Stir-fry* *Kickin' Chicken* *Chicken & Vegetables…* *Creamy Chicken Enchiladas* *Crockpot® Fajitas* *Chicken Cacciatore* *Sweet & Sour Chicken*
_____	1	**Chicken leg quarters optional (thigh and drumsticks, pkg. of 4)**	**To accompany** *Oven Fries and Ratatouille*
_____	4	**Turkey, extra-lean ground breast (1 lb. pkgs.)**	*Unstuffed Peppers* *Veggie Sghetti* *Tantalizing Turkey-Loaf* *3-Bean Chili* *Turkey Joes*

Restock	Par Stock	Item and size	For use in …
_____	1	**Turkey tenderloin boneless (1 lb.)**	*Turkey Vegetable Stew*
_____	1	**Turkey tenderloin boneless, slices or cutlets (1 lb.)**	*Parmesan Turkey Cutlets…*
_____	1 - 2	**Lean sirloin or flank steak (1 ± 2 lbs.)**	*Easy Pepper Steak Stir-Fry* *Beef Barley Soup* *Beef Stroganoff*
_____		**Pork tenderloin (2 lbs.)**	*Cranberry Pork Roast* *Optional in Sweet & Sour…* *Gypsy Stew* *Crockpot® Fajitas*

Alcohol for Cooking

Purchase small bottles.

Restock	Par Stock	Item and size	For use in …
_____	1	**White Wine**	*Chicken and Vegetables…* *Oven-Baked Lentils and Rice*
_____	1	**Amaretto**	*Chocolate Amaretto …*
_____	1	**Banana Liqueur**	*Flaming Bananas Foster*
_____	1	**White Rum** **Frozen or Bottled Juices**	*Flaming Bananas Foster*

Will I need to buy a deep freezer?

Definitely a plus on owning a deep freezer. But if you don't have one, simply plan on extra strict cleaning and organizing to optimize capacity. Either way, be sure to reserve a separate area for vegetables, meats, juices, etc. so you can keep things rotated (first in, first out) and find things FAST.

Remember:

- Use your fresh produce early in the week and frozen later in the week.

- A full variety of frozen vegetables is nice to have on hand.

- A one pound bag of vegetables should serve 3-4, not 5-6.

- Frozen fruits are a delicious snack eaten frozen or just partially thawed.

- Try chocolate syrup drizzled over frozen cherries for "healthy" chocolate covered cherries!

Grocery List

Restock	Par Stock	Item and size	For use in ...
		Frozen Veggies	

(Yes, I do suggest having all these on hand, in addition to having a full drawer of fresh. Use the fresh early in the week and the frozen later in the week).

Restock	Par Stock	Item and size	For use in ...
_____	1	**Corn (16 oz)**	**Various entrees**
_____	1	**Peas (16 oz)**	**Various entrees**
_____	1	**Lima beans (16 oz)**	**Various entrees**
_____	1	**Mixed vegetables (16 oz)**	**Various entrees**
_____	1	**Cut green beans (16 oz)**	**Various entrees**
_____	1	**Whole green beans (16 oz)**	**Various entrees**
_____	1	**California blend (16 oz) broccoli, cauliflower and carrots**	
_____	1	**Mixed stir-fry vegetables (16 oz)** *Freshlike*® **Oriental Blend or Pepper Stir-fry**	*Easiest Stir-Fry Ever*
_____	4	**Spinach, chopped (10 oz)**	*Veggie Sghetti* *Unstuffed Peppers* *Gypsy Stew* *Spinach Dip*

Restock	Par Stock	Item and size	For use in ...
_____	1	**Peas pods or snow peas (10 oz)**	**Various entrees**
_____	1	**Carrots, crinkle cut (10 oz)**	**Various entrees**
_____	1	**Asparagus (10 oz) use fresh if you prefer**	*Chicken Dijon Stuffed…* *Creamy Chicken Dijon*
_____	1	**Hash browns with onions and peppers, *Ore Ida*® O'Brien Potatoes**	*Breakfast Casserole* *Scrambled Omelette* *Cheesy Potato Skillet* *Cheesy Scrambled Tofu*
_____	1	**Potato Wedges with skins *Ore Ida*®**	*Kickin' Chicken w/Fries*

Frozen or Bottled Juices

Restock	Par Stock	Item and size	For use in ...
_____	4	**Orange juice concentrate (cans)**	**Snacks**
_____	1	**V-8® juice, low-sodium (1 qt. jar)**	*Miracle Soup* *3 Bean Chili*
_____	1	**V-8® juice, low-sodium (6 pack of 6 ounce cans)**	**Snacks**
_____	4	**100% fruit juice, your choice of flavors, *Dole*®**	**Snacks**

Grocery Store Checkout
One minute Stress Buster

Whew! Aren't you glad you're done? Now for the torturous checkout. While waiting there (instead of musing about the slow line, reading tabloids or drooling over the chocolate bars), refresh your body by doing some deep breathing, stretching and strengthening exercises.

1. Lift your hands straight up over your head and stretch. Take a deep breath in. Exhale. (Care not what others think of you!) Repeat twice.

2. Raise up on your toes, hold and lower, (calf-raises). Once you get good, stand on one foot at a time and work each calf separately.

3. Lift your leg straight out behind you, (look first!). Feel the muscle in your buttocks contract. Alternate legs.

4. Standing with feet shoulder width apart, curl your foot up to almost kick your behind. Feel the muscle in the back of your leg contract. Alternate feet back and forth.

Before you know it, it will be time to start unloading your cart, and you will hardly have noticed that the line was slow, or that the candy bars were a temptation.

P.S. No matter what you've been doing all day, chained to your computer, running errands, chasing children, or flying from airport to airport, give these 1 minute stress busters a try!

Grocery List

Restock	Par Stock	Item and size	For use in ...

Frozen Fruit

_____	1	**Strawberries (12 oz bag)**	Snacking *Smoothies*
_____	1	**Blueberries (12 oz bag)**	Snacking *Smoothies* *Blueberry Buckle*
_____	1	**Cherries (12 oz bag)**	Snacks

Frozen Miscellaneous

_____	1	**Honey-wheat bread dough (pkg. of 3)**	*Glazed Cinnamon Nut Buns*
_____	1	**Cheese ravioli (25 oz bag)**	*Ravioli Stew*

Choose 1 or 2 of the following:

_____	1	**Ice cream or frozen yogurt low-fat or fat-free, *Edy's*® or *Healthy Choice*® Vanilla**	*Blueberry Buckle* *Flaming Bananas Foster* *Applesauce Dumplings*
_____	optional	**Lemon or Raspberry Sorbet**	Dessert
_____	optional	**Fudgesicles**	Dessert
_____	optional	**Frozen yogurt bars**	Dessert

Restock	Item and size

Cleaning Supplies

_____ _____
_____ _____
_____ _____
_____ _____

Personal Hygiene

_____ _____
_____ _____
_____ _____
_____ _____

Paper Goods

_____ _____
_____ _____
_____ _____
_____ _____

Restock	Item and size

Laundry Supplies

_____ _____
_____ _____
_____ _____
_____ _____

Pet Supplies

_____ _____
_____ _____
_____ _____
_____ _____

Optional Items

_____ _____
_____ _____
_____ _____
_____ _____

Lickety-Split Meals

Grocery List
43

Frozen Fruit / Frozen Miscellaneous / Personal Items

Breakfast

"Breakfast is your most important meal of the day."

I know you've heard this a million times before. (I even bet I know from *who*!) I also balked at my mother's advice for the first 22 years of my life. But then in a college classroom, Mom's advice

took on new appeal. A study found different rates of weight loss between two groups of people, although their calorie intakes were identical. The group who ate their calories across breakfast, lunch and dinner lost more weight than the group eating their

calories across lunch and dinner only. This shows how our gastrointestinal tract burns calories simply by digesting food. Starting that process early in the morning (when your metabolism is high) means a higher total calorie burn for the day.

I don't know how this sounds to you, but it sounds to me like breakfast is the most important meal of the day!

Try these great recipes to make your most important meal of the day, the most delicious meal of the day!

Great ideas from people like you!

"The day I turned 65, something told me I would feel a lot younger if I lost weight. So with guidance from Zonya, I embarked step by step upon my new way of life. I did not follow a diet, just ate nutritious food and didn't deprive myself of anything. By the time I ate all the recommended fruits and vegetables, I was too full to eat junk foods. I felt then, as I do now, that I can eat so many tasty things, all without counting calories. I also began walking over my lunch hour for 30 minutes; raincoat, umbrella and all. Now that I'm retired, my husband and I walk 3 miles, 4 days a week. I absolutely love my new way of life!"

—BETTY S., 67
maintaining a 60 pound
weight loss for 18 months
and counting

Breakfast Casserole

Here's a special breakfast recipe that's not labor-intensive like pancakes or omelettes, yet is every bit as delicious. Ideal to put in the oven before you head out to do your morning exercise. Be sure to keep this in mind for when you have overnight company—(They'll love it!)

4 OR 8

BREAKFAST CASSEROLE
ENGLISH MUFFINS
STRAWBERRIES, MELONS OR GRAPES

Preheat oven to 375°.
Spray baking dish with nonstick spray.
(Be sure to coat the sides of the dish too).

Great as a morning Oven • Exercise • Eat!

For 4	For 8	
½ bag	1 bag	(24 oz) frozen *Ore Ida*® O'Brien Potatoes (hash browns with onions & peppers)
½ c	1 c	reduced-fat shredded cheddar cheese
2 oz	4 oz	lean ham *or* Canadian bacon *or* lowfat smoked sausage (*Healthy Choice*©)
2	4	whole eggs
3	6	egg whites
15 grinds	30 grinds	fresh ground pepper

Use an 8" x 8" pan for 4 servings, a 9" x 13" pan for 8 servings.

Place the frozen potatoes in the bottom of the baking dish. Break up large chunks. Cut the meat into small chunks. Sprinkle the meat and cheese over the potatoes.

Whip lightly with a fork in a small bowl. Pour evenly over the potatoes.

Top casserole with pepper. Place in oven uncovered and set timer for 40 minutes (4 servings) or 45 minutes (8 servings). No, don't read the paper, how about using one of those aerobic videos you have?

Serve with English muffins and fresh fruit.

EXCHANGE VALUES

1 Starch	2 Meat	— Veg.	— Fruit	— Milk	— Fat

Nutrition information for — 1 cup of casserole | Preparation Time —5 min. | Oven Time — 40 or 45 min.

Calories 160	Fat .... 4.5 g	Fiber .... 2 g	Sodium .... 340 mg	Total Carbohydrate .... 16 g
Calories from Fat 26%	Saturated Fat .... 2 g	Cholesterol .... 117 mg	Protein .... 13 g	Sugars .... < 1 g

The Vegetarian Omelette: Friend or Foe?

Did you know that a "restaurant" vegetarian omelette, made with 3 eggs and cheese, served with buttered toast and hash browns, *racks up 50 grams of fat?* That's equivalent to ½ stick of butter!

Thank goodness, knowledge is power and you have choices! Next time you're at a restaurant for breakfast, try ordering my recommendation: vegetarian omelette, made with egg substitute or egg whites; hold the cheese, double the veggies (don't forget the spinach!), dry whole-wheat toast, with jam, jelly or honey and fruit. If I'm exercising that day, I'll order the hash browns (11 grams of fat) and eat only ½ of the portion. (5 grams of fat.) Better yet, stay home and make *Scrambled Omelette*.

Either way, you will have slashed 50 grams of fat down to 10, and you'll feel lighter and more alert all day!

Super Time Saving Tip

Skip microwaving the potatoes and chopping the pepper and onion by using 2 cups of *Ore Ida® Potatoes O'Brien* (a frozen hash brown product called for in previous recipe). It has no fat, just chopped potatoes, onions and peppers, and saves you loads of time!

Scrambled Omelette

Not patient enough to make an omelette, but crave the taste?
Here's the compromise — and they're healthy too!

Delegate Someone to: Chop onion, green peppers and tomato Slice and peel cantaloupe Make toast

2 med	potatoes*

Scrub thoroughly and pierce each potato with a fork. Microwave on high for 7 minutes. (If you prefer your omelette without potatoes, then skip this step.)

¹/₂	green pepper, chopped*
1 sm	onion, chopped*

Chop (or save time and use pre-prepped frozen!)

4 slices	Canadian bacon, chopped *or*
	2 turkey sausage patties† (optional)

Spray a nonstick skillet with nonstick spray. Sauté onion and pepper with sausage over medium high heat. Break sausage patty into chunks.

4 slices	whole-wheat bread *or*
	4 English muffins

Put in toaster.

When potatoes finish, chop and add to sauté.

4	eggs
6	egg whites (yes, throw those yolks away!)
¹/₄ cup	skim milk

Whip together with a fork in small bowl. Add to sauté and stir constantly.

1	tomato, chopped
¹/₂ cup	reduced-fat shredded cheddar cheese
15 grinds	fresh ground pepper

Fold in when eggs are almost completely done. Cover and let set 1 minute. Top with fresh ground pepper. Serve with toast and fresh cantaloupe.

Note: If not using meat, you may wish to sprinkle on ¹/₄ tsp. of salt.

EXCHANGE VALUES

2 Starch	3 Meat	— Veg.	— Fruit	— Milk	— Fat

* See my Super Time Saving Tip above.
† See recipe on page 50.

Nutrition information for — 1 cup omelette made with Homemade Turkey Sausage† and 1 slice of toast   Preparation Time — 20 min.

Calories 300	Fat .... 9 g	Fiber .... 4 g	Sodium .... 540 mg	Total Carbohydrate .... 29 g
Calories from Fat 27%	Saturated Fat .... 3.5 g	Cholesterol .... 236 mg	Protein .... 27 g	Sugars .... 3 g

If I eat breakfast, I'm hungry again mid-morning, again at lunch, and I seem to eat all day long...

It amazes me that people think this is bad. This is good! This is eating to match your metabolism. I promise that after a day of this, you'll find it's much easier to eat a light dinner with only a little evening snack.

Scrumptious Swiss Oats 'n Fruit

Think you don't like oatmeal 'cause it's gloppy? Have you tried uncooked oats, the Swiss way? You won't believe how absolutely delicious this dish is! Thanks to Elizabeth Wagner (culinary wizard, caterer and new-found friend) for this dish you'll be proud to serve your family. It saves time on the morning rush and is perfect for overnight guests. This also makes a great "dish to pass" for a morning meeting. Bye-bye doughnuts!

SWISS OATS N' FRUIT
ENGLISH MUFFINS (OPTIONAL)

Needs to soak for at least 4 hours.

For 4	For 8	
1½ c	3 c	**dry oats** (quick-cooking *or* old fashioned)
1¼ c	2½ c	**skim, ½% milk *or* soy milk**
2 T	¼ c	**honey**
½ tsp	1 tsp	**cinnamon**
3 c	6 c	**any variety of fresh *or* dried fruit that fancies you:**
		• sliced banana
		• sliced kiwi
		• strawberries, cut in half
		• blueberries
		• raspberries
		• bite-size chunks of apple
		• raisins
		• craisins (dried cranberries)
		• dried cherries
		• dried chopped apricots
¼ c	½ c	**chopped walnuts, pecans *or* almonds**

Night before:

Stir together in a large bowl and allow to soak in the refrigerator overnight.

In the morning:

Add and gently mix together.

Serve in a large attractive bowl with matching small bowls. Include English muffins on the side if you wish.

EXCHANGE VALUES

1.5 Starch	1 Meat	— Veg.	2 Fruit	— Milk	1 Fat

Nutrition information for — 1-1/2 cup serving   Preparation Time —p.m. 5 min. — a.m. 15 min.

Calories 300	Fat .... 7 g	Fiber .... 7 g	Sodium .... 42 mg	Total Carbohydrate .... 53 g
Calories from Fat 21%	Saturated Fat .... < 1 g	Cholesterol .... 1 mg	Protein .... 9 g	Sugars .... 27 g

Don't have time for breakfast?

Trust me, breakfast doesn't have to be time-consuming. Here are 5 *fast* breakfasts you can count on:

- *The Eat While You Drive—*
  1 banana, 1 bagel or 3 *Breakfast in a Cookie* cookies, 1 juice box

- *The Eat at Your Desk While the Boss Isn't Looking—*
  8 oz light yogurt with ¼ cup of *Grapenuts*® mixed in and 1 *Breakfast in a Cookie* cookie

- *The 3-Minute Favorite—*
  Cereal & skim or soy milk and a piece of fresh fruit

- *The "Stick to Your Ribs" When You Know You Won't Be Getting Lunch Until Late—*
  Bagel with a thin spread of natural peanut butter, glass of skim or soy milk, or juice.

- *The Quickie—*
  A glass of skim or soy milk, and a glass of orange juice. (Although this may not seem ideal, it gives you 30% of your calcium needs, good carbohydrates and protein to fuel your body, and 160% of your vitamin C needs). **Throw in 3 *Breakfast in a Cookie* cookies and you really do have a meal!**

Breakfast in a Cookie

Very low-fat cookies that are full of good nutrition — you can eat them for breakfast! This recipe makes a lot so you can freeze plenty for weeks of quick breakfasts, desserts and snacks.

MAKES 5 DZ.
(THAT'S 60 COOKIES!)

3 BREAKFAST COOKIES
GLASS OF SKIM MILK OR JUICE

Preheat oven to 375°.

Make ahead for the freezer!

1 cup	oatbran
³/₄ cup	orange juice

Mix together in a small bowl and set aside to soak for 10 minutes.

1 cup + 1 T	applesauce, unsweetened
1 T	canola oil
1 cup	honey
¹/₃ cup	firmly packed brown sugar
3	eggs
1¹/₂ T	vanilla
1 T	grated orange rind

Meanwhile… combine in a large bowl, using an electric mixer.

5pts per 3 cookies

3 cups	whole-wheat pastry flour*
1 T	baking powder
1¹/₂ tsp	baking soda

Measure into a sifter and sift into the large bowl.

1 cup	non-fat dry milk
3 cups	dry oats (quick-cooking *or* old fashioned)
1 cup	nuts
1 cup	raisins

Add the soaked oatbran and remaining ingredients to the large bowl and mix thoroughly with a strong wooden spoon.

Spray baking sheets with nonstick cooking spray.

Drop by slightly heaping tablespoons, a full 2" apart.

Bake for 12 to 14 minutes.

EXCHANGE VALUES

2 Starch	1 Meat	— Veg.	1 Fruit	— Milk	— Fat

* If you don't have whole-wheat pastry flour, you can substitute with 1¹/₂ cups whole-wheat and 1¹/₂ cups all-purpose flour.

Nutrition information for — 3 cookies | **Preparation Time — 30 min.** | **Oven Time — 30 min.**

Calories 265	Fat .... 6 g	Fiber .... 4 g	Sodium .... 200 mg	Total Carbohydrate .... 46 g
Calories from Fat 21%	Saturated Fat .... 4 g	Cholesterol .... 32 mg	Protein .... 8 g	Sugars .... 23 g

Freezing Bananas

Do your bananas sometimes over-ripen before you can eat them all? Try this—peel them and slip them into a *Ziplock®* bag to freeze. Later, add the bananas while still frozen, to the *Smoothie* recipe for a frosty-fruity sensation.

You can also thaw and mash the bananas to use in *Nana' Bread/Cake or muffins* (pages 195 and 199).

P.S. A *Smoothie* is an ideal energy booster after a workout!

Smoothies

These nutrition-packed drinks are very dessert-like. Kids and adults alike love them for breakfast or a snack. *Smoothies* are especially good for an after exercise pick-me-up. Use blueberries instead of strawberries for your kids and call them "Smurf" *Smoothies*. The smoothies can be made with yogurt, skim milk or soymilk, based on your personal nutrition goals.

1 cup	skim milk, soy milk *or* non-fat plain yogurt
1 T	sugar
2 cups	frozen strawberries (roughly 1/2 of a 20 oz. bag)
1	banana (a ripe frozen one is especially good)
3 T	wheat germ (optional)
3	ice cubes (if your strawberries aren't frozen)

Buzz together in a food processor or blender. This produces a thick, frozen consistency, perfect for eating with a spoon.

1/2 - 1 cup	orange juice

Add fruit juice to attain the desired consistency, perfect for sipping through a straw.

Serve with a bagel or a *Breakfast in a Cookie* (page 48) for a complete meal or snack.

EXCHANGE VALUES

— Starch	— Meat	— Veg.	1 Fruit	1/2 Milk	— Fat

Nutrition information for — 1-1/4 cup serving   **Preparation Time — 3 min.**

Calories 125	Fat .... < 1 g	Fiber .... 3 g	Sodium .... 34 mg	Total Carbohydrate .... 27 g
Calories from Fat 6%	Saturated Fat .... < 1 g	Cholesterol .... 1 mg	Protein .... 4 g	Sugars .... 21 g

Why go to the effort to make *Homemade Turkey Sausage?*

Regular Pork Sausage .... 20-24 grams of fat/serving .... 75-84% of calories from fat

Commercial Turkey Sausage .... 8-11 grams of fat/serving .... 60-70% of calories from fat

Homemade Turkey Sausage .... 1 gram of fat/serving .... 7% of calories from fat

And it's more than just for breakfast...

This homemade turkey sausage is called for in the following recipes: *Scrambled Omelette, Herbed Italian Sausage over Pasta* and *Hot & Spicy Pizza with Sausage.* So make some up for the freezer today!

Money saving tip!

Watch for turkey breast to go on sale. Skin it, bone it and grind it yourself for delicious turkey sausage—the guilt-free way!

Homemade Turkey Sausage

Since truly lowfat sausage is so hard to find, here's one you can make yourself. This sausage is rock bottom low in fat and delicious. It's easy to make and you can enjoy it for months to come. The larger recipe makes enough to serve sausage every Sunday morning for a family of 4 for 3 months!

MAKES 16 OR
48 2-OUNCE
PATTIES

HOMEMADE TURKEY SAUSAGE
SCRAMBLED EGGS
TOAST

For 16	For 48	
2 lbs	6 lbs	extra lean ground turkey breast*
1 tsp	1 T	black pepper†
1½ tsp	1½ T	sage
1½ tsp	1½ T	thyme
1½ tsp	1½ T	rosemary
¼ tsp	1 tsp	red pepper flakes
¼ tsp	1 tsp	cayenne†
10 grinds	30 grinds	fresh black pepper†
¾ tsp	2 tsp	salt
½ cup	1 cup	applesauce, unsweetened

Make ahead for the freezer!

Mix all ingredients together very thoroughly. Use your hands if necessary.

Stack up (16) or (48) 10" squares of freezer wrap or wax paper.

Divide the sausage into 4 equal quadrants in the bowl.

From each quadrant, make 4 (small batch) or 12 (large batch) 2" size balls. Place each ball in the center of the paper squares.

Fold the square up from the bottom, the sides, then the top. This will flatten the ball into a patty.

Put 4 to 8 patties each in a Ziplock® freezer bag and freeze.

To cook:

Spray a nonstick skillet with cooking spray. Place skillet over medium high heat.

Unwrap frozen patties (no need to thaw) and place on skillet.

Cook patties 3 minutes on each side or until they are no longer pink.

Serve with scrambled eggs and toast.

* If grinding turkey yourself, use either cutter for fine or coarse sausage, depending on which you like best.
† Three types of pepper are used to enhance flavor.

EXCHANGE VALUES

— Starch	1 Meat	— Veg.	— Fruit	— Milk	— Fat

Nutrition information for — 1 turkey sausage **Preparation Time — 30 min.**

Calories 25	Fat .... < 1 g	Fiber .... < 1 g	Sodium .... 110 mg	Total Carbohydrate .... < 1 g
Calories from Fat 7%	Saturated Fat .... < 1 g	Cholesterol .... 9 mg	Protein .... 4.5 g	Sugars .... 0 g

But I'm never hungry in the morning!
The mere thought of food makes me nauseous...

As soon as I hear this from a client, I quickly ask about their nighttime nibbling. If you eat at night, very little digestion occurs during sleep. You wake up with a full stomach, so of course you are not going to feel hungry. When you start matching your eating to your metabolism and eat less at night, you will be hungry in the morning.

Whole-Grain Pancakes

While you may think you love the white flour pancakes you grew up with, wait 'til you change over to whole grain. These offer texture without being too grainy. And talk about nutrition packed! A great way to start your day!

2 cups	whole-wheat pastry flour*
1/2 cup	wheat germ (or just use more flour)
2 tsp	baking powder
1 T	sugar

In a medium-size bowl, stir together until baking powder is well distributed.

1	egg
2	egg whites
2 1/2 cups	skim milk or soy milk

Add all at once to the flour and mix just until combined.

Heat griddle over medium-high heat. Spray with nonstick cooking spray. (It should be hot enough so that when you sprinkle drops of water on the surface, they dance.)

Use a 1/4 cup measuring cup to measure and pour the cakes. Turn when bubbles come to the surface and pop, and the edges are slightly dry.

Serve with applesauce or light syrup and fresh fruit.

Makes approximately 18 pancakes. Left-over pancakes can be re-warmed in the microwave the next day, or frozen for another day.

EXCHANGE VALUES

| 2 Starch | 1 Meat | — Veg. | — Fruit | — Milk | — Fat |

* If you don't have whole-wheat pastry flour, you can substitute with 1 cup whole-wheat and 1 cup all-purpose flour.

Nutrition information for — 3 pancakes   **Preparation Time — 40 min.**

| Calories .... 200 | Fat .... 2.5 g | Fiber .... 4 g | Sodium .... 245 mg | Total Carbohydrate .... 35 g |
| Calories from Fat .... 10% | Saturated Fat .... < 1 g | Cholesterol .... 37 mg | Protein .... 12 g | Sugars .... 8 g |

Changing Your Sweet Tooth

It *is* possible for you to change your sweetness acuity. For instance, if you like to pour ¹/₂ cup of syrup on your pancakes, you can gradually reduce the amount. Soon, you are topping pancakes with only fruit. Likewise, if you like 3 teaspoons of sugar on cereal or oatmeal, you can slowly cut back to 1. Sprinkling cinnamon, raisins and other fruits on your cereal sweetens it while adding nutritional value.

Banana-Oat Pancakes

Since we are big fans of pancakes, I thought you'd like both of our favorite recipes. If we have bananas, we make these. If not we make the previous *"Whole-Grain" Pancakes*. Enjoy!

³/₄ cup	dry oats (quick-cooking *or* old fashioned) *or* oatbran
2 cups	skim milk *or* soy milk

Mix these together in a medium size bowl, and let them sit for 5 minutes to give them some extra "soaking" time.

1 cup	whole-wheat pastry flour*
1 T	baking powder

Mix together with a fork in another bowl. Be sure the baking soda is evenly distributed. Add to the soaking oats and stir.

1	egg (*or* 2 egg whites)

Gently mix in.

2	bananas
¹/₄ cup	chopped walnuts (optional)

Slice bananas very thin. Fold with nuts into the batter.

Heat griddle over med-high heat, spray with cooking spray. (It should be hot enough so that when you sprinkle drops of water on the surface, they dance.)

Use ¹/₄ cup of batter for each pancake, cooking over medium heat. After spooning the batter onto the pan, give the pan a quick shake to spread the batter out slightly. Cook for about 2 minutes or until bubbles appear on the surface. Flip the pancakes and cook for another minute or so.

Serve with reduced calorie syrup, fruit spread or applesauce on top, and fresh cantaloupe or berries. Makes approximately 12 pancakes.

EXCHANGE VALUES

2 Starch	1 Meat	— Veg.	1 Fruit	— Milk	— Fat

* If you don't have whole-wheat pastry flour, you can substitute with ¹/₂ cup whole-wheat and ¹/₂ cup all-purpose flour.

Nutrition information for — 3 pancakes   **Preparation Time — 45 min.**

Calories 295	Fat .... 7.5 g	Fiber .... 5 g	Sodium .... 445 mg	Total Carbohydrate .... 48 g
Calories from Fat 22%	Saturated Fat .... 1 g	Cholesterol .... 55 mg	Protein .... 13 g	Sugars .... 15 g

Favorite Exercise Videos

Speaking of buns, one of my favorite exercise videos is "8-Minute Buns." These are very effective exercises for firming up. Also available are the "8-Minute Abs," "8-Minute Arms" and "8-Minute Legs," all of which are excellent and worthwhile. Call Collage Video at 1-800-433-6769 to order.

Glazed Cinnamon Nut Buns

	SERVES	MENU
What a delicious holiday treat! You'll especially enjoy serving these for your overnight guests. Waking them up to this winning aroma will make you a favorite host/hostess!	9 (CAN BE DOUBLED)	GLAZED CINNAMON NUT BUNS FRESH FRUIT YOGURT

Set frozen dough out the night before to rise.

1 **frozen honey wheat bread dough** (1 lb.) (unbaked loaf)	**Night before (about 10:00 p.m.)** Remove dough from freezer and plastic bag. Place in a medium-size bowl. Cover with plastic wrap. Set out to thaw and rise overnight.

In the morning (about 7:30 a.m.)
Prepare a clean work surface and dust with flour. *(I use the countertop or a cutting board.)* Punch down dough and roll out until it reaches a 10" x 12" rectangle.

3 T **light corn syrup***	Evenly spread across dough.

Recipe continued on next page.

* **1 T of light margarine can be substituted.**

What's your secret to fitness?

"As a mother of 3 (all under the age of 6) you can guess, time to myself is a rarity. What works for me is to work-out before the kids wake up. Five mornings each week, I'm up at 6:30 a.m. and on my stepper by 6:40. At 7:00 I change to my treadmill. At 7:20 I cool down and do 100 sit-ups. At 7:30 I'm in the shower. (If any child wakes up early, my husband knows he's on duty). I am both physically and mentally prepared for my children when my husband leaves for work and they wake up by 8:00."

—DIANE PETERSEN, 35
Attaining and maintaining
her ideal weight
(and flat stomach!),
despite 3 C-sections.
Wow!

Glazed Cinnamon Nut Buns (Con't.)

3 T	sugar
1½ tsp	cinnamon
¼ cup	chopped almonds, pecans

Preheat oven to 350°.

½ cup | powdered sugar
2½ tsp | skim milk
¼ tsp | vanilla

Mix together in a 1 cup measuring cup and sprinkle across dough.

Begin rolling, starting on the long side, to form a long cylinder. Pinch the seams together to seal.

Spray an 8" x 8" baking dish with nonstick spray.

Cut roll into 9 equal slices and place in baking dish with spirals facing up and sides touching.

Cover the rolls and allow to sit on top of the stove for 45 minutes to 1 hour while the oven preheats to 350°. The warmth of the oven will help facilitate the 2nd rise. *(I use this time to grab a shower!)*

About 8:45 or 9:00 a.m.

Place in oven to bake 15 to 17 minutes.

Meanwhile… slice fresh fruit, set out yogurt, juice & coffee.

Cool the rolls 5 minutes before removing them from the pan.

Mix together the glaze in a small cup.

Transfer rolls to a serving platter. Drizzle with glaze.

About 9:15 a.m.

Serve with yogurt and fresh fruit, and watch your guests' eyes pop!!

EXCHANGE VALUES

2.5 Starch — Meat — Veg. — Fruit — Milk — Fat

Nutrition information for — 1 Cinnamon Nut Bun			Preparation Time — 30 min.	Oven Time — 15-17 min.
Calories 210	Fat .... 4 g	Fiber .... 2.5 g	Sodium .... 290 mg	Total Carbohydrate .... 40 g
Calories from Fat 16%	Saturated Fat .... < 1 g	Cholesterol .... < 1 mg	Protein .... 7 g	Sugars .... 15 g

This sleepy head's goof-proof method of getting up early to exercise:

1. The night before, I lay out exercise clothes in the bathroom. (Not beside the bed; that NEVER worked!) I also lay out clothing appropriate for both indoor and outdoor temperatures. (You know how plans may change, depending upon what the morning brings).

2. I set my alarm beside my bed for 5:55 a.m., and a second alarm in the bathroom for 6:00 am. (The first alarm warns me before I actually have to get up). The screaming bathroom alarm is my insurance to be up by 6:00 am. And there, low and behold, are my exercise clothes, waiting for me!

3. While brushing my teeth, I focus on how good it feels to get my workout in before work, and how disappointed I would be if I don't. (This is key—associating more pleasure with my new habit, and pain to my old).

4. Once downstairs, I drink diluted juice to rehydrate and provide carbohydrates to get me going.

5. Music is my next saving grace. It does wonders for waking me up and energizing me. Out the door I go, or onto my exercise equipment.

While you may still feel groggy the first couple of days, your body will adjust. Be persistent! Before you know it you'll be a die-hard morning exerciser too!

Ambrosia Rice

The next time you find yourself with 2 cups of leftover plain rice, turn it into this! Not only does it make a delicious breakfast, but also a delight for the lunch box, picnic basket, or dessert table.

Great use for leftover cooked rice.

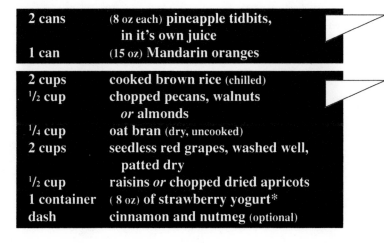

2 cans	(8 oz each) **pineapple tidbits, in it's own juice**
1 can	(15 oz) **Mandarin oranges**

Open cans and drain.

Reserve pineapple juice for another use.

2 cups	**cooked brown rice** (chilled)
1/2 cup	**chopped pecans, walnuts** *or* **almonds**
1/4 cup	**oat bran** (dry, uncooked)
2 cups	**seedless red grapes, washed well, patted dry**
1/2 cup	**raisins** *or* **chopped dried apricots**
1 container	(8 oz) **of strawberry yogurt***
dash	**cinnamon and nutmeg** (optional)

Add and mix gently.

Serve now or later. Will keep in fridge for 2 days.

EXCHANGE VALUES

1 Starch — Meat — Veg. 2 Fruit — Milk 1 Fat

* If all you have is plain yogurt, simply stir in 2 T of strawberry jam or preserves to 1 cup of plain yogurt. Other flavors like raspberry and peach work great as well.

Nutrition information for — 1 cup

Preparation Time — 10 min.

Calories 240	Fat .... 6 g	Fiber .... 3 g	Sodium .... 20 mg	Total Carbohydrate .... 44 g
Calories from Fat 21%	Saturated Fat .... < 1 g	Cholesterol .... 0 mg	Protein .... 4.5 g	Sugars .... 29 g

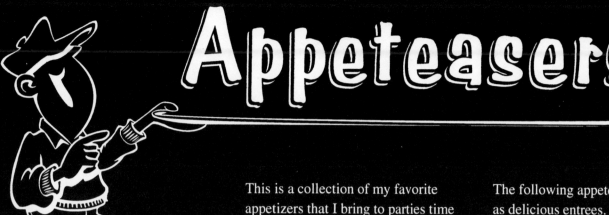

Appeteasers

You're invited over to friends on Friday night. Great! You've been asked to bring an appetizer. Hmmm! What should you bring? The pressure can be quite nerve racking to bring something everyone will like, and that you'll be proud of. You want it to be attractive, delicious, unsuspectingly healthy, and above all, FAST. Wonder no more; it's all right here!

This is a collection of my favorite appetizers that I bring to parties time and time again. No more shuffling through mounds of recipes to find something tasty and easy, just thumb through these. *That's* a time saver in itself! And if you've used the *"Lickety-Split"* grocery list, you have all the ingredients you need.

Keep in mind these other recipes, which also make great appeteasers. There is a special note on the recipes, as well as I've listed them here.

- *Guiltless Nachos Supreme* (15-Minute Meals, page 87)
- *Shrimp Pizza* (Pizza page 142) or any of the pizzas

The following appeteasers can be made as delicious entrees. There is a special note on the recipes as well as I've listed them here:

- *Benito Bean Dip* (for burritos)
- *7-Layer Bean Dip*
- *Marinated Sesame Chicken Kabobs*
- *Simple Tofu Bites* (to stuff pitas or top salads)
- *Oklahoma Bean Dip* (to stuff pitas or top salads)
- *Herbed Salmon Spread* (to make sandwiches)

Enjoy these appeteasers, they are fast, fun and tasty!

Food Processor Cleaning Tip

When processing dips, spreads or cheese-cake batter that clings to the metal blade, try this cleaning tip:

1. Scrape most of the food out of the work-bowl with a rubber spatula, leaving the blade in place.

2. Put the bowl, with the blade, back in place on the base. Cover and process for about 2 seconds.

The excess food will spin off, leaving a clean blade!

Benito Bean Dip

My husband makes this up almost as soon as we run out. Also perfect for making *Benito Bean Burritos* and *Chicken and Bean Enchiladas*.

A favorite at parties!

3	**green onions** (optional)

5 minutes before serving:

Chop in the food processor.

1 jar	**(48 oz) pinto beans, rinsed and drained**
1 cup	**salsa**
¹/₂ tsp	**cumin *or* chili powder** (optional)

Add to processor and blend thoroughly.

Serve at room temperature or slightly chilled.

Serve with *Baked Tostitos®* or *Bagel Chips* (page 62).

EXCHANGE VALUES

2 Starch — Meat — Veg. — Fruit — Milk — Fat

Nutrition information for — 1/3 cup dip with 10 baked corn chips   Preparation Time — 5 min.

Calories 180	Fat .... 1 g	Fiber .... 10 g	Sodium .... 500 mg	Total Carbohydrate ....37 g
Calories from Fat 5%	Saturated Fat .... 0 g	Cholesterol .... 0 mg	Protein ....7 g	Sugars ....1 g

Party Survival Tip #1: Plan ahead

Eat a low-fat breakfast and lunch to save-up
a few extra fat grams to spend at the party.
However, do NOT arrive at the party
overly hungry either! In fact, eating a
small snack before you go is a good idea.

7-Layer Bean Dip

Thanks to our neighbors, Dan & Karen Hettel, you can make this popular party appetizer which has been a hit at many of our get-togethers. It's both attractive and delicious!

Also makes a delicious, yet healthy, Friday night meal!

2 cups	*Benito Bean Dip* (see previous recipe)

3	green onions, chopped
2 cups	shredded lettuce
1	green pepper, seeded and chopped
2	tomatoes, chopped
4 oz	reduced-fat shredded cheddar cheese
15 slices	black olives (optional)

1 large bag	baked tortilla chips (*Tostitos®*)

20 minutes before serving:

Spread this mixture all across a large decorative serving platter.

Layer on in the order listed.

Open chips, it's party time!

EXCHANGE VALUES

2 Starch	— Meat	— Veg.	— Fruit	— Milk	— Fat

Nutrition information for — approximately 1/4 cup of dip with 10 baked corn chips   Preparation Time — 20 min.

Calories 160	Fat .... 3 g	Fiber .... 5 g	Sodium .... 365 mg	Total Carbohydrate ....30 g
Calories from Fat 14%	Saturated Fat .... < 1 g	Cholesterol .... 5 mg	Protein .... 6 g	Sugars ....1 g

Party Survival Tip #2:
Include exercise before you go

Let's face it, parties generally mean
a few more calories than you usually eat.
Overindulge on a day you don't exercise
and your fat cells will grow all night long!
To prevent this from happening, be sure to
exercise before you go.

Oklahoma Bean Dip

My thanks to Gloria Edwards for this tasty recipe that has become a regular at our family get togethers. Great as dip with *Baked Tostitos*®, rolled up in a flour tortilla or stuffed into a pita pocket for a quick sandwich. For a real change, try this served on top of tossed salad. You won't need dressing, since it's already in it!

Also makes a quick meal!

1 can	(14 oz.) **black-eyed peas**
2 cans	(15½ oz) **garbanzo beans**

2 or more hours before serving:

Drain and rinse. Place in a medium size bowl.

2 medium	**tomatoes**
4	**green onions**
2 cloves	**garlic**
2	**jalapeno peppers** (optional)
½ cup	**fresh parsley**

Chop and place in bowl.

1 bottle	(8 oz) **lite** *or* **fat-free Italian dressing**
1 tsp	**oregano**

Add to mix.

Mix all ingredients well.

Let stand for 2 hours or more before serving. This will keep for 5 days in your refrigerator.

Just before serving:

1 bag	**baked tortilla chips** (*Tostitos*®)

Toss beans gently and serve with chips.

EXCHANGE VALUES

3 Starch	— Meat	— Veg.	— Fruit	— Milk	— Fat

Nutrition information for — approximately 1/2 cup of dip with 10 baked corn chips		Preparation Time — 12 min.	
Calories 215	Fat .... 3 g	Fiber .... 7 g	Sodium .... 665 mg	Total Carbohydrate ....42 g
Calories from Fat 13%	Saturated Fat .... < 1 g	Cholesterol .... < 1 mg	Protein .... 7 g	Sugars .... 5 g

Party Survival Tip #3:
Bring a low-fat dish

In addition to picking a recipe from this chapter, a vegetable tray or a platter of sliced fruit are also great ideas. My favorite quick fruit dip is lemon yogurt. You can mix it up yourself, using $1/2$ tsp. of lemon extract and $1^1/_2$ T of sugar per 8 ozs. of plain non-fat yogurt. For a vegetable dip, I simply use bottled low-fat or fat-free Ranch dressing.

Herbed Salmon Spread

This makes an excellent party appetizer. Serve inside a hollowed out loaf of round pumpernickle bread and eat with the bread cubes. This is also wonderful served with bagel or pita chips, or crackers. Try it as a lunchtime sandwich spread!

2 cups	plain non-fat yogurt

10 to 16 hours before serving:

Line a strainer with a paper coffee filter or cheesecloth. Place over a bowl. Spoon yogurt onto coffee filter, cover and refrigerate for 10 to 16 hours.

Yogurt will now be thick. Discard the collected liquid beneath or use it in soups or breads. Remove yogurt from the filter and place in a small bowl.

1 can	(15 oz) **red** *or* **pink salmon packed in water, drained**
1 T	*Miracle Whip*® **Light**
1 T	**fresh parsley, chopped**
1 T	**green onion, tops and bottoms, chopped**
¼ tsp	**dill**
¼ tsp	**thyme**

Gently mix into yogurt. Serve now or refrigerate 4 hours before serving.

Serve with *Bagel Chips* (page 62).

Note: If "water puddles" appear after the dip has sat awhile, simply stir.

EXCHANGE VALUES

1 Starch	1 Meat	— Veg.	— Fruit	— Milk	— Fat

Nutrition information for — approximately 4 T spread on 4 *Bagel Chips*			Preparation Time — 12 min.	
Calories 140	Fat .... 4 g	Fiber .... .5 g	Sodium .... 260 mg	Total Carbohydrate .... 16 g
Calories from Fat 23%	Saturated Fat .... < 1 g	Cholesterol .... 24 mg	Protein .... 12 g	Sugars .... 2 g

Party Survival Tip #4: Use a plate

One thing that puts on weight, is eating more than you're aware of. Anytime you nibble on things directly from the bowl, you can end up eating more than if you put all the food on a plate. Therefore, **make a rule for yourself: everything goes on a plate.** Make it a small plate for even better results!

Holiday Crab Dip

So simple and delicious yet very low in fat and calories.
Serve with homemade bagel chips or whole-wheat crackers.

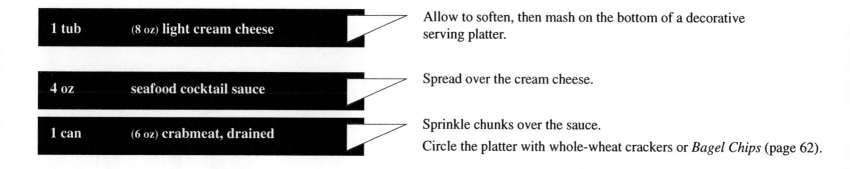

1 tub	(8 oz) **light cream cheese**	Allow to soften, then mash on the bottom of a decorative serving platter.
4 oz	**seafood cocktail sauce**	Spread over the cream cheese.
1 can	(6 oz) **crabmeat, drained**	Sprinkle chunks over the sauce. Circle the platter with whole-wheat crackers or *Bagel Chips* (page 62).

EXCHANGE VALUES

| 1.5 Starch | 1 Meat | — Veg. | — Fruit | — Milk | — Fat |

Nutrition information for — approximately 4 T of dip and 4 *Bagel Chips*   Preparation Time — 5 min.

| Calories .... 195 | Fat .... 5.5 g | Fiber .... 1 g | Sodium .... 590 mg | Total Carbohydrate .... 24 g |
| Calories from Fat .... 26% | Saturated Fat .... 3 g | Cholesterol .... 35 mg | Protein .... 10 g | Sugars .... 4 g |

Party Survival Tip #5: Put foods to the "pinch, slip and shine" test

One way to scout out fat is to look and do the pinch test for its "slip and shine." The following are appetizers that will undoubtedly give you a positive reading on that very test, therefore alerting you to avoid them:

- Egg rolls

- Buttery crackers

- Potato chips

- Pigs-in-a-blanket

- Chicken wings

- Meatballs

- Anything wrapped in bacon

These bagel chips pass the test with no sign of "slip and shine." On the contrary, a bag of commercial bagel chips has enough "slip" to shine several pairs of shoes!

Bagel Chips

Looking for a snack that's a hit? These are absolutely terrific served with any dip, but most importantly, *Herbed Salmon Spread, Holiday Crab Dip* or *Benito Bean Dip.* Also makes a delicious "road trip" munchie all by itself.

Preheat oven to 350°.

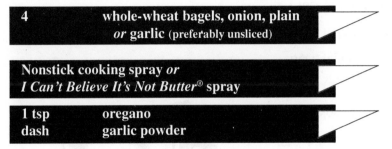

4	**whole-wheat bagels, onion, plain** *or* **garlic** (preferably unsliced)

Using a sharp serrated knife, slice bagel vertically (from top to bottom) into very thin slices. Arrange in single layer on baking sheet.

Nonstick cooking spray *or* ***I Can't Believe It's Not Butter*® spray**

Lightly spray bagel slices.

1 tsp	**oregano**
dash	**garlic powder**

Sprinkle on bagel slices.

Bake for 12 minutes.

Let cool and enjoy! Store in an airtight container for up to 1 week.

EXCHANGE VALUES

1 Starch	— Meat	— Veg.	— Fruit	— Milk	— Fat

Nutrition information for — approximately 4 *Bagel Chips*   **Preparation Time — 20 min.**   **Oven Time — 12 min.**

Calories 95	Fat .... .5 g	Fiber .... 1 g	Sodium .... 190 mg	Total Carbohydrate .... 19 g
Calories from Fat 5%	Saturated Fat .... 0 g	Cholesterol .... 0 mg	Protein .... 4 g	Sugars .... 0 g

Party Survival Tip #6:
Avoid drinking all your calories

"But I hardly ate a thing all holiday season!
How did I gain weight?"

Think before you drink:

Egg Nog (4 oz.) 355 calories

Wine (3 oz.) 85 calories

Beer, regular (12 oz.) 150 calories

Beer, light (12 oz.) 100 calories

Cider (12 oz.) 180 calories

Fruit punch (12 oz.) 180 calories

Piña colada (6 oz.) 325 calories

Opt for: club soda or sparkling water to
dilute punch or fruit juice, mineral water,
low-calorie soda or diet tonic water.

Spinach Dip in Pumpernickel

Here's that delicious dip that is always a hit at parties, minus the hit on your hips! Don't tell anyone it's lowfat; they'll never guess on their own.

Also good with rye bread.

1½ cups	plain non-fat yogurt *or* light sour cream
1 cup	*Miracle Whip*® **Light**
1 pkg	**dried vegetable soup mix** *(Knorr or Mrs. Grass)*

3 hours before serving:

Mix together so the dried soup can begin rehydrating.

3 pkg	(10 oz each) **frozen chopped spinach**

Thaw the spinach in the microwave. Squeeze out all excess water. Stir into mixture.

1 can	(8 oz) **sliced water chestnuts, drained**

Chop into small pieces. Stir into mixture. For best results, refrigerate 3 hours before filling the pumpernickel loaf and serving.

Just before serving:

1 large	**round loaf of pumpernickel bread***

Using a knife, hollow out a large hole. Fill the hole with dip. Cube the bread you've removed to serve on the side for dipping. When the cubes are gone, invite guests to tear bread from the "bowl".

EXCHANGE VALUES

1 Starch	— Meat	2 Veg.	— Fruit	— Milk	1 Fat

* If you can't find a large round unsliced loaf of pumpernickel bread, simply buy sliced pumpernickel, cube it and serve with the dip.

Nutrition information for — 4 T of dip on 6 cubes of bread (or 1 slice of bread) Preparation Time — 30 min.

Calories 160	Fat .... 4 g	Fiber .... 4.6 g	Sodium .... 580 mg	Total Carbohydrate .... 26 g
Calories from Fat 23%	Saturated Fat .... < 1 g	Cholesterol .... < 1 mg	Protein .... 6 g	Sugars .... 4 g

Party Survival Tip #7:
Mingle AWAY from the food

Standing beside a big bowl of cashews or Spanish peanuts can really throw a monkey wrench into your weight loss efforts. Think I'm kidding? Just try to stand or sit near an enticing bowl of nuts and NOT unconsciously eat a little handful here, another handful there. Although you swear it wasn't much, it was an unconscious downing of 10 grams of fat per handful!

Suggestion:

Take out 5 whole cashews (equivalent to 5 grams of fat) and line them up on your napkin or plate. Enjoy them one-by-one, with lots of time in between. Take a break and enjoy other foods like raw vegetables and fruit. Repeat with 5 more if you really want them. Decide that you're finished and move away from them!

South of the Border Roll-ups

Thanks to my neighbor Suzy Crossley for the recipe to this popular appetizer. It has been a hit at many neighborhood parties.

16 (4 PINWHEEL BITES EACH)

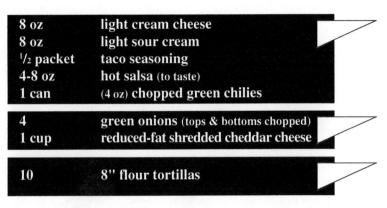

8 oz	light cream cheese
8 oz	light sour cream
1/2 packet	taco seasoning
4-8 oz	hot salsa (to taste)
1 can	(4 oz) chopped green chilies

4	green onions (tops & bottoms chopped)
1 cup	reduced-fat shredded cheddar cheese

10	8" flour tortillas

4 hours before serving:

Mix together in a medium size bowl.

Gently stir in.

Lay out 5 tortillas at a time. Using 1/2 the cheese mixture, divide and spread evenly across the 5 tortillas. Roll up creating spirals inside. Repeat with remaining 5 tortillas.

Lightly dampen 10 sheets of paper towel. Wrap each roll in one. Refrigerate 3 to 4 hours.

Just before serving:

Unwrap each roll and slice 1" apart.

Arrange on decorative platter.

EXCHANGE VALUES

1 Starch	1 Meat	— Veg.	— Fruit	— Milk	— Fat

Nutrition information for — 4 pinwheel bites			Preparation Time — 30 min.	
Calories 142	Fat ....6 g	Fiber ....1.7 g	Sodium ....655 mg	Total Carbohydrate ....15 g
Calories from Fat 35%	Saturated Fat ....3 g	Cholesterol ....14 mg	Protein ....8 g	Sugars ....4 g

Party Survival Tip #8:
Keep your focus away from the food

While good food is certainly an important part of an enjoyable party, be sure you keep it in perspective. Be sure to appreciate the other great things: socializing, the beautiful decorations, the music, games and activities.

Why tofu?

See page 83 to find out!

Simple Tofu Bites

Serve these at your next party. When your guests ask what these delicious little cheese chunks are, watch their jaws drop when you tell them it's tofu!

Use as meatslices for sandwiches or sprinkle the chunks on a tossed salad.

16 oz	firm tofu

2 or more hours before serving:

Slice the tofu into small bite size chunks, or into ⅛" "lunchmeat" slices for sandwiches.

2 T	soy sauce, reduced-sodium *or* Tamari sauce
½ tsp	low-sodium *Spike®* or *Mrs. Dash®* seasoning mix

Mix the soy or Tamari sauce with the seasoning. Marinate the tofu chunks in the mixture for 2 or more hours.

Preheat oven to 425°.

45 minutes before serving:

When marinating time is almost up, heat oven to 425°. Spray a nonstick baking sheet with cooking spray. Place the tofu on the baking sheet. Bake 30 minutes. Tofu should become slightly browned.

Line platter with red tipped lettuce leaves and layer on the chunks. Stab chunks with toothpicks and serve hot or cold.

Note: This simple marinade works great with chicken too.

EXCHANGE VALUES

— Starch	1 Meat	— Veg.	— Fruit	— Milk	— Fat

Nutrition information for — approximately 8 chunks			Preparation Time — 5 min.	Oven Time — 30 min.
Calories 75	Fat .... 3 g	Fiber .... not available	Sodium .... 310 mg	Total Carbohydrate .... 4 g
Calories from Fat 37%	Saturated Fat .... 0 g	Cholesterol .... 0 mg	Protein .... 9 g	Sugars .... 1 g

Party Survival Tip #9: Stop Eating Early

Even if you stay late, decide in your mind *when* you will quit eating. This strategy can do wonders to prevent that continuous "just because it's there" munching, saving you hundreds of calories.

Tzatziki & Vegetables

My thanks to Carol Brickenden and Stacy Rafalko for this simple and delicious dip for vegetables. It is also the traditional Greek sauce used in pita sandwiches. Try using this instead of butter or mayonnaise in a sandwich.

12 to 24 hours before serving:

Line a strainer with a paper coffee filter or cheesecloth. Place over a bowl. Spoon yogurt onto coffee filter, cover and refrigerate for 12 to 24 hours.

Yogurt will now be thick. Discard the collected liquid beneath or use it in soups or breads. Remove yogurt from the filter and place in a small bowl.

1 hour before serving:

Mix into yogurt.

Serve with a variety of fresh vegetables like: fresh green beans (lightly steamed), green, red or yellow pepper, carrots, celery, zucchini, yellow squash, tomatoes, cucumbers, radishes, broccoli and cauliflower. Also delicious with pita triangles and bagel chips.

2 cups	plain non-fat yogurt
1/2	cucumber, peeled, seeded & shredded
2 large	cloves of garlic, minced
1/2 tsp	dill* (dried)
1/4 tsp	salt
2 tsp	lemon juice
1 tsp	olive oil

EXCHANGE VALUES

— Starch	— Meat	— Veg.	— Fruit	.5 Milk	— Fat

* Can use 1 tsp of fresh dill instead.

Nutrition information for — approximately 4 T			Preparation Time — 8 min.	
Calories 40	Fat .... < 1	Fiber .... < 1	Sodium .... 115 mg	Total Carbohydrate .... 5 g
Calories from Fat 15%	Saturated Fat .... < 1	Cholesterol .... 1 mg	Protein .... 3 g	Sugars .... 3 g

Party Survival Tip #10:
No matter what, stay positive

Even if you did overdo it at the party, keep
things in perspective. You do not need to
be "perfect" all the time, and one event
does not make you an overweight person,
or give you high cholesterol. Say "It's no
big deal", and start your next day back on
your healthy fitness regime.

Marinated Sesame Chicken Kabobs

Here's a great way to add a lean protein source to your finger-food party menu. Festive, delicious and easy to eat, your guests will love them!

Preheat BBQ grill or oven broiler.
Position oven rack 6 inches from broiler.

¼ cup	Tamari *or* soy sauce (reduced-sodium)
1 tsp	sesame oil
1 T	firmly packed brown sugar
½ tsp	ginger (fresh grated is best)
8 grinds	fresh ground pepper
¼ tsp	minced garlic
2 T	sesame seeds

6	skinless, boneless, chicken breast (halves)

Optional additions
Whole mushrooms, green & red pepper chunks, onion wedges, cherry tomatoes, pineapple chunks

Kids' Favorite

5 hours before serving or night before:

Mix together in a large bowl for marinating.

Slice the chicken into small 2" x ½" strips. Thoroughly coat with marinade, cover and refrigerate for 5 hours or overnight.

If using these, mix with the chicken and marinate a few minutes before assembling (over-exposure to the salty marinade causes vegetables to "wilt.")

Using 6" bamboo skewers for appetizers* and 12" for dinner entrees, begin assembling K-bobs. Pierce 1 end of the chicken strip, then hook it around and pierce the other end. Or pierce the whole strip lengthwise (use a weaving motion if desired). Alternate with the colorful vegetables if using.

Broil or grill 6 to 8 minutes or until chicken is fully cooked.

Serve warm or cold on a lined tray of red tipped lettuce leaves.

* Simply cut 12" skewers in ½.

EXCHANGE VALUES

— Starch	2 Meat	— Veg.	— Fruit	— Milk	— Fat

Nutrition information for — (2) 6-inch skewers (without optionals)			Preparation Time — 40 min.	
Calories 85	Fat .... 2 g	Fiber .... < 1 g	Sodium .... 217 mg	Total Carbohydrate .... 2 g
Calories from Fat 20%	Saturated Fat .... < 1 g	Cholesterol .... 33 mg	Protein .... 14 g	Sugars .... 2 g

1-Minute Mini-Meals

We've all been there. It's 6:50 p.m., and you're walking in the door. You have a 7:00 meeting to go to and it takes 5 minutes to get there. You have 5 minutes, so frantically you scrounge through the fridge and cupboards for anything to eat. The only thing you're thinking is "FOOD NOW!"

There's no time for cooking anything, you'll just have to "grab." Is there something you can throw together in 1 minute, that suffices as a meal and happens to be healthy *and* taste good? In the past, a $^1/_2$ a bag of *Doritos*® would have done the trick. But not anymore! Assuming you've shopped using the *Lickety-Split* grocery list, you're in business to make ANY of these tasty and "good for you" 1-Minute Mini-Meals!

True or False?

"Popcorn should be reserved as a snack and a snack only. It would be unhealthy to serve popcorn as the grain in your meal."

Answer: FALSE!

Popcorn is corn and corn is a healthy contribution to a meal, right? Corn is actually a grain (sorry, not a vegetable) and grain or starch should be a major part of every meal. Who says potatoes, rice, pasta and bread are the only grains allowed at meal time? As long as your popcorn is healthfully prepared (including the truly low-fat versions of microwave popcorn), it's fine to include popcorn in a meal. My personal combination favorites are beans and popcorn, and soup and popcorn!

Quick Nachos

Spread 20 *Baked Tostitos®* on a microwave safe plate.

Sprinkle with ¼ cup of reduced fat shredded cheddar cheese.

 Microwave on high 45 to 60 seconds.

Eat with fat-free refried beans and salsa along with baby carrots and fruit juice.

SERVES 1

Quick Quesadilla

Place a flour tortilla on a plate.

Sprinkle with 2 T reduced-fat shredded cheddar cheese.

 Microwave 20 seconds on high.

Meanwhile, chop a tomato for topping. (Salsa may also be used).

 Roll-up and eat.

SERVES 1

Cheese Pita Pizza

Spread 2 T of spaghetti sauce on a pita.

Sprinkle with 2 T reduced-fat shredded mozzarella cheese and 2 tsp Parmesan cheese.

(Add any vegetables you have lying around too!)

 Microwave until cheese is melted.

SERVES 1

Zon's Stress Reliever: Beans and Popcorn

Place a bag of *Orville Redenbacher® Smart Pop* in the microwave on high.

Open a single serving can of *Eden®* flavored beans.

 Eat the beans while waiting for the popcorn.

 Chase beans with ½ a bag of popcorn.

SERVES 1 TO 2

Lovers tip: Prepare separate sleeping quarters for evening to follow.

Beans & Crackers

Open a can of baked beans and eat with crackers.

 Any baked beans are OK, however *Eden®'s* baked beans can't be beat for being the most nutritionally smart. And their single serving size pop-top can is so convenient.

SERVES 1 TO 2

Fiesta Bean Burrito

Spread ½ cup fat-free refried beans and 1 T salsa in a flour tortilla.

 Roll-up and eat.

SERVES 1

Great ideas from people like you!

How do you eat right when your job has you on the road ALL the time?

"Restaurants used to be my downfall, but not anymore. My secret is I no longer look at the menu. That took care of the fried mozzarella sticks and chicken wings staring me in the face. Now, instead of ordering from the menu, I ask the server, 'Can you make me a broiled chicken breast, with lots of steamed vegetables, no butter, some marinara sauce and a baked potato?' No more surprises and it's NEVER too much fat."

—SUE KLOC, 41,
Management Analyst
Celebrating the loss of 20 pounds and
normalization of her high blood pressure
without drugs.

See page 169 for the steps Sue took!

Snappy Sandwich Roll

Spread mustard on 1 flour tortilla or Lavash flat bread.

Add 2 oz of 97% fat-free lunch meat *or* low-fat cheese.

Place in a couple carrots and celery sticks lined up end to end.

 Roll and eat.

SERVES 1

Low-Fat Yogurt & Grapenuts

Pour ⅓ cup of *Grapenuts*® into 8 ozs of flavored yogurt.

 Stir and eat.

Tip: *If all you have is plain yogurt, simply stir in 1 to 2 T of fruit jam or preserves.*

SERVES 1

English Muffin Melt

Toast an English muffin

Lay ½ a slice of low-fat cheese on each ½.

 Microwave 15 seconds.

Add a tomato slice, if you like. Eat with an apple.

SERVES 1

Cottage Cheese & Fruit

Open a can of pineapple, peaches or apricots.

Place fruit over a scoop of low-fat cottage cheese.

 Eat with wheat crackers.

SERVES 2

Applesauce and Cottage Cheese

Place a plop of each side by side.

Sprinkle with cinnamon, if desired.

 Slightly mix together as you eat.

SERVES 1

Easy Cheesy Tomatoes

Open a 14½ oz can of stewed tomatoes.

Pour into a bowl with 1 oz. of reduced-fat shredded mozzarella cheese, 1 tsp. Parmesan cheese and a dash each of oregano and pepper.

 Microwave until hot and cheese is melted.

 Eat with crackers.

SERVES 1 TO 2

Pop Quiz!

Your fruit bin and baskets are typically:

A. Stocked with the season's best selection, replenished at least once if not twice each week.

B. Full after shopping, but empty for days between trips, since it's hard to get to the store.

C. Home to a few apples or oranges, or other fruits with a long shelf life.

D. What bin or drawer?

Correct Answer: A.

With all the anti-aging compounds in fresh fruit, it's hard to name a habit more beneficial to your health than eating 3 to 4 pieces of fruit each day. And in order to eat fruit, you have to BUY fruit. Establish the habit of making a midweek stop at a produce market so you'll always have enough!

P.S. Fruit is fast food!

Pepper Strips and Low-fat Cottage Cheese

Slice 1 red or green pepper.

Pour a puddle of light Thousand Island dressing.

Plop ½ cup of cottage cheese beside that for 2-step dipping.

 Eat with a nectarine, pear or orange.

SERVES 1

Pita Wedges and Veggies Dipped in Hummus

Rinse some fresh broccoli flowerets and baby carrots.
Slice a pita into 8 triangles.

 Dip pita triangles and veggies into hummus and eat.

Note: *You buy the ready-made hummus in a case near the deli-section of your grocery store.*

AN 8 OZ. TUB OF HUMMUS SERVES 2 TO 4

Bagelwich

Slice a bagel and throw on 2 oz of turkey with some mustard.

 Eat with a handful of baby carrots and radishes.

SERVES 1

Sardines and Crackers

Pop open a 3¾ oz can of sardines in mustard sauce.

 Eat with reduced fat *Triscuits*® or *Wheat Thins*® and a handful of baby carrots.

SERVES 1

Garden Lentil Salad and Crackers

Eat salad directly from container with a fork.

 Eat with 6 to 10 crackers.

Note: *You buy this delicious ready-made salad from the deli section of your grocery store. (I like the* Oasis Mediterranean Cuisine's *Garden Lentil Salad).*

SERVES 1 TO 2

Mediterranean Lavash Roll-up

Spread ¼ cup hummus and ½ cup tabouli on a Lavash flat bread (or flour tortilla).

 Roll-up and eat.

Note: *You buy the ready-made hummus and tabouli in a case near the deli-section of your grocery store.*

SERVES 1

Pop Quiz!

Which best describes your vegetable consumption yesterday?

A. Cup of vegetable soup, large stir-fry including peppers, broccoli and carrots

B. Small iceberg salad with tomato fragment, 1/2 cup overcooked green beans

C. Ketchup, pickles and French fries

If you answered anything besides A, you're in big trouble! With all the cancer and heart disease fighting compounds in vegetables, your body needs the help of these protectors to stay disease free. Say yes to a double serving of vegetables at dinner, and munch on raw vegetables at lunch. Your body will thank you with a reduced risk of cataracts, clogged arteries and cancer!

P.S. Raw veggies are fast food!

Turkey Rolls with Potato Chips

Lay out 2 slices of 97% fat-free turkey lunchmeat.

Spread with hot mustard.

Place a couple carrots lined up end to end.

 Roll up and eat.

Chase with 15 *Baked Lay's*® potato chips and a juice box.

SERVES 1

Quick Chicken Sandwich

Open a 10 oz can of cooked chicken.

Mix with 2 to 3 T of *Miracle Whip*® Light and 1 T of Dijon mustard.

 Spread ⅓ of chicken mixture on bread and eat with an apple, pear or nectarine.

SERVES 3

Baked Tostitos® and Spicy Pintos

Pop open a single serving can of *Eden*® *Spicy Pintos* and eat with *Baked Tostitos*®.

 Chase with 5 spoonfuls of applesauce.

SERVES 1

Simple Salad Supper

Pour a bowl full of pre-cleaned salad greens.

Pop open a single-serving can of *Eden*® garbanzo beans.

 Drain and sprinkle on top of salad.

Add a plop of low-fat cottage cheese, a bunch of canned beets and other fresh veggies.

Top with light Thousand Island dressing and croutons.

SERVES 1

String-Cheese Standby

Eat 1 *or* 2 string-cheese pieces with crackers and an apple, orange or pear.

SERVES 1

Salmon Pita Sandwich

Open a 7 oz can of salmon and drain.

Mix with 2 T of *Miracle Whip*® Light. (Smash bones with a fork).

 Stuff into a pita.

Add lettuce and tomato, and eat.

SERVES 2 TO 3

Lickety-Split Meals

Pop Quiz!

Which best describes the high calcium foods you consumed yesterday?

A. Milk on cereal, 6 oz. yogurt and 1 oz. of low-fat cheese on broccoli

B. Cheese on pizza, ice cream

C. No dairy; you avoid it because of allergy or intolerance.

Correct Answer: A.

Calcium is a VERY important anti-aging food. It helps prevent osteoporosis, (weak and porous bones), a common disease of aging. If you answered A, great. If you answered B, the amount of calcium is not only insufficient, but it also contains excessive saturated fat and calories.
C means you just plain need to start taking a calcium supplement. Don't delay. Start doing it now!

Tuna Cracker Sandwiches

Pop open a single serving can of tuna and drain.

 Make cracker sandwiches and eat with a can of low-sodium *V-8®*.

SERVES 1

Left-Over Rice and Veggie Salad

Chop green or red pepper and carrots.

Add to bowl with left-over rice.

Toss with a salad dressing like *Henri's® Private Blend TAS-TEE®* low-fat dressing. This is a coleslaw type, which works great.

ABOUT 1½ CUPS SERVES 1

Hard-Boiled Egg with Crackers

Crack and peel 1 *or* 2 of the eggs you've previously cooked.

 Eat with 8 reduced-fat *Triscuits®* and an apple.

SERVES 1

Tuna in a Pita

Spread 1 T of *Miracle Whip®* Light inside a pita.

Pop open a single serving can of tuna and drain. Stuff into pita.

 Add any vegetables that you have.

SERVES 1

Peanut Butter Rice Cake

Spread 1 T peanut butter thinly on a couple of rice cakes.

 Eat with a banana.

SERVES 1

Corny Chicken Salad

Rinse and drain a 10 oz can of cooked chicken and a 15 oz can of corn.

Flake chicken and toss together in a bowl with 3 T of lite *or* fat-free Italian dressing.

 Eat with widely cut strips of red pepper.

SERVES 2 TO 3

Dashboard Dining Tip

Keep a *Ziplock*® bag full of napkins, plastic forks, spoons and one sharp knife in your car's glove box. You are now in a better position to grab and eat a healthy lunch from a grocery store. (Bye-bye fast food restaurants)! I recommend the following favorites:

- Low-fat deli salads

- Pre-packaged salads like lentil or garbanzo bean

- Bagel with sliced low-fat deli meat

- Yogurt

- Low-fat cottage cheese and low-fat crackers

- Fresh fruit

- Veggies off the salad bar

Quick 2-Bean Salad

Rinse and drain a 15 oz can of kidney beans and a 14½ oz can of green beans in a colander.

Transfer to a bowl and toss with ¼ cup of lite *or* fat-free Italian dressing.

 Eat with crackers.

SERVES 2

Quick Black Bean and Corn Salad

Open a 15 oz can each of black beans and corn.

 Rinse and drain in a colander.

Transfer to a bowl and toss with 2 cups of salsa.

 Eat as a salad, rolled up in a tortilla, or as a dip with *Baked Tostitos®*.

SERVES 2 AS A MAIN MEAL SALAD, *OR*
SERVES 4 AS A TORTILLA ROLL-UP

5-Minute Meals

I t just astounds me how many people go out to eat. "I don't have time to cook" they say. But eating out takes SO MUCH time! Even going through a drive-through takes time. My husband and I firmly believe that the fastest way to get a meal is to make it yourself. The secret is keeping the right ingredients on hand, and of course, use *this* book!

When we want a meal in 5 minutes, we mentally pick from these 3 things:

- **Roll-ups** (bean burrito or a lavash rollup) or
- *Quick Pita Sandwich* or *Pita Pizza* (see Pizza chapter page 135) or
- **Canned beans** (mix with canned corn or tuna)

Once you decide, you'll be eating 5 minutes later!

What is fiber and where do you find it?

Fiber is the portion of plant foods that you can not digest, also known as "roughage." It is not found in any animal foods.

Yes	No
Plant foods	**Animal foods**
Fruits	Chicken
Vegetables	Beef
Grains	Pork
Whole grain flours	Veal
Whole grain baked goods	Fish
Dried beans and peas	Milk
Nuts and seeds	Eggs

Benito Bean Burritos

Burritos without the *refried* beans. Soon to be a household favorite!

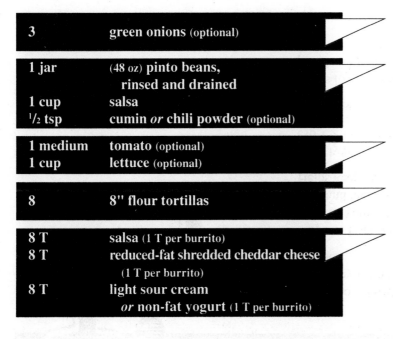

3	green onions (optional)

Chop in the food processor.

1 jar	(48 oz) **pinto beans, rinsed and drained**
1 cup	salsa
½ tsp	cumin *or* chili powder (optional)

Add to processor and blend thoroughly.*

Heat the spread in the microwave for 2 or more minutes.

1 medium	tomato (optional)
1 cup	lettuce (optional)

Rinse and chop for extra toppings, if desired.

8	**8" flour tortillas**

Microwave for about 5 seconds per tortilla.

8 T	salsa (1 T per burrito)
8 T	**reduced-fat shredded cheddar cheese** (1 T per burrito)
8 T	**light sour cream** *or* **non-fat yogurt** (1 T per burrito)

Use as desired for topping your burrito.

Assemble by spreading approximately ¼ cup Benito Spread on tortilla and layer on any additional ingredients you choose. Fold in the ends and roll up.

Slice 2 apples into wedges and place on table with baby carrots.

If you must eat on the run, just roll your burrito up in a paper towel, and take it with you. Don't forget your apples & carrots.

EXCHANGE VALUES

2 Starch	— Meat	1 Veg.	— Fruit	— Milk	— Fat

* This step can be replaced by simply opening a can of fat-free refried beans. My husband and I still prefer the flavor of this old fashion method.

Nutrition information for — 1 burrito

Calories 255	Fat .... 4 g	Fiber .... 14 g	Sodium .... 800 mg	Total Carbohydrate .... 42 g
Calories from Fat 14%	Saturated Fat .... 1.6 g	Cholesterol .... 6 mg	Protein .... 15 g	Sugars .... 4 g

Why is fiber so important?

- Yields no calories! Helps control your weight by filling you up on fewer calories.

- Plays an important role in intestinal health. (Your intestinal tract is 24 feet long and needs to be kept clean!) Helps keep you "regular."

- Greatly reduces your risk of cancer, especially colon cancer.

- Helps lower blood cholesterol.

- Helps lower blood sugar levels for people with diabetes.

Great Northern Tuna Salad Stuffer

Quickly mix this up for a delicious pita pocket stuffer, flour tortilla roll-up, or on top of a tomato or bed of salad greens. Friends will rave!

Keeps in refrigerator for 4 days. Use for lunches all week.

1 large can	(12 oz) water packed tuna	
1 jar	(24 oz) Great Northern beans, rinsed	

Drain tuna, rinse and drain the beans.
Toss together in a medium sized bowl.

¹/₂ tsp	dill
¹/₄ cup	light Thousand Island dressing

Add and mix gently.

Optional:

1	green onion, chopped
¹/₂	red pepper, chopped
¹/₄	cup fresh parsley, chopped

Add if you have time.

Serve ³/₄ cup stuffed into 2 pita halves, rolled in a flour tortilla, on top of a tomato or salad greens, or simply eat with crackers.

EXCHANGE VALUES

1 Starch	2 Meat	1 Veg.	— Fruit	— Milk	— Fat

Nutrition information for — 3/4 cup including the optional veggies

Calories 185	Fat .... 2 g	Fiber .... 8 g	Sodium .... 535 mg	Total Carbohydrate ....21 g
Calories from Fat 10%	Saturated Fat .... .2 g	Cholesterol .... 18 mg	Protein .... 21 g	Sugars ....0 g

How much fiber do you need?

The recommended intake is 20-30 (or more) grams per day.

On the average, people eat only 11 grams of fiber per day, with some people eating even less than that. (YIKES!)

Almond Chicken Salad

This makes a very special luncheon dish served in a 1/2 of a cantaloupe.
It's also great for sprucing up a brown bag lunch.

1 can	(8 oz) **pineapple tidbits** (in it's own juice)	Open cans and drain. Reserve pineapple juice for another use.
1 can	(15 oz) **Mandarin oranges***	
2 cups	**diced cooked chicken *or* turkey *or* 1 can (10 oz) white chicken rinsed & drained**	Place in a medium bowl with the fruit.
¼ cup	*Miracle Whip*® **Light**	Mix together in a 2 cup measuring cup. Fold into fruit and chicken.
¼ cup	**non-fat plain yogurt**	
¼ cup	**slivered almonds**	Gently mix in.

Use to make a sandwich, stuff a pita, top lettuce greens
or a cantaloupe ½.

EXCHANGE VALUES

— Starch	3 Meat	— Veg.	1.5 Fruit	— Milk	— Fat

*** Try substituting 1 cup of grape halves for variety.**

Nutrition information for — approximately 1 cup

| Calories .... 315 | Fat .... 10 g | Fiber .... 1.4 g | Sodium .... 195 mg | Total Carbohydrate .... 25 g |
| Calories from Fat .... 30% | Saturated Fat .... 1.3 g | Cholesterol .... 72 mg | Protein .... 30 g | Sugars .... 22 g |

How can you get all 20-30 grams of fiber each day?

Think "10 + 10 + 10" .... **To achieve this each day, EAT:**

10 grams from fruit .... 3 or more pieces of fruit

10 grams from vegetables .... 3 or more ½ cup servings of vegetables

10 grams from whole grains .... 4 or more servings of whole grain bread, cereals, brown rice, oatmeal, etc.

Also include beans on a weekly basis:

Pinto, kidney, garbanzo, navy, lima beans, and lots of peas and corn.

This *Black Bean and Corn Salad* at 7 grams of fiber per serving helps get you to your daily goal of 20-30 grams in a hurry!

Black Bean & Corn Salad

This is so simple, it's almost obscene! Thanks to Karen Pender for this incredibly simple and delicious dish! She brought it to a 4th of July potluck picnic where so many of us fell in love with it.

2 cups	**frozen corn** *or* **1 can** (16 oz) **corn**

Place in a strainer to drain. If using frozen corn, run warm water over it to thaw. Transfer to a medium bowl.

1 can	(16 oz) **black beans**

Rinse in a strainer, then add to bowl.

1 cup	**fresh tomato salsa***

Add to bowl and mix contents gently.

Eat it as a salad, or rolled up in a tortilla as a quick sandwich.

Also makes a wonderful accompaniment for outdoor-grilled chicken or fish.

Optional additions
¹/₂ tsp	cumin
¹/₂ tsp	chili powder
3 dashes	cayenne pepper

EXCHANGE VALUES

2 Starch	— Meat	1 Veg.	— Fruit	— Milk	— Fat

* If you only have canned salsa, try adding some chopped fresh tomatoes and minced parsley for fresh color and flavor.

Nutrition information for — approximately 1 cup

Calories 150	Fat .... .5 g	Fiber .... 7 g	Sodium .... 516 mg	Total Carbohydrate ....35 g
Calories from Fat 2%	Saturated Fat .... < 1 g	Cholesterol .... 0 mg	Protein .... 7 g	Sugars .... 4 g

Why buy Lavash?

1. It's very nutritious since you can buy 100% whole-wheat Lavash bread that has no added fat.

2. It allows you to make a sandwich out of leftover stir-fry or just about anything!

3. It's a nice change from eating "sandwiches" all the time.

4. It allows you to easily include all kinds of vegetables.

5. It's perfect for eating on the run!

Turkey & Hot Mustard Roll-ups

I don't know what we would do without these Lavash breads. Be sure to try this.
A great way to get a meal on the run!

Also an excellent party appetizer.

1	10" Lavash flat bread*
2 T	light cream cheese
2 tsp	Honeycup mustard (*or* to taste) (any spicy mustard will do)
2 oz	home-cooked turkey breast
2	baby carrots, cut into fours lengthwise
¼	cucumber, cut lengthwise
½	tomato, cut into wedges
¼	cup alfalfa sprouts

Lay bread out on flat surface.

Spread across entire bread.

Spread this on top the cream cheese.

Place each in a row side by side.

Get ready to roll! Starting from the edge of a long row, roll it up.
If eating later, wrap in plastic wrap.

To neatly eat as a sandwich peel back a few inches of plastic wrap, eat,
peel some more, eat… you get the idea!

To eat as an appetizer it works best to let them "set" in the refrigerator
for 2 or 3 hours. Then remove the plastic wrap. Slice the rolls, 1 to
1½" apart using a sawing motion.

Serve on a platter garnished with red tipped lettuce or purple kale.
P.S. Make more!

Note: If you use a processed turkey instead of home-made,
the sodium for this sandwich soars to 1,225 mgs!

EXCHANGE VALUES

4 Starch	3 Meat	1 Veg.	— Fruit	— Milk	— Fat

* Find Lavash (sometimes spelled lawash) in the deli section, or bakery section of your
grocery store. It's a large flat bread like a tortilla.

Nutrition information for — 1 entire roll-up

Calories 490	Fat .... 9 g	Fiber .... 5 g	Sodium .... 760 mg	Total Carbohydrate .... 73 g
Calories from Fat 16%	Saturated Fat .... 4 g	Cholesterol .... 62 mg	Protein .... 31 g	Sugars .... 10 g

Go Mediterranean!

The Mediterranean Diet has become increasingly popular, spotlighting the health benefits of legumes, vegetables, olive oil and garlic. Purchasing ready-made hummus and tabouli is a great way to conveniently reap these benefits.

Hummus: Ground chickpeas, sesame seed paste, lemon and garlic. Excellent for dipping with pita bread triangles or crackers.

Tabouli: Bulgur (wheat kernels that have been steamed, dried and crushed), parsley, lemon, olive oil and garlic. Excellent as a side salad or stuffed into a pita or rolled in a lavash.

The combination of hummus and tabouli together in these sandwiches is awesome! You must try it!

Mediterranean Roll-ups

You'll never be saying "Where's the meat?" in this delicious super fast vegetarian sandwich. Just stop by the specialty section of your grocery store deli for prepared Tabouli and Hummus, and a package of Lavash.

Also an excellent party appetizer.

1	10" Lavash flat bread*	Lay bread out on a flat surface.
¼ cup	ready made Hummus (*Oasis* brand)	Pile on each in a long row, side by side.
¼ cup	ready made Tabouli (*Oasis* brand)	
	Romaine lettuce leaves whole *or* chopped (I use the pre-cleaned *Dole Salad Creations*®)	Add generously.
	Alfalfa *or* bean sprouts (optional)	Add as desired.
½	tomato, chopped	

Get ready to roll! Starting from the edge of a long row, roll it up. If eating later, wrap in plastic wrap.

To neatly eat as a sandwich peel back a few inches of plastic wrap, eat, peel some more, eat… you get the idea!

To eat as an appetizer it works best to let them "set" in the refrigerator for 2 or 3 hours. Then remove the plastic wrap. Slice the rolls, 1 to 1½" apart using a sawing motion.

Serve on a platter garnished with red tipped lettuce or purple kale.
P.S. Make more!

EXCHANGE VALUES

5 Starch	1 Meat	1 Veg.	— Fruit	— Milk	— Fat

* Find Lavash (sometimes spelled lawash) in the deli section, or bakery section of your grocery store. It's a large flat bread like a tortilla.

Nutrition information for — 1 entire roll-up

Calories 478	Fat .... 8 g	Fiber .... 10 g	Sodium .... 800 mg	Total Carbohydrate .... 91 g
Calories from Fat 14%	Saturated Fat .... < 1 g	Cholesterol .... 0 g	Protein .... 14 g	Sugars .... 5 g

Test Your Weight Loss IQ:

If you change from drinking 2 cups of 2% milk each day, to drinking 2 cups of ¹/₂% milk each day, you'll lose:

    A. 6 pounds in a year

    B. 10 pounds in a year

    C. 12.5 pounds in a year

Answer: C. 12.5 pounds in a year!

Vegetable & Spinach Dip Roll-ups

Have leftover spinach dip? Here's the perfect way to use it.

Also excellent as a party appetizer.

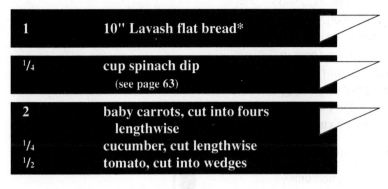

1	**10" Lavash flat bread***
¹/₄	**cup spinach dip** (see page 63)
2	**baby carrots, cut into fours lengthwise**
¹/₄	**cucumber, cut lengthwise**
¹/₂	**tomato, cut into wedges**

Lay bread out on a flat surface.

Spread across entire bread.

Line up the vegetables each in a row, side by side.

Get ready to roll! Starting from the edge of a long row, roll it up. If eating later, wrap in plastic wrap.

To neatly eat as a sandwich peel back a few inches of plastic wrap, eat, peel some more, eat… you get the idea!

To eat as an appetizer it works best to let them "set" in the refrigerator for 2 or 3 hours. Then remove the plastic wrap. Slice the rolls, 1 to 1¹/₂" apart using a sawing motion.

Serve on a platter garnished with red tipped lettuce or purple kale. **P.S. Make more!**

EXCHANGE VALUES

4 Starch — Meat 2 Veg. — Fruit — Milk — Fat

* Find Lavash (sometimes spelled lawash) in the deli section, or bakery section of your grocery store. It's a large flat bread like a tortilla.

Nutrition information for — 1 entire roll-up

Calories 410	Fat .... 6 g	Fiber .... 7 g	Sodium .... 800 mg	Total Carbohydrate .... 80 g
Calories from Fat 12%	Saturated Fat .... < 1 g	Cholesterol .... < 1 mg	Protein .... 13 g	Sugars .... 12 g

What IS tofu?

Tofu is made from soymilk by adding a coagulant and pressing the curds into blocks like cheese. It's high in protein and happens to be the staple meat alternative in Asian countries.

Why should we eat tofu?

Soybeans contain a powerhouse of antioxidants and other disease-fighting agents. Thirty-four studies have shown that soy protein lowers cholesterol by 15% or more. In study after study, consumption of soy foods is associated with lower risk of heart disease, breast and prostate cancers, and osteoporosis.

Eating soy is like taking a sip from the fountain of youth!

More ways to incorporate beneficial soy:

Soy milk on your cereal (I personally like the *EdenSoy® Extra,* both vanilla and original). Try cooking your oatmeal in it. Makes pudding too!

Black soy beans (you can buy these canned and ready to eat from *Eden®*). Rinse and drain, and add to chili or any dish you that would use beans. They are very much like black beans, but black soy beans are incredibly high in the healthful soy compounds.

Tofu (see the recipes in this book).

Commercial soy burgers (these have had most of the beneficial soy compounds removed, however, they are still healthier than eating meat).

Eggless Salad Sandwiches

You can make this great summertime salad with chicken and tofu, or only tofu. Never tried tofu? Combined with the chicken, it's a tasty way to become a tofu believer!

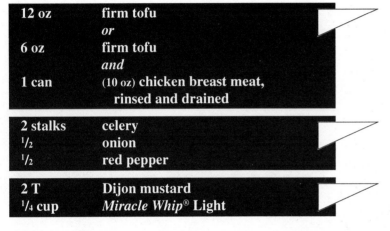

12 oz	**firm tofu**
	or
6 oz	**firm tofu**
	and
1 can	(10 oz) **chicken breast meat, rinsed and drained**

Drain water from tofu. Crumble the tofu with a fork in a medium bowl. If using chicken, add it to the bowl and flake it apart.

2 stalks	**celery**
¹/₂	**onion**
¹/₂	**red pepper**

Chop vegetables. Add them to the bowl and mix.

2 T	**Dijon mustard**
¹/₄ cup	*Miracle Whip*® **Light**

Add to the bowl and mix well.

Serve in a pita pocket or on whole-wheat bread with lettuce and tomatoes. This is also delicious, as a dip for crackers or celery sticks.

EXCHANGE VALUES

— Starch	1 Meat	1 Veg.	— Fruit	— Milk	— Fat

Nutrition information for — approximately 1/2 cup of salad (without bread)

Calories 110	Fat .... 4 g	Fiber .... 1 g	Sodium .... 250 mg	Total Carbohydrate .... 5 g
Calories from Fat 35%	Saturated Fat .... < 1 g	Cholesterol .... 21 mg	Protein .... 12 g	Sugars .... 2 g

15-Minute Meals

It's a quarter to 6 and the family is starved. You were planning on having chicken, but you forgot to thaw it out. Is it still humanly possible to get a hot and satisfying chicken dinner on the table in 15 minutes?

Welcome to 15-Minute Meals! You'll discover how to turn frozen chicken breasts into *Crispy Chicken Dijon* or *Creamy Chicken Dijon over Noodles* all within 15 minutes! Or how about stuffed baked potatoes, sloppy joes, or nachos? They're all here, and you'll know how to get the complete meal on the table in 15 minutes or less. Guaranteed!

Remember: If it takes a bit longer than 15 minutes, refer back to the introduction about how to speedisize your kitchen. To really achieve this kind of efficiency, it's imperative to have every drawer, cupboard and utensil in full cooperation.

Why make the effort to eat less fat?

1. To lower your risk of heart disease

2. To lower your risk of cancer

3. To control your weight

4. To have MORE energy!

Veggie & Cheese Stuffed Baked Potatoes

Here's what we serve most often in our house. It's a real "no-brainer."

1 large	potato

Scrub thoroughly and pierce 3 or 4 times with a fork. Place in microwave on high for 4 to 5 minutes. Make sure it's done by piercing with a fork. Cook more if necessary.

1 cup	frozen California blend broccoli, cauliflower & carrots

Place vegetables in a microwave safe dish. Cover and cook with potato for 6 to 8 minutes on high heat.

Split potato open and top with vegetables (overflowing the spud!)

¼ cup	reduced-fat shredded cheddar cheese

Sprinkle on top and microwave the entire potato for 1 more minute until melted.

Top potato with pepper if desired and serve with a side of cottage cheese, a dollup of plain yogurt or light sour cream, and light canned peaches.

EXCHANGE VALUES

2 Starch	1 Meat	2 Veg.	— Fruit	— Milk	— Fat

Nutrition information for — potato with vegetables and cheese, no toppings

Calories	235	Fat	3 g	Fiber	5 g	Sodium	280 mg	Total Carbohydrate	37 g
Calories from Fat	13%	Saturated Fat	2 g	Cholesterol	9 mg	Protein	14 g	Sugars	1 g

How many fat grams can I have each day?

It is recommended to consume between 30 and 60 grams of fat per day depending on your health needs*.

If you are less active and/or want to lose weight, choose closer to 30 grams.

If you are more active and/or want to maintain weight, choose closer to 60 grams.

* Studies by Dean Ornish, MD, author of *Reversing Heart Disease Without Drugs or Surgery*, suggests that a vegetarian diet as low as 15 grams of fat in combination with exercise and meditation, can reverse heart disease in diseased patients.

Did you know?

Every 5 grams of fat on a label you see = 1 teaspoon of lard or shortening!?!

Some Americans eat over 100 grams of fat per day!

That's almost a $^1/_2$ cup of lard or shortening EACH DAY!

Chicken Dijon Stuffed Baked Potatoes

SERVES	**MENU**
3	STUFFED BAKED POTATOES
	APPLESAUCE

Here's another great way to make a quick meal out of a baked potato. The sour cream replaces the mayonnaise for a perfect complement atop a potato.

3 large   baking potatoes

Scrub thoroughly and pierce each potato 3 or 4 times with a fork. Microwave on high for 8 minutes. Cook more if necessary.

Place a steamer with water on high heat.

1 bunch   asparagus (about 18 spears)
           or broccoli
1   red pepper

Rinse vegetables. Cut off asparagus ends. Slice pepper into long strips. Place all in the steamer, which should be boiling by now. Steam 8 to 10 minutes.

1 can   (10 oz) white chicken meat, drained

Drain and place in a medium-size microwave safe bowl. Flake meat with a fork.

¼ cup   light sour cream *or* non-fat
           plain yogurt
1 T   Dijon mustard
1   green onion, chopped *or* 1 tsp dried
           onion flakes

Add to chicken along with sour cream and mustard. Mix well.

When potatoes are done, microwave the chicken mixture for 1½ to 2 minutes on high.

To serve, cut potatoes in ½, spoon the chicken salad into the middle of the potatoes and top with the steamed vegetables.

Serve with applesauce.

EXCHANGE VALUES

2 Starch	3 Meat	2 Veg.	— Fruit	— Milk	— Fat

Nutrition information for — 1 stuffed baked potato

Calories 300	Fat .... 4.5 g	Fiber .... 4 g	Sodium .... 300 mg	Total Carbohydrate .... 40 g
Calories from Fat 8%	Saturated Fat .... 2 g	Cholesterol .... 48 mg	Protein .... 27 g	Sugars .... 3 g

True or False?

Nachos are a fattening appetizer, and could never pass as a "healthy dinner".

TRUE for most restaurant nachos, FALSE for your own homemade!

Sitting down to a mounding plate of nachos covered with beans, cheese and sour cream sounds like a major binge, right? Not at all, thanks to all the new low-fat foods available. Baked tortilla chips (like *Tostitos*®) can count as a healthful serving of grain. Add vegetables, beans, salsa and non-fat sour cream or yogurt, and you have a *most* delicious, satisfying and completely guilt-free meal!

Compare this to a *restaurant* serving of *Nachos Supreme,* at 800 calories and 55 grams of fat!

Note: To achieve the recommended vegetable quota at dinner, munch on raw vegetables while you're making this up.

Guiltless Nachos Supreme

Here's my favorite Friday night "veg-out" dinner. My husband and I munch on raw carrots, broccoli and cauliflower as we're making this up.

2
DOUBLES &
TRIPLES EASILY

NACHOS
RAW VEGGIES
GRAPES

Also a great party appetizer!

Turn broiler on and keep oven door ajar.

1 T	water
¼ cup	onion *or* 2 green onions, chopped
½ cup	green pepper, chopped
1 cup	pinto *or* black beans (drained, rinsed)
1 tsp	chili powder

Chop vegetables, then sauté all ingredients in a nonstick pan for about 3 minutes.

30	(3 oz) **baked tortilla chips** (*Tostitos®*)

Spread out onto a baking sheet.

Layer sauté over chips.

½ cup	**reduced-fat shredded cheddar cheese**

Sprinkle on top of nachos.

Broil 6" from heating element for 4 to 6 minutes, or until cheese melts and browns slightly.

Play "Macho, Macho Man" by the Village People, dance around and sing, "Nacho, Nacho Man." Throw in a few jumping jacks and sit-ups while you're at it.

¼ cup	salsa
¼ cup	**light sour cream** *or* **non-fat plain yogurt**

Serve on the side for dipping. Fresh grapes make the ideal dessert.

Sodium alert! While 1,145 mg of sodium can work into a day's guideline of 3,000 mg, it is a bit much for other people needing to stay under 2,000. Therefore, to reduce sodium, use *Eden®* brand canned beans (which are low in sodium). Other sodium saving options are fresh (low sodium) salsa and unsalted baked corn tortillas.

EXCHANGE VALUES

4 Starch	2 Meat	2 Veg.	— Fruit	— Milk	— Fat

Nutrition information for — ½ the recipe, 15 chips with salsa and light sour cream

Calories 430	Fat .... 8 g	Fiber .... 15 g	Sodium .... 1,145 mg	Total Carbohydrate .... 70 g
Calories from Fat 16%	Saturated Fat .... 4 g	Cholesterol .... 20 mg	Protein .... 22 g	Sugars .... 5 g

"The Clean-Plate-Club Syndrome"

Try to refrain from asking your children to clean their plates. Insisting they finish their food when their stomachs are full, is teaching them to ignore their innate "obesity fighting" signal. Instead, say to them, "When your stomach tells you you've had enough, you can be excused." Then cover unused portions and refrigerate for the next meal or snack time.

Turkey Joes

These Joes are fast and healthy. You can make your own Sloppy Joe sauce to save on the sodium, but when you need it fast, the can will do.

Kids' Favorite

1 lb.	extra-lean ground turkey breast	Brown in a nonstick skillet.
1	onion, chopped	
1 can	(16 oz) Sloppy Joe sauce (*Manwich®*)	Add to the skillet. Cover and cook over medium high heat and simmer for 3 more minutes.
6	whole-wheat hamburger buns	Ladle $\frac{1}{6}$ of the batch on top of each hamburger bun.

Serve with *Sunshine Carrot-Raisin Salad* (page 173) and applesauce on the side.

EXCHANGE VALUES

2.5 Starch	2 Meat	1 Veg.	— Fruit	— Milk	— Fat

Nutrition information for — 1 Turkey Joe with bun

Calories 275	Fat .... 2.5 g	Fiber .... 4.5 g	Sodium .... 795 mg	Total Carbohydrate .... 40 g
Calories from Fat 8%	Saturated Fat .... < 1 g	Cholesterol .... 36 mg	Protein .... 25 g	Sugars .... 4 g

Buying chicken:
Save yourself time, money and headaches

I've found buying bags of *individually frozen*, skinless, boneless chicken breasts saves a lot of time, money and effort. This product is so convenient because you can reach into the *Ziplock*® bag and grab however many you need. The chicken breasts are a uniform size and thickness. No need to plan ahead; they thaw in minutes on your cutting board. For even quicker results, add to the pan while still frozen. (They will thaw *and* cook in no time). How terrific!

Look for this type of chicken in the freezer section of your grocery store.

Sodium Alert

Check the label and avoid brands containing over 200 mg of sodium per serving. (Sometimes they go overboard injecting with a salt-water solution to promote juiciness.)

Crispy Chicken Dijon

Add this to your "must try" list. It's absolutely terrific!

SERVES | MENU

4

CRISPY CHICKEN DIJON
BAKED SWEET POTATOES
GREEN BEANS AND CARROTS
GRAHAM CRACKER ICE CREAM
SANDWICHES (OPTIONAL)

2 medium	sweet potatoes (or 4 regular potatoes)

Scrub and place in microwave for 12 minutes on high.

| 1 box | (10 oz) frozen green beans, broccoli, or pea pods |
| 1 box | (10 oz) frozen sliced carrots |

Place steamer basket in a pan and add 1" of water. Place over medium-high heat. Add vegetables and cover. When you notice it's boiling, set timer for 8 minutes.

| 1/2 cup | dry bread crumbs, unseasoned |
| 1/4 cup | Dijon mustard |

Take out 2 cereal bowls and place the bread crumbs in one, the mustard in the other.

| 1 T | olive oil |

Heat over medium heat in a non-stick skillet.

| 4 | (4 oz each) boneless skinless chicken breast (halves) |

Dip chicken in mustard, then roll in the crumbs. Brown each side in the skillet 4 to 5 minutes.

If vegetable timer goes off before you're ready, remove from heat and partially remove lid (to allow steam to escape but to still keep them warm.)

Check to see if the chicken is done.

Serve with vegetables and a potato.

EXCHANGE VALUES

2 Starch	4 Meat	2 Veg.	— Fruit	— Milk	— Fat

Nutrition information for — 1 chicken breast half, 1/2 sweet potato, 1 cup vegetables

| Calories .... 380 | Fat .... 8.5 g | Fiber .... 6 g | Sodium .... 360 mg | Total Carbohydrate .... 42 g |
| Calories from Fat .... 20% | Saturated Fat .... 1.7 g | Cholesterol .... 73 mg | Protein .... 32 g | Sugars .... 13 g |

Simple Cutting Tip

Cutting chicken into strips is easy when the chicken is still mostly frozen. Set individually frozen chicken breasts out on your cutting board to thaw for about 5 minutes. A chef's knife (the kind with a big wide blade) works quickly and easily. Be careful, they can be a little slippery!

Creamy Chicken Dijon over Noodles

SERVES | MENU

Unexpected guests? Proudly serve this delicious 15 minute "company food" meal. Guests will rave and family will feel like guests!

4 OR 6

CREAMY CHICKEN DIJON

EGG NOODLES

ASPARAGUS

SLICED TOMATOES & CUCUMBERS

FRESH FRUIT CUP

Place a large kettle full of water on to boil.

For 4	For 6	
1 T	1½ T	olive oil
1 tsp	1½ tsp	minced garlic (2 cloves)
1 lb	1½ lb	skinless, boneless, chicken breast strips

Sauté 7 or 8 minutes until chicken is no longer pink.

8 oz	12 oz	dry egg noodles

Meanwhile… add to boiling water. Set timer for 6 minutes.

1 small	1 large	bunch fresh asparagus

Meanwhile… wash asparagus. Trim off ends, cut diagonally into 1½" slices, set aside.

1 can	2 cans	(7 oz each) mushrooms, drained

Add to chicken and cook 1 minute.

¼ cup	⅓ cup	*Dijon* mustard
½ cup	¾ cup	light sour cream *or* non-fat yogurt

Meanwhile… mix together using a 2 cup measuring cup. Add to bubbling chicken and mushrooms.

When timer goes off, toss asparagus in with the bubbling noodles. Set timer 2 minutes. Quickly drain.

Serve the Creamy Chicken Dijon over the noodles with asparagus, sliced tomatoes and cucumbers and a fresh fruit cup.

Delegate Someone to: Prep asparagus, tomatoes, cucumbers and fruit.

EXCHANGE VALUES

2 Starch	4 Meat	2 Veg.	— Fruit	— Milk	— Fat

Nutrition information for — 1 chicken breast half, 1-1/2 cups noodles & asparagus, 1/4 cup sauce

Calories 460	Fat .... 11 g	Fiber .... 4 g	Sodium .... 440 mg	Total Carbohydrate ....48 g
Calories from Fat 22%	Saturated Fat .... 3.5 g	Cholesterol .... 130 mg	Protein .... 40 g	Sugars .... 6 g

Pop Quiz!

Which of the following best describes your consumption of cooked dried beans?

A. Each week: A cup of bean soup, garbanzo beans on a salad, a bean burrito, and a serving of mixed vegetables (including lima beans).

B. 2 bean entrées per week including another serving from the left-overs for lunch on the following day. (4 servings per week).

C. Refried beans in Mexican food, once a week.

D. Chili twice a year, baked beans twice a year.

E. Beans? Are you crazy? I tasted them when I was 7 years old and I didn't like them!

Correct answer: A and B

Dried beans are among the best foods on the planet! They are jam-packed with disease fighting phyto-chemicals, vitamins, minerals and cholesterol-lowering fiber. They are rich in protein and are, therefore, a wonderful meat alternative. When beans *replace* meat at a meal, the benefit is magnified even more.

Do yourself a favor: Think beans, 4 times a week!

White Beans with Tomato, Basil & Parmesan

SERVES	MENU
4 AS A MAIN COURSE	WHITE BEANS WITH TOMATO, BASIL & PARMESAN
8 AS A SIDE DISH	CORNBREAD OR 9-GRAIN BREAD
	RAW VEGETABLES & DIP
	LEMON SORBET

Serve this hot or cold, as a main dish or a side dish.
Great with cornbread or whole-grain bread and raw veggies.

**Note: If you're planning to have *Cornbread,* mix that up first.
Start this recipe once you have the cornbread in the oven.**

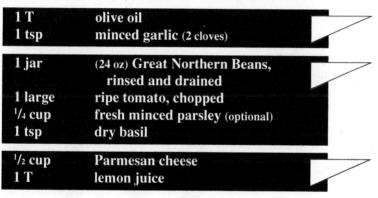

1 T	olive oil
1 tsp	minced garlic (2 cloves)

In a 12" nonstick skillet, sauté over medium heat for 3 minutes.

1 jar	(24 oz) Great Northern Beans, rinsed and drained
1 large	ripe tomato, chopped
¼ cup	fresh minced parsley (optional)
1 tsp	dry basil

Stir in and cook about 7 minutes longer.

Meanwhile… slice bread and prep raw veggies.

½ cup	Parmesan cheese
1 T	lemon juice

Mix in just before serving.

Serve with *Cornbread* or 9-grain bread, raw vegetables and dip.
Try lemon sorbet for dessert.

EXCHANGE VALUES

2 Starch	1 Meat	— Veg.	— Fruit	— Milk	— Fat

Nutrition information for — maincourse serving, 1 cup

Calories 240	Fat .... 6.5 g	Fiber .... 13 g	Sodium .... 550 mg	Total Carbohydrate ....32 g
Calories from Fat 24%	Saturated Fat .... 2.5 g	Cholesterol .... 8 mg	Protein .... 14 g	Sugars .... 1 g

White Beans with Tomato, Basil & Parmesan

Lickety-Split Meals

"The Big Eater"

Do you remember being praised for eating more food than anyone else?

When your child does eat a big meal, avoid the temptation to say, "good boy" or "good girl." Instead, keep your comments low-key and focused on their "gut" feelings, like, "Wow, you were hungry tonight, weren't you?" Responses like these go a long way in preventing the overeating habit.

Cheesy Potato Skillet with Mixed Vegetables

Talk about a "no-brainer", this is fast and satisfying after a super hectic day.

CHEESY POTATO SKILLET WITH MIXED VEGETABLES

WHOLE-WHEAT GARLIC CHEESE TOAST (OPTIONAL)

SLICED APPLES, ORANGES OR KIWIS

1 T	**oil** (olive *or* canola)
16 oz	**frozen mixed vegetables**
	(peas, corn, carrots)

Place in a non-stick skillet over medium-high heat for 4 minutes. Stir frequently.

(During this time, consider making the *Whole-Wheat Garlic Cheese Toast* (page 183).

16 oz	**frozen *Ore Ida*® O'Brien Potatoes** (hash browns with onions and peppers)

Add and cook 6 minutes longer, stirring frequently.

(Look for fruit to serve like oranges, apples and kiwi.)

½ cup	**reduced-fat shredded mozzarella cheese**
10 grinds	**fresh ground pepper**
2 T	**Parmesan cheese**

Sprinkle over all, turn off heat, cover and let stand 1 minute.

Serve with orange sections, apple wedges or kiwi slices and *Whole-Wheat Garlic Cheese Toast.*

EXCHANGE VALUES

3 Starch	1 Meat	2 Veg.	— Fruit	— Milk	— Fat

Nutrition information for — one generous serving (1/2 the recipe) NOTE: If serving with *Whole-Wheat Garlic Cheese Toast*, serve less.

Calories 436	Fat 11	Fiber .... 15 g	Sodium .... 450 mg	Total Carbohydrate .... 70 g
Calories from Fat 21%	Saturated Fat 3.5	Cholesterol .... 14 mg	Protein .... 20 g	Sugars .... 11 g

Beans, Beans the Magical Fruit...

I suppose it's time to talk about ... GAS. If you find yourself avoiding beans because of this problem, try these tips:

1. Many people's digestive tracts gradually adjust in their ability to produce the necessary enzymes to digest beans. **Therefore, add beans to your diet in *small* servings several times per week.** Not eating beans on a consistent basis and then digging into a big batch of chili and beans is what shocks your system, causing excessive gas.

2. Start with easier-to-digest beans like lentils and split peas.

3. **Consider a supplement like *"Beano."*** It provides the enzyme that your body is not sufficiently producing. Available at your pharmacy.

4. If all else fails, take frequent walks.

Whatever it takes, get your body used to eating a small portion of beans, FOUR times per week!

Gingered Black Beans with Squash

I'm always on the lookout for recipes using the nutrition dynamo Winter squash. This recipe comes from *Easy Eden*® by Lorna Sass and is delightful served over rice.

3 cups	instant whole-grain brown rice
2½ cups	water (adjust according to package directions, brand vary)

Place rice and water in a 2 quart microwave safe dish. Cover and cook on high for 12 minutes.

2 cans	(15 oz) *Eden*® *Black Beans with Ginger & Lemon*
½ cup	water
½ tsp	salt *or* 1 tsp lite salt

In a large saucepan, place over medium-high heat.

1 medium	butternut squash

Peel, seed and cut into chunks. Place in a food processor and pulse a few times to create pieces slightly larger than the beans.

Add squash to the beans and simmer 5 minutes or until squash is done.

3 T	white wine
½ cup	sliced green onions (tops & bottoms)

Stir in and serve over rice.

Serve with apple wedges.

EXCHANGE VALUES

4 Starch	1 Meat	1 Veg.	— Fruit	— Milk	— Fat

Nutrition information for — ⅙ of the recipe

Calories 338	Fat .... 1 g	Fiber .... 5.5 g	Sodium .... 440 mg	Total Carbohydrate .... 68 g
Calories from Fat 3%	Saturated Fat .... 0 g	Cholesterol .... 0 mg	Protein .... 13 g	Sugars .... 5 g

What does tofu taste like?

No one can say tofu tastes bad. It simply has no taste at all! The good news is, tofu takes on the flavors of whatever spices or flavorings you use with it. In fact, a good rule of thumb is to increase spices and seasonings by one-half whenever using tofu.

See page 83 for information about what tofu is and its benefits.

*Super Time Saving Tip

Skip microwaving the potatoes and chopping the pepper and onion by using 2 cups of *Ore Ida® Potatoes O'Brien*. (A frozen hash brown product, called for in previous recipe). It has no fat, just chopped potatoes, onions and peppers, and saves you loads of time!

Cheesy Scrambled Tofu

This is the very first recipe I learned to make (and like!) using tofu. Makes a great dinner or breakfast. You can save a lot of fat grams by using your favorite fat-free cheese.

SERVES 4

MENU

CHEESY SCRAMBLED TOFU

WHOLE-WHEAT GARLIC CHEESE TOAST OR ENGLISH MUFFINS

GRAPES AND STRAWBERRIES

2	potatoes*

Scrub potatoes clean. Poke each twice with a fork. Wrap them in damp paper towels. Microwave on high 6 to 8 minutes.

1/2	green pepper*
1/2	onion*

Meanwhile… chop vegetables and begin to sauté in a nonstick pan using nonstick spray.

Optional extras

1 cup	frozen corn
1	chopped tomato
1 cup	sliced mushrooms
1 cup	fresh *or* frozen snow peas

Add any optional extras.

4 slices	whole-wheat bread, *or*
	4 English muffins

Make toast.

12 oz	firm tofu
1 tsp	cumin, dill *or* oregano
	(pick your favorite)

Crumble tofu and add it to the sauté. Add tofu and your choice of spice to the pan. It is important for the tofu to absorb the flavors from the vegetables and spice. When potatoes are done, chop them and add to sauté 5 minutes.

1/4 cup	reduced-fat shredded cheddar cheese
1/4 cup	reduced-fat shredded mozzarella cheese

Sprinkle both kinds of cheese on top. Cover and cook 2 minutes more.

Meanwhile… set the table, set out fresh fruit, toast and jam.

EXCHANGE VALUES

2 Starch	2 Meat	— Veg.	— Fruit	— Milk	— Fat

* See my Super Time Saving Tip above.

Nutrition information for — 1 serving, including optional extras and 1 slice of bread

Calories 265	Fat .... 5.5 g	Fiber .... 6 g	Sodium 385	Total Carbohydrate .... 40 g
Calories from Fat 17%	Saturated Fat .... 1.2 g	Cholesterol .... 5 mg	Protein .... 17 g	Sugars .... 5 g

30-Minute Meals

While researching the needs of families, I heard several common wishes:

- "Easy meals for more quality dinner time at home"
- "Can unnecessary steps be eliminated?"
- "Can less mess be created?"
- "Can the entire meal be on the table in 30 minutes?"

Are you also in need of the Wizard? Welcome to the Land of Oz, where there's no place like home. It's back to the family, gathered around the table for a home cooked meal. All in only 30 minutes!

Money Saving Tip for Brown Rice

While instant whole-grain brown rice combines nutrition with convenience, it can also be a bit pricey. Try this tip: On any day that you are going to be around the house for an hour, cook 3 cups of brown rice in 6 cups of water for 45 minutes to 1 hour. The rice will then keep in the refrigerator for 4 days, or in the freezer for up to 3 months. Either way, reheating the rice in the microwave is as fast as using instant rice, without the cost!

Curried Chickpeas & Gingered Black Beans

SERVES | MENU

Ready for a nice twist for the old taste-buds? You know, I never thought I liked curry and avoided every recipe with it. What a mistake! The ginger and curry are awesome together and the presentation is beautiful. Try it!

4

CURRIED CHICKPEAS W/RICE
BROCCOLI & CARROTS
LEMON SORBET

2 cups	instant whole-grain brown rice
1¾ cup	water (adjust according to package directions, brands vary)

Place in microwave safe dish.

1 head	broccoli (cleaned & cut into flowerettes)
12	baby carrots

Add to rice. Cover and place in microwave.
Cook on high for 10 minutes.

1 small	onion
1 T	olive oil
2 tsp	ginger (fresh grated is best)
2 tsp	curry

Cut onion into small wedges. Heat oil on medium-high in a nonstick skillet. Add onion and spices. Cook 2 minutes. Meanwhile… open cans. Drain and rinse beans for next step.

1 can	(14.5 oz) stewed tomatoes
1 can	(15 oz) chickpeas, rinsed and drained
1 can	(15 oz) blackbeans, rinsed and drained
⅓ cup	chopped fresh parsley (optional)

Add to skillet and simmer 5 minutes.

1 T	lemon juice (optional)

Stir in just before serving.

Serve beans over the rice and vegetables, with lemon sorbet for dessert.

EXCHANGE VALUES

5 Starch	1 Meat	2 Veg.	— Fruit	— Milk	— Fat

Nutrition information for — approximately 1 cup over 1 cup rice with 1 cup vegetables

Calories 440	Fat .... 6 g	Fiber .... 15.5 g	Sodium .... 766 mg	Total Carbohydrate ....87 g
Calories from Fat 11%	Saturated Fat .... < 1 g	Cholesterol ....0 mg	Protein .... 17 g	Sugars .... 10 g

Married with children?

Finding it hard to get a sitter for that once-a-week date your marriage desperately deserves? Follow the advice of my friends, Jay and Art Johnson. Pick 1 night a week for date night. Make the kids their favorite dinner while the two of you munch on raw veggies and dip. Get the kids to bed promptly at 8:00. Light candles. Make a simple yet light and elegant dinner. Rent a movie. Presto! You have date night, without hiring a sitter!

Romantic dinner for two suggestions:

Skillet Chicken and Vegetables in Wine (this page!)

Crispy Chicken Dijon (page 89)

Chicken Marsala with Brown Rice and Peas (page 98)

White Beans with Tomato, Basil & Parmesan (page 91)

Our favorite, *Guiltless Nachos Supreme* (page 87)

Skillet Chicken & Vegetables in Wine

Serve this scrumptious meal with a tossed salad and whole grain bread.

SERVES | MENU

4 | SKILLET CHICKEN IN WINE
TOSSED SALAD
WHOLE-GRAIN BREAD
FROZEN YOGURT

4	potatoes, sweet *or* regular

Scrub thoroughly and pierce each potato 3 or 4 times with a fork. Microwave on high for 10 minutes. Cook more if necessary.

1 T	olive oil (garlic flavored if you have it)
4	skinless, boneless, chicken breasts (halves)

Heat oil in nonstick pan on medium high. Add chicken to pan and cook until browned. Turn and brown other side.

1	onion
1	red *or* yellow pepper
1½	cups frozen peas

Meanwhile… cut peppers into strips and onion into wedges. Add to chicken, saute for 2 minutes.

¼ cup	white wine
¼ tsp	thyme
¼ tsp	rosemary
¼ tsp	poultry seasoning
5 grinds	fresh ground pepper
½ tsp	salt

Add to pan and cover. The wine should entirely evaporate in only a few minutes. When "brown bits" begin collecting in the pan, the dish is done.

Serve with potatoes, salad and whole grain bread.

If you still have room for dessert, treat yourself to a small scoop of vanilla frozen yogurt with chocolate syrup on top.

EXCHANGE VALUES

2 Starch	4 Meat	1 Veg.	— Fruit	— Milk	— Fat

Nutrition information for — 1 chicken breast half, 1 potato, 3/4 cup vegetables

Calories 340	Fat .... 5 g	Fiber .... 7 g	Sodium .... 430 mg	Total Carbohydrate .... 36 g
Calories from Fat 14%	Saturated Fat .... 1 g	Cholesterol .... 68 mg	Protein .... 34 g	Sugars .... 5 g

Germ-Free Cooking

The Center for Science in the Public Interest recommends that we assume *all* raw meat, poultry and fish are contaminated with bacteria, and therefore handle it properly. To prevent even a mild case of food poisoning "flu" in your home, do not allow any uncooked meat to come in contact with cutting boards, plates or utensils-that will touch foods that will be eaten uncooked.

Follow these important safe handling tips:

- Own 2 cutting boards. Reserve one for meats, the other for vegetables. This helps reduce the chances of cross contamination.

- Thoroughly wash your cutting boards and knifes immediately after prepping your meat. (Delaying this chore is an invitation for cross contamination to occur).

- Use a CLEAN plate for serving meat off the grill. (Not the plate you used to bring the meat *to* the grill). Use a clean utensil as well.

- Discard meat marinade after its use. (However if you boil it, you can serve it as a dipping sauce).

Chicken Marsala

This is worth the extra effort to buy Marsala cooking wine. You'll think you're eating restaurant food! And you'll be glad to know this really only takes 20 minutes.

4

2 cups	instant, whole-grain brown rice
1³/₄ cup	water (adjust according to package directions, brand vary)
2 cups	frozen peas

Combine in a microwave safe dish. Cover and cook on high 9 to 10 minutes.

1	onion, cut into wedges
1 T	olive oil
1 tsp	minced garlic (2 cloves)
1 can	(7 oz) mushrooms, drained

Meanwhile… prep the onion. Then heat oil in a nonstick skillet. Add all to the skillet and begin sautéing.

4	skinless, boneless, chicken breast (halves)

Add to the skillet. Brown on each side 5 minutes.

¹/₃ cup	Marsala wine

Add to skillet. It will begin evaporating quickly.

²/₃ cup	chicken broth, ¹/₃ less sodium
¹/₄ tsp	salt (optional)
4 tsp	cornstarch
4 grinds	fresh ground pepper

Mix together using a measuring cup. Add to skillet. Reduce heat to low. Simmer 5 minutes until chicken is done.

Serve the chicken and the sauce over the rice and peas with *Where's the Lettuce? Salad* (page 171) and sliced fruit for dessert.

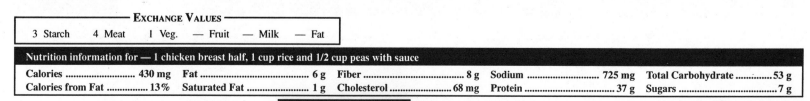

EXCHANGE VALUES

3 Starch	4 Meat	1 Veg.	— Fruit	— Milk	— Fat

Nutrition information for — 1 chicken breast half, 1 cup rice and 1/2 cup peas with sauce

Calories .... 430 mg	Fat .... 6 g	Fiber .... 8 g	Sodium .... 725 mg	Total Carbohydrate .... 53 g
Calories from Fat 13%	Saturated Fat .... 1 g	Cholesterol .... 68 mg	Protein .... 37 g	Sugars .... 7 g

How to combat the afterwork snack attacks

A good way to prevent coming home ravenous and out of control, is take a banana (or similar snack) to work with you. Save it to eat later in the afternoon or on your drive home. Eating a snack at this time allows for the nourishment to "hit your stomach," so you will feel energized, instead of famished, upon arriving home. Chasing it with a bottle of water is also very filling and supplies needed hydration which many people are lacking at this time of day.

Hungarian Chicken Paprikash

SERVES | MENU

This is a nutri-sized version of Katherine Buss' original Hungarian recipe and you won't believe how delicious it is. Katherine's granddaughter, Stacy Rafalko and I were able to save 15 grams of fat per serving off the original recipe. Grandma, can you tell?

6

CHICKEN PAPRIKASH
EGG NOODLES
TOSSED SALAD
GREEN BEANS
GINGER SNAPS AND GRAPES

3 medium	onions, chopped
1½ T	olive *or* canola oil

Sauté in oil over medium-high heat for 8 to 10 minutes.

Meanwhile… place a large kettle of water on to boil.

6	skinless, boneless, chicken breast (halves)
3 T	paprika (Yes, that's T's, not tsp's)
10 grinds	fresh ground pepper
2 T	low-sodium chicken bouillon
1½ tsp	salt
¾ cup	water

Add to onions and mix to coat chicken. Cover and cook 15 minutes, turning chicken occasionally.

12 oz	egg noodles

Meanwhile… add to boiling water. Set timer for 10 minutes.

2 boxes	(9 oz each) frozen whole green beans

Place in a microwave safe dish, cover and microwave on high for 8 minutes. Use this time to prepare a tossed salad and set the table.

1½ cups	light sour cream

Remove chicken from heat and stir in sour cream.

Drain noodles. Pour chicken mixture over noodles and toss.

Serve with the green beans and salad.

EXCHANGE VALUES

3 Starch   4 Meat   1 Veg.   — Fruit   — Milk   — Fat

Nutrition information for — 1 chicken breast half with 1-1/2 cups of noodles and 1/2 cup of green beans

Calories 500	Fat .... 12 g	Fiber .... 4.3 g	Sodium .... 721 mg	Total Carbohydrate .... 53 g
Calories from Fat 23%	Saturated Fat .... 5 g	Cholesterol .... 142 mg	Protein .... 40 g	Sugars .... 9 g

Attention Macaroni and Cheese Fans!

Rescue a high-fat, high-calorie, low-fiber meal with the following 2 simple changes:

1. Use skim milk.

2. Reduce the margarine to 1 T (eventually none!) and make up the reduced liquid in extra milk. (Numerous clients agree that even finicky children, do not notice this change).

2. Reduce the portion of macaroni and cheese and serve ample vegetables and sliced fruit with the meal. (This helps increase the fiber while reducing your sodium intake). You may choose to add vegetables right to the macaroni and cheese to get twice the benefit from the cheesy sauce.

Easy Succotash Dinner

You may think I'm crazy that I call this dish a meal, but think about it! It's protein, grain and vegetables all in one dish. It's as fast as macaroni and cheese, and much more delicious and nutritious.

1 cup	water
1 bag	(16 oz) **frozen corn**
1 bag	(16 oz) **frozen lima beans**

Bring water to a boil in medium pan. On medium heat, cover and simmer for 13 minutes. Be sure to set your timer, this is the exact time before all the water boils away.

Search your refrigerator for some lettuce, vegetables or fruit to make a salad. Raw carrots will do if that's all you can find.

1 cup	**reduced-fat shredded cheddar cheese**
10 grinds	**fresh ground pepper**

At the sound of the timer, remove from heat and stir-in. The cheese will melt in seconds.

Serve with salad or carrot sticks and frozen yogurt.

EXCHANGE VALUES

3 Starch	2 Meat	— Veg.	— Fruit	— Milk	— Fat

Nutrition information for — 1-1/4 cup serving

Calories 270	Fat .... 4 g	Fiber .... 9 g	Sodium .... 310 mg	Total Carbohydrate .... 44 g
Calories from Fat 13%	Saturated Fat .... 2 g	Cholesterol .... 9 mg	Protein .... 18 g	Sugars .... 5 g

Can you think of any foods that may have contributed to your youthfulness?

"For 30 years, we raised sweet potatoes, and boy did we eat a lot of them. I've always cooked up a pot of beans weekly (yes with a ham bone)! But probably the biggest thing, has been my years of home cooked meals, not processed restaurant foods."

—My grandmother
MINNIE BURGESS, 90
still climbing the stairs
of her home effortlessly,
countless times a day

Broiled Orange Roughy

Let's face it, who wants to cook on Friday night? (And it's time you had a break from pizza!) This meal comes together so fast—you won't even know you cooked!

BROILED ORANGE ROUGHY
VEGETABLE MEDLEY
BAKED POTATOES
5 GINGERSNAPS

Turn broiler on. Don't forget to leave oven door ajar.

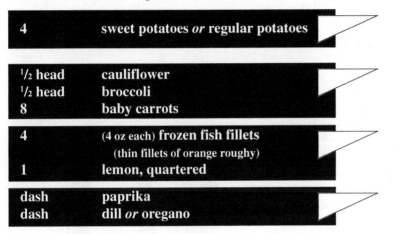

4	sweet potatoes *or* regular potatoes

Scrub thoroughly and pierce each potato 3 or 4 times with a fork. Microwave on high for 8 minutes. Cook more if necessary.

¹/₂ head	cauliflower
¹/₂ head	broccoli
8	baby carrots

Clean and cut into pieces or save time and use frozen. Place in a steamer on top of the stove to cook for 8 to 10 minutes.

4	(4 oz each) **frozen fish fillets**
	(thin fillets of orange roughy)
1	**lemon, quartered**

Place frozen fillets on broiling pan. Squeeze ¹/₄ of the lemon over each fillet.

dash	paprika
dash	dill *or* oregano

Sprinkle as you wish, onto each fillet.

Broil 6" from heating element for 7 to 10 minutes.

Place potatoes and vegetables on the table and serve fish.

Note: Fish will not need to be turned, to cook all the way through if fillets are thin. Fish is done when it flakes easily with a fork.

EXCHANGE VALUES

3 Starch   3 Meat   3 Veg.   — Fruit   — Milk   — Fat

Nutrition information for — 1 fish fillet, 1 potato, 1 cup vegetables

Calories 325	Fat .... 1.5 g	Fiber .... 10 g	Sodium .... 137 mg	Total Carbohydrate ....57 g
Calories from Fat 4%	Saturated Fat .... 0 g	Cholesterol .... 23 mg	Protein .... 23 g	Sugars ....27 g

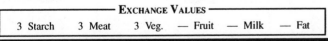

Fish Facts

It all started with studies showing that fish-loving Eskimos hardly ever get heart disease. Now we know the oil in fish reduces heart attack risk by warding off blood clots, lowering blood pressure and bringing down high triglycerides (blood fats). Other associations are being made about fish oil being helpful to arthritics.

A smart move: Replace prime rib with salmon to boost your health. Also, for convenience at home, consider cracking open a can of salmon, just as you would tuna, for salmon salad sandwiches.

Aim to eat fish 2-3 times per week!

Salmon Burgers

These are delicious! A simple and tasty way to eat salmon, which is so good for you! Serve on hamburger buns, with lettuce and tomato as burgers, or serve with baked potato and green vegetables for a salmon patty dinner.

1 can	(15 oz) **red** *or* **pink salmon, packed in water, drained** (*or* 2 cups flaked)

In a medium sized bowl, remove skin from fish and flake with a fork, mashing bones (great calcium).

8	**crackers** (whole-wheat saltines)
¼ cup	**diced red pepper**
3 T	*Miracle Whip*® **Light**
1 tsp	**lemon juice** (bottled *or* fresh squeezed)
4 drops	**Tabasco sauce**

Crush the crackers and add to the bowl. Add remaining ingredients. Mix well. Set aside.

| 1 bunch | **Fresh asparagus** *or* **green beans** |

Clean and place in a microwave-safe dish. Cover and microwave on high for 7 minutes.

Return to the salmon mix. Shape into 4 patties. Spray a nonstick skillet with cooking spray and place over medium heat. Cook salmon cakes, turning once, until lightly browned on each side.

4	**hamburger buns** (preferably whole-wheat)
4	**lettuce leaves**
1	**tomato, sliced**

Assemble into burgers.

| 40 | *Baked Tostitos*® |

Serve with asparagus and 10 chips on the side.

Don't forget the fudgesicle for dessert!

EXCHANGE VALUES

3 Starch	3 Meat	1 Veg.	— Fruit	— Milk	— Fat

Nutrition information for — 1 Salmon Burger with whole-grain bun, 6 asparagus spears and 10 baked corn chips

Calories	415	Fat	13.5 g	Fiber	6 g	Sodium	795 mg	Total Carbohydrate	50 g
Calories from Fat	27%	Saturated Fat	2 g	Cholesterol	76 mg	Protein	28 g	Sugars	4 g

Pepper power!

Among the vegetable superstars stands sweet peppers. Red, yellow, orange and green, they pack a powerful punch of valuable nutrition. Even the natural "color" of the peppers is tremendously valuable to your body and its defenses against cancer and heart disease.

My advice to you: Buy, cook and snack on them as often as possible!

Super Time and Money Saving Tip:

When you find peppers on sale (particularly the red, yellow and orange ones which can be quite pricey), buy as many as you can. Wash, seed and chop them. Place them in zip-lock bags and freeze. (Add chopped onions if you'd like). Every 20 minutes over the next hour, reach in and shake the bags. (This keeps them from freezing in one big chunk. Set the timer to remind you).

You will now have fast and economical chopped peppers ready in your freezer for directly adding to any stir-fry or vegetable sauté. They keep up to 3 months. (However, use fresh peppers for raw dishes like salads).

Unstuffed Peppers

Who has time for fancy stuffed peppers? This recipe skips that step, yet delivers the characteristic flavor in a fast and simple skillet dish.

SERVES	MENU
6	UNSTUFFED PEPPERS
	TOSSED SALAD
	MULTI-GRAIN BREAD
	SLICED FRUIT

1 box	(10 oz) **frozen chopped spinach**

Take spinach out of freezer and thaw most of the way in the microwave. Set aside.

1 each	**green, red and yellow pepper**
2 tsp	**minced garlic** (4 cloves)
20	**baby carrots**

Cut all the vegetables into small wedges.

1 T	**olive oil** (garlic *or* red pepper flavored is good)

Heat oil in a large nonstick kettle and sauté the vegetables and garlic.

1 lb	**extra-lean ground turkey breast**

Crumble the turkey, break up the spinach and add both to the sauté.

2 tsp	*Mrs. Dash*® or *Spike*® **seasoning**
2 tsp	**oregano**
$\frac{1}{4}$ tsp	**salt** (optional)
2 cans	(14.5 oz) **stewed *or* crushed tomatoes**
1 can	(14.5 oz) **chicken broth,** $\frac{1}{3}$ **less sodium**

While waiting for the meat to brown, add seasonings to sauté. Open the cans. Once the meat is completely brown, add broth and tomatoes.

2 cups	**instant whole-grain brown rice**
$\frac{1}{2}$ cup	**Parmesan cheese**

Once the mixture comes to a boil, add rice and cheese. Stir well. Cover and set timer for 5 minutes.

Meanwhile… search through the refrigerator for tossed salad fixins. Slice up bread. Slice apples, kiwi, oranges or any other fruit you have. When timer goes off, dinner is ready!

EXCHANGE VALUES

2 Starch	3 Meat	2 Veg.	— Fruit	— Milk	— Fat

Nutrition information for — 1-1/2 cup serving

Calories 320	Fat .... 6 g	Fiber .... 5.2 g	Sodium .... 800 mg	Total Carbohydrate .... 40 g
Calories from Fat 17%	Saturated Fat .... 2 g	Cholesterol .... 40 mg	Protein .... 28 g	Sugars .... 9 g

Tip

"Because cancer fighting compounds from my foods are of utmost importance to me, I focus on dried beans, whole grains, fruits, vegetables and plenty of soy foods, including a pound of tofu every week. I assure this with my ritual morning shake, consisting of tofu, soy milk, carrots, fruit, fruit juice, wheat bran, wheat germ and flax seeds. I developed this shake after my third cancer, as a way to get as many phytochemicals in my diet as possible."

—DIANA DYER, MS, RD, CNSD
Dietitian
Vibrant and healthy
3-time cancer survivor

P.S. To follow an example for creating your own cancer recovery and healing program, order Diana's book, *A Dietitians Cancer Story: Information and Inspiration for Recovery and Healing from a 3-Time Cancer Survivor.* From diet to meditation, exercise, supplements, alternative and conventional cancer therapies, Diana shares it all in this wonderful and personal book. Order by sending a check for $6.30 made out to Diana Dyer at P.O. Box 130221, Ann Arbor, MI 48113. And tell her I said hello!

Why tofu?

See page 83 to find out!

Tofu Fiesta

You can have this delicious, meatless/cheeseless meal on the table in no time at all!

SERVES	MENU
4	TOFU FIESTA TOSSED SALAD MULTI-GRAIN BREAD FRUIT BOWL

2	potatoes	Scrub thoroughly and pierce each potato 3 or 4 times with a fork. Microwave on high for 7 minutes. Cook more if necessary.

1	onion
¹/₂	green pepper
¹/₂	red pepper
1 tsp	minced garlic (2 cloves)
1 cup	frozen corn
¹/₂ cup	chopped fresh parsley *or* cilantro (reserve ¹/₄ cup for garnish)

Spray frying pan with nonstick cooking spray. Chop onion and peppers into wedges or strips. Sauté vegetables in pan over medium-high heat for 3 minutes.

12 oz	firm tofu
2 cups	(canned) pinto beans, rinsed and drained
1¹/₂ tsp	chili powder
¹/₂ tsp	cumin

Add crumbled tofu and spices to the pan. Drain and rinse beans. Add to pan. Sauté 5 minutes more.

Meanwhile… retrieve cooked potatoes. Chop into small pieces and add to sauté.

2 cups	salsa (fresh salsa is best)
¹/₄ cup	reserved chopped parsley *or* cilantro

Add salsa. Cover and cook 3 minutes more. Sprinkle on any additional parsley or cilantro for garnish.

Serve with warm bread and a tossed salad.

EXCHANGE VALUES

2 Starch	2 Meat	2 Veg.	— Fruit	— Milk	— Fat

Nutrition information for — approximately 1 cup

Calories	310	Fat	3 g	Fiber	14 g	Sodium	840 mg	Total Carbohydrate	58 g
Calories from Fat	8%	Saturated Fat	0 g	Cholesterol	0 mg	Protein	16 g	Sugars	8 g

What do you think is the secret to your youthfulness?

"Since I feel my best on the days I get out and about, I sure think that's important. Each day I always eat 3-4 pieces of fruit and always have. I drink a lot of water, 2 glasses of $1/2$% milk and hot water instead of coffee."

—CHARLOTTE BROWNELL, 82
Still volunteering
at the thrift store
15 years and
counting

Grilled Beef or Chicken Teriyaki

When I was growing up, I remember mom let us pick what we wanted to have for our Birthday dinner. I always chose "Beef Teriyaki." It's now my husband's favorite recipe for venison. This marinade is so versatile you can use it for any of your favorite meats or even tofu!

4

GRILLED TERIYAKI

BROWN RICE

BROCCOLI & CARROTS

SLICED NECTARINES OR SIMPLE SUMMER FRESH FRUIT PIE

Night before or in the early morning

¼ cup	soy sauce, reduced-sodium
1 T	firmly packed brown sugar
2 T	water
2 tsp	sesame oil
½ tsp	ginger (fresh grated is best)
5 grates	fresh black pepper
¼ tsp	minced garlic (1 clove)

Mix together in a bowl big enough to hold the meat you will be marinating.

1 lb	lean trimmed sirloin, flank steak, chicken breasts, venison, fish *or* 2 tubs (12 oz each) tofu cut into chunks *or* strips

Add and toss to coat. Allow to marinate in the refrigerator 8 hours or overnight.

Consider making *Simple Summer Fresh Fruit Pie* (page186).

Preheat gas grill or broiler.

30 minutes before dinner

2 cups	instant whole-grain brown rice
1¾ cups	water (adjust according to package directions, brands vary)

Place in microwave-safe dish.

1 head	broccoli (cleaned and cut into flowerets)
12	baby carrots

Add to rice. Cover and place in microwave. Cook on high for 10 minutes.

Remove meat from marinade and grill or broil. Check meat frequently for doneness. Discard marinade.

Serve with rice, vegetables & fruit or fruit pie for dessert.

EXCHANGE VALUES

2 Starch	4 Meat	2 Veg.	— Fruit	— Milk	— Fat

Nutrition information for — 4 oz. of beef, 1 cup rice, 1 cup vegetables

Calories 475	Fat .... 16 g	Fiber .... 4.5 g	Sodium .... 390 mg	Total Carbohydrate .... 44 g
Calories from Fat 30%	Saturated Fat .... 5.6 g	Cholesterol .... 94 mg	Protein .... 39 g	Sugars .... 7 g

Oven · Exercise · Eat

The road to dinner

You've just gotten home. Only this time there's still an hour to go before dinner. Your early morning meeting kept you from exercising this morning. How are you going to fit in your workout, before you're too pooped? Your personal experience tells you that inertia is five times stronger in the hours after dinner. If only you could fit exercise in BEFORE dinner.

Well, now you can, with Oven • Exercise • EAT! This is a collection of complete meal recipes that are quick to go in the oven, so you can exercise during the baking time and dinner is ready when you are done. Just flip through and see what looks good tonight. Note the length of prep-time and oven/exercise-time that works best for you. And assuming you've shopped using the *Lickety-Split* grocery list, you will have all the ingredients you need!

Keeping the Exercise in Oven/Exercise/Eat

If you're like most of us, you'll probably be tempted to use your bake time to do other seemingly important things, like laundry or housekeeping. But unless you've already exercised today, DON"T GIVE IN! A clean house has nothing over a clear mind and healthy body!

Have a great workout and enjoy a healthy and delicious meal, hot out of the oven when you're done!

Oven-Baked Lentils & Rice

Yes, this recipe makes a huge batch. That's because you're going to enjoy it so much that you'll be glad you made the extra for lunch "planned overs." It keeps in the refrigerator for 5 days and freezes well too. Serve with steamed vegetables, salad and whole grain bread.

LENTILS & RICE
STEAMED VEGETABLES
SALAD
WHOLE-GRAIN BREAD

Preheat oven to 350°.

2 small	onions
2 cans	(14.5 oz each) **chicken broth,** **¹/₃ less sodium**
1³/₄ cups	water
¹/₂ cup	white wine
1¹/₂ cups	lentils
1 cup	brown rice (not quick-cooking)
1 small jar	(2 oz) **chopped pimentos**
1 tsp	dried basil
1 tsp	dried oregano
¹/₂ tsp	dried thyme
¹/₄ tsp	garlic powder
15 grinds	fresh ground pepper

Chop onions. Mix together in a large baking dish. Set timer for 90 minutes and bake uncovered.

Meanwhile... how about 9 holes of golf? Remember, you don't need a cart!

1¹/₂ cups	reduced-fat shredded mozzarella *or* Swiss cheese

After 90 minutes of baking, sprinkle on and bake 15 minutes longer.

Use this time to steam vegetables, make a salad, slice some bread and set the table.

EXCHANGE VALUES

2 Starch	1 Meat	— Veg.	— Fruit	— Milk	— Fat

Nutrition information for — 1/6 of the recipe		Preparation Time — 10 min.	Oven / Exercise Time — 90 min.
Calories 240	Fat .... 3.5 g	Fiber .... 3 g	Sodium .... 665 mg	Total Carbohydrate .... 33 g
Calories from Fat 13%	Saturated Fat .... 1.7 g	Cholesterol .... 10 mg	Protein .... 15 g	Sugars .... 2 g

Exercising Consistently: Here's How to Make Your Good Intentions Come True!

If you are just getting into an exercise routine, it's important to establish positive feelings of accomplishment, so you will want to continue and be consistent.

WEEK #1

Try starting with only 5 minutes* of easy exercise, but **do it 5 times that week**. Perhaps marching in place in front of the TV, or spinning on your exercise bike. (Keep your intensity low). You can always find 5 minutes! What's important is to do it **5 times per week. Do it at the same time each day, which will become your routine exercise time.**

WEEK #2, 3, 4 and 5

How does it feel to have exercised 5 times last week? Pretty good, huh?

Now, over the next 4 weeks, **increase your exercise time.** Up to 7 minutes, then 10, 12, 15, 20, 25, 30. Keep your intensity fairly low. Be sure to keep up 5 times a week!

WEEK #6

Now, don't you feel GREAT having exercised 5 times a week for 5 weeks? Congratulations!

Now you're ready to add intensity. Increase your walking speed or turn up the resistance on the stationary bike. Try to increase this by 10% each week.

*If you are particularly fit, you can start with 10 minutes, but not more. The point is NOT to do all you are physically capable of doing, but rather to establish the concrete habit for CONSISTENCY. Most people agree, *consistency* is the hardest part!

Reminder: ALWAYS CHECK WITH YOUR DOCTOR FIRST BEFORE STARTING ANY EXERCISE PROGRAM!

Pizzucchini

Here's a delicious summer dish, that uses up your extra zucchini and tomatoes. *Pizzucchini* gets it's name from smelling like pizza while baking. We serve this with corn on the cob and cantaloupe.

SERVES	MENU
6	PIZZUCCHINI WITH REDSKINS CORN ON THE COB CANTALOUPE

Popular summer feast!

Preheat oven to 375°.
Spray a 9" x 13" baking pan with nonstick cooking spray.

3 small	zucchini
1 medium	onion
4 medium	tomatoes

Slice vegetables ¹/₈ inch thick.
Separate onion slices into rings.

6 T	**Parmesan cheese**
1¹/₂ cups	**reduced-fat shredded** **mozzarella cheese**
2 tsp	**dried oregano**
1 tsp	**garlic powder**

Mix together in a medium size bowl.

Make 2 layers in the baking dish, using half the ingredients each time in the order listed: zucchini, onion, tomatoes, cheese mixture (repeat).

6 small	**red-skin potatoes, cut in ¹/₂**

Scrub potatoes and slip in around the edges of the casserole.

Cover and bake for 1 hour. (Remember to set timer.)

How about swimming?

After 1 hour, remove cover and bake 15 minutes more. Use this time to cook some corn on the cob and slice some cantaloupe. Enjoy!

EXCHANGE VALUES

1 Starch	1 Meat	2 Veg.	— Fruit	— Milk	— Fat

Nutrition information for — 1/6 of the recipe			Preparation Time — 20 min.	Oven / Exercise Time — 60 min.
Calories 200	Fat .... 4.5 g	Fiber .... 4 g	Sodium .... 335 mg	Total Carbohydrate .... 26 g
Calories from Fat 20%	Saturated Fat .... 2.5 g	Cholesterol .... 14 g	Protein .... 14 g	Sugars .... 5 g

Tip

Don't let the weather control your workout.

Always have a back-up plan for nasty weather. If the weather is nice, I walk, jog, rollerblade or ride my bike. If not, I work out indoors doing aerobics, the *Health Rider®,* indoor bike or *Nordic Track®*. Develop a plan that works best for you.

Tuna Noodle Casserole

SERVES | MENU

4 OR 8 | TUNA NOODLE CASSEROLE
TOSSED SALAD
WHOLE-WHEAT ROLLS
FUDGESICLE

Yes, it's your all-American favorite! This time it's made lower in fat and sodium, and without the time wasting step of boiling the noodles first. Plan on a good workout tonight with 50 minutes of oven time!

Preheat oven to 375°.

For 4	For 8	
1 can	2 cans	(10¾ oz each) **cream of mushroom soup** (*Campbell's® Healthy Request®*)
1¼ c	2½ c	**skim milk** (fill the empty soup can)

Mix together in a casserole dish. Use a medium dish for serving 4 and a large dish for serving 8.

For 4	For 8	
1 can	2 cans	(6 oz each) **water packed tuna drained and flaked**
1 tsp	2 tsp	**dried onion flakes**
½ tsp	1 tsp	**dill**
¼ c	½ c	**Parmesan cheese**
1½ c	3 c	**frozen peas**
3 c	6 c	**uncooked shells *or* noodles**

Add and mix.

Put in oven covered. Set timer for 50 minutes.

 How about heading outside for some "active" gardening or yard work?

Check refrigerator for salad making possibilities, or try sliced cucumbers, tomatoes and carrots.

Prepare salad or simply serve sliced cucumbers and tomatoes. Serve with whole-wheat rolls.

EXCHANGE VALUES

3 Starch   2 Meat   — Veg.   — Fruit   — Milk   — Fat

Nutrition information for — 1/4 of the small batch, 1/8 of the large batch		Preparation Time — 10 min.	Oven / Exercise Time — 50 min.
Calories 315	Fat .... 4.6 g Fiber .... 4 g	Sodium .... 620 mg	Total Carbohydrate ....45 g
Calories from Fat 13%	Saturated Fat .... 1.8 g Cholesterol .... 18 mg	Protein .... 23 g	Sugars .... 9 g

Want to create some fun and support between you and your spouse?

In a conspicuous place, hang 2 calendars side by side. Designate 1 for you and 1 for your spouse. Record your minutes of exercise each day. On Saturday or Sunday night, total up your minutes. The person with the least minutes gives a back-rub to the other. What competitive (and slightly romantic) fun!

Tantalizing Turkey Loaf Dinner

This dinner is a far cry from the traditional artery-clogging classic. It's fast and tasty too! The applesauce replaces the moisture lost by using extra-lean ground turkey.

Preheat oven to 350°.

4	baking *or* 4 sweet potatoes

Scrub potatoes and place in oven.

1 small	onion

Chop and place in a medium sized bowl.

1 lb	extra-lean ground turkey breast
2	egg whites
1/2 - 1 tsp	Italian seasoning (young children prefer less seasoning)
1/4 tsp	crushed red pepper (optional)
1/2 cup	applesauce, unsweetened
1/2 tsp	salt
1/2 cup	dry unseasoned bread crumbs
2 T grated	Parmesan cheese

Add and mix together thoroughly, using your hands if necessary. *(Wash them first!)*

Spray an 8" x 8" baking dish with nonstick cooking spray.

Form meat into a loaf and place in the middle of the pan.

1 cup	spaghetti sauce (*Healthy Choice®*)

Pour sauce over top. Place in oven and set timer for 45 minutes.

Head out for 40 minutes of exhilarating exercise.

4 cups	broccoli

Upon returning from exercise, place into a microwavable dish, cover and cook on high for 5 minutes. *Stretch those muscles!* When the oven timer goes off, slice loaf into 8 equal parts. It's time to eat!

EXCHANGE VALUES

3 Starch	3 Meat	2 Veg.	— Fruit	— Milk	— Fat

Nutrition information for — 2 slices turkey loaf, 1 small potato, 1 cup broccoli   Preparation Time — 20 min.   Oven / Exercise Time — 45 min.

Calories 415	Fat .... 3 g	Fiber .... 7 g	Sodium .... 780 mg	Total Carbohydrate .... 58 g
Calories from Fat 7%	Saturated Fat .... < 1 g	Cholesterol .... 56 mg	Protein .... 38 g	Sugars .... 13 g

Tantalizing Turkey Loaf Dinner

Oven • Exercise • Eat
110

Lickety-Split Meals

Eat the skin on your potato because it's good for you... Or is it?

While nutritionists have advised to eat the potato skin because of its extra vitamins, minerals and fiber, new findings are causing a second look at this advice. These days most commercial potatoes have been sprayed, to slow their sprouting and extend their shelf life. This spray has raised safety concerns. **Therefore, the advice to "eat the skin on your potato because it's good for you," holds true only for potatoes bought at your local farmers market or organically grown.**

And what about all those extra vitamins, minerals and fiber that you'll be throwing away? It's not enough to fret over, there is good nutrition throughout the potato.

Oven Fries

I can't begin to tell you how much my husband loves these! Easy to make, inexpensive and delicious
low-fat versions of the high fat American favorite. I'll leave it up to you what to serve them with.
Perhaps baked chicken legs and steamed vegetables?

4

BAKED CHICKEN LEGS
OVEN FRIES
STEAMED VEGETABLES

Preheat oven to 375°.

4 large	**baking potatoes**
	(try sweet potatoes, they're great!)

Thoroughly wash and scrub—peel if commercial potatoes. (See tip above.)
Cut lengthwise into wedges. Place in bowl.

Husbands and kids love these!

1 T	**oil** (canola *or* olive)

Drizzle over potatoes and toss.

Spray a cooking sheet with nonstick cooking spray.

Spread potato wedges on cooking sheet.

Set timer and bake for 50 minutes or until tender.

*Now head out the door
for a 20 minute brisk walk or jog!*

At the sound of the timer, transfer to a serving dish.

Salt, pepper and ketchup

Sprinkle salt and pepper on potatoes to taste. Serve with ketchup.

Note: *Ore Ida®* now makes frozen Potato Wedges, which are almost exactly the same as these. Buying their product will save you from scrubbing and slicing potatoes (about 10 minutes), but are of course more costly than buying plain potatoes. The choice is up to you!

EXCHANGE VALUES

3 Starch	— Meat	— Veg.	— Fruit	— Milk	— Fat

Nutrition information for — 1/4 of the recipe, without ketchup, salt and pepper			Preparation Time — 10 min.	Oven / Exercise Time — 50 min.
Calories 250	Fat .... 3.5 g	Fiber .... 5 g	Sodium .... 16 mg	Total Carbohydrate .... 50 g
Calories from Fat 13%	Saturated Fat .... .5 g	Cholesterol .... 0 mg	Protein .... 5 g	Sugars .... 3 g

Oven Fries

Oven • Exercise • Eat
111

Lickety-Split Meals

Why aren't you lifting weights?

Don't have time? This book takes care of that!

Don't want clunky equipment cluttering up the living room? All it takes is 2 pair of dumbells and you can store them under the coach.

Don't know how? Buy a video! Find one in "The Complete Guide to Exercise Videos," a catalog put out by Collage Video (1-800-433-6769). I highly recommend the "8-Minute Arms" video as well as the other 8-Minute tapes they offer.

Attention women. Afraid you'll get big muscles? Don't worry! You'd have to lift heavy weights for 3 hours a day, every day for a year, before that could even possibly become a problem!

LaZonya

My lasagna has lots of veggies, low-fat cheese and unboiled noodles (to save time). Double the recipe and freeze one pan for another time (freeze <u>after</u> baking). The sauce is so tasty, I have you make extra. Freeze the extra sauce for a quick meal (topping a baked potato or pasta).

(1) 9 x 13	(2) 9 x 13	
½	1	green and red pepper
2	4	carrots
2	4	small onions
1 c	2 c	fresh mushrooms *or* zucchini (optional)
1 tsp	2 tsp	minced garlic (2 or 4 cloves)
1 T	2 T	olive oil
¼ c	½ c	fresh chopped parsley
1 lb.	2 lbs.	extra-lean ground turkey breast (optional)
1 block	2 blocks	(12 oz) firm tofu crumbled (optional)
1 tsp	2 tsp	oregano
¼ tsp	½ tsp	red pepper flakes
2 jars	4 jars	(26 oz each) spaghetti sauce (*Healthy Choice®*)
1 box	2 bxs	(10 oz) frozen spinach
1 tub	2 tubs	(15 oz) light Ricotta cheese (*or* low-fat cottage cheese)
½ tsp	1 tsp	dried onion flakes
1 T	2 T	fresh parsley (from earlier)
1 T	2 T	Parmesan cheese

THE SAUCE...

Clean. Chop peppers, chop or shred carrots, dice onions, and slice mushrooms/zucchini.

Heat oil on medium-high in your largest nonstick kettle and add garlic and vegetables.

Chop. Reserve 1 to 2 T for later in recipe. Add to kettle.

Add turkey and/or tofu by crumbling. (A good idea for first time tofu users, use ½ tofu and ½ turkey. Your guests will never be able to tell the difference.) Add spices. Cook, stirring frequently for 5 minutes or until turkey is done.

Add sauce and spinach. Simmer on medium while you prepare the cheese mixture. When ready, move sauce to assembly line and place a measuring cup near it for scooping.

THE CHEESES...

Mix together in a medium bowl. Divide into 3 equal parts (1 for each layer) for use during the *LaZonya* assembly process. Place a tsp in the bowl.

Recipe continued on next page.

The benefits of lifting weights are endless!

1. Helps fight off osteoporosis.

2. Raises your metabolism (muscle burns more calories than fat does).

3. Helps you lose inches, look firmer and feel great.

4. Helps reverse the aging process.

LaZonya (Con't.)

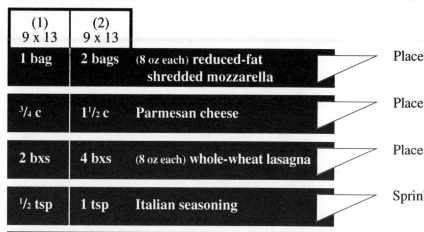

(1) 9 x 13	(2) 9 x 13		
1 bag	2 bags	(8 oz each) **reduced-fat shredded mozzarella**	Place opened bags in assembly line.
³/₄ c	1¹/₂ c	**Parmesan cheese**	Place in bowl. Place a T in bowl for use in assembly line.
2 bxs	4 bxs	(8 oz each) **whole-wheat lasagna**	Place opened boxes in assembly line.
¹/₂ tsp	1 tsp	**Italian seasoning**	Sprinkle on top layer when assembly is complete.

THE ASSEMBLY

1. Spray (1) or (2) 9" x 13" pans with nonstick cooking spray. Place 1³/₄ cups sauce in the bottom of each pan.

2. Layer 3 hard noodles; 1³/₄ cups sauce, spread evenly; 12 rounded tsps Ricotta cheese; ¹/₂ cup mozzarella sprinkled evenly and 3 T Parmesan cheese sprinkled. (repeat layering 3 times)

3. After the third Parmesan cheese sprinkle, complete the fourth and final layer with 3 hard noodles; 1¹/₂ cups sauce spread evenly; ¹/₂ cup mozzarella sprinkled evenly; 3 T Parmesan cheese and ¹/₂ tsp Italian seasoning. **Remember, there should be leftover sauce for you to freeze for a quick meal later!**

4. Pour ¹/₄ cup of water (for each pan) all around the edges of the pan. This provides the needed steam to cook the noodles.

5. Cover with aluminum foil and bake 45 minutes.

Capitalize on this time to get in a thorough resistance exercise workout.

Uncover and bake 10 minutes longer. Meanwhile… prepare a salad and garlic toast.

Allow 10 minutes to set before serving.

Use this time to stretch and set the table!

EXCHANGE VALUES

2 Starch	3 Meat	2 Veg.	— Fruit	— Milk	— Fat

Nutrition information for — 1 square (1/12 of the pan) made with ground turkey and tofu | Preparation Time — 60 min. | Oven / Exercise Time — 50 min.

Calories 335	Fat .... 7.5 g	Fiber .... 7.5 g	Sodium .... 713 mg	Total Carbohydrate .... 43 g
Calories from Fat 19%	Saturated Fat .... 3.5 g	Cholesterol .... 36 mg	Protein .... 29 g	Sugars .... 10 g

Be sure to stretch! It only takes a minute!

Benefits of stretching:

1. Improves flexibility, mobility and range of motion.

2. Helps prevent injuries.

3. Promotes better circulation.

4. Reduces tension.

5. Helps prevent muscle stiffness and soreness after exercise.

(Doesn't this sound like a great way to slow aging)?

Rules for stretching:

1. Gently hold a stretch for about 20 seconds.

2. Stretch only until you feel a comfortable stretch in the muscle.

3. Breathe normally. Do not hold your breath.

4. Never force a muscle to stretch too far when true pain is felt.

5. Never bounce while stretching! You want a constant, steady stretch.

Mexican LaZonya

(A.K.A. Bean and Vegetable Enchilada Bake) Teenagers will love how this dish resembles "Taco Bell" type food. If you have small children, you may want to $\frac{1}{2}$ the cumin and chili powder.

Preheat oven to 375°. Note: If serving *Cinnamon Butternut Squash* (page 182), get it started first.

2	onions, chopped
2	peppers (one green, one red), chopped
$\frac{1}{2}$ head	cauliflower florets
1 medium	zucchini *or* 3 carrots, chopped

Prep the vegetables.

2 T	olive oil
1 tsp	chopped garlic (2 cloves)

Heat skillet and add oil. Add the garlic and the chopped vegetables, (or frozen vegetables straight from the bag).

1 jar	(16 oz) salsa
1 can	(16 oz) low-sodium tomato puree

Add and set timer for 5 minutes.

1 T	ground cumin
1 T	chili powder
1 can	(15 oz) pinto, black *or* kidney beans, rinsed and drained

Meanwhile… add to the simmering skillet.

When the timer goes off, it's time to assemble.

12	corn tortillas (flour tortillas work fine too)
1$\frac{1}{2}$ cups	reduced-fat shredded cheddar cheese

TO ASSEMBLE…

Layer evenly; $\frac{1}{3}$ of the sauce in a 9" x 13" baking dish; 4 tortillas; $\frac{1}{2}$ cup cheese on top of tortillas (repeat 2 more times), **but wait to add last layer of cheese.** Cover with aluminum foil and place in oven. Set timer 25 minutes.

How about jumping rope? Start with 5 minutes, working up to 20 when you can.

Remove foil, add the remaining cheese and bake 5 more minutes. *Stretch!*

Serve with Cinnamon Butternut Squash, tossed salad or fresh vegetables with dip. Olé!

EXCHANGE VALUES

2 Starch	1 Meat	2 Veg.	— Fruit	— Milk	— Fat

Nutrition information for — 1 square (1/8 of the pan) — Preparation Time — 40 min. — Oven / Exercise Time — 20 min.

Calories 280	Fat .... 7 g	Fiber .... 10.5 g	Sodium .... 675 mg	Total Carbohydrate .... 41 g
Calories from Fat 22%	Saturated Fat .... 2 g	Cholesterol .... 7 mg	Protein .... 14 g	Sugars .... 8 g

Calories burned during exercise

Don't get depressed when you think…
I exercised for 20 minutes and all I burned
was 160 calories??? Just remember the
secret to consistency over time:

Twenty minutes of exercise 3 times a
week for a full year burns 24,960 calories,
which translates to **7 pounds of fat
burned in a year**!

Thirty minutes of exercise 5 times a week
for a year burns 62,400 calories, which
translates to **18 pounds of fat burned
in a year**!

Forty-five minutes of exercise 5 times a
week for a year burns 93,600 calories,
which translates to **27 pounds of fat
burned in a year**!

*As you can see,
consistency pays!*

Kickin' Chicken with Fries

Check this out! You get your workout in *and* your family fed all in less than 45 minutes! Your family will ask for this again and again!

Preheat oven to 450°.
Arrange oven racks to accommodate both a cookie sheet and a 9" x 13" pan.

Kids' Favorite

1 cup	salsa *or* Picante sauce
1 T	firmly packed brown sugar
½ T	Dijon mustard

Mix together in a 2 cup measuring cup.

4	skinless, boneless, chicken breast (halves)

Place chicken in a 9" x 13" baking dish. Pour sauce over chicken. Put in oven.

1 bag	(24 oz) *Ore Ida*® potato wedges*

Spread out on cookie sheet. Place in oven. Set timer for 25 minutes.

1 bag	(16 oz) mixed vegetables
2 T	water

Place in microwave safe dish, cover and set to cook on high for 12 minutes. (You will be allowing the vegetables to sit in the oven 10 minutes longer.)

Jump on your treadmill (or stationary bike) for a quick 22 minutes. (Take the first 2 minutes to warm up.)

16 oz	applesauce, unsweetened

At the sound of the timer, check chicken to see if it's done. Cook 5 more minutes if necessary. Open the applesauce and set the table.

It's Kickin' Chicken time!

EXCHANGE VALUES

4 Starch	3 Meat	2 Veg.	— Fruit	— Milk	— Fat

* If you prefer, make the home-made version of *Oven Fries* (page 111).

Nutrition information for — 1 chicken breast half, 1 cup fries, 1 cup mixed vegetables			Preparation Time — 15 min.	Oven / Exercise Time — 22 min.
Calories 490	Fat .... 7 g	Fiber .... 10 g	Sodium .... 460 mg	Total Carbohydrate .... 73 g
Calories from Fat 12%	Saturated Fat .... 15 g	Cholesterol .... 68 mg	Protein .... 35 g	Sugars .... 24 g

How is it that people who can never find time to exercise can always find time to eat?

The wonder of 336

You may find it interesting that there are 336 30-minute time segments in EVERY week. You need ONLY 3 to 5 of these 30-minute time segments each week for exercise.

This requires less than 5% of your time each week!

(Eating on the other hand, takes much more time)!

Delicate Baked Trout

SERVES | MENU

The next time you walk by the fresh seafood counter, check out their fresh trout. My dear friend Jay Johnson taught me how the milk in this recipe does wonders to keep the flavor delicate and mild. (Not at all fishy!)

4

BAKED TROUT
OVEN FRIES
CALIFORNIA VEGETABLES
9-GRAIN ROLLS

Preheat oven to 350°.

1 bag	(24 oz) *Ore Ida*® potato wedges*

Spread out on cookie sheet.
Place in oven.

1½ lbs	fresh trout fillet

Rinse clean and place in a 8" x 8" baking dish.

½	lemon (*or* 1 T from a bottle)
1 tsp	oil (canola *or* olive)
1 cup	skim milk

Drizzle or pour over the fish in the order given.

Kids' Favorite

⅛ tsp	salt
6 grinds	fresh ground pepper
3 dashes	paprika

Sprinkle as needed.

Place in oven. Set timer for 35 minutes.

2 bags	(16 oz each) **frozen California blend vegetables**
1 T	water

Place in microwave safe dish, cover and let set.

Pop in an exercise video for 30 minutes of aerobic work. Remember to warm up.

When the timer goes off, put vegetables in microwave on high for 10 minutes. Allow fish to continue baking until microwave finishes.

Step in place for 1 minute for a cool down. Grab 2 soup cans and do bicept curls & overhead presses. Follow with some sit-ups and 2 minutes of stretching.

Set table. When vegetables are done, it's time to eat!

* If you prefer, make the home-made version of *Oven Fries* (page 111).

EXCHANGE VALUES

2 Starch	3 Meat	3 Veg.	— Fruit	— Milk	— Fat

Nutrition information for — 4 oz. trout, 1 cup fries, 1-1/2 cups vegetables | Preparation Time — 10 min. | Oven / Exercise Time — 35 min.

Calories 420	Fat .... 11 g	Fiber .... 10 g	Sodium .... 221 mg	Total Carbohydrate .... 51 g
Calories from Fat 24%	Saturated Fat .... 2.6 g	Cholesterol .... 62 mg	Protein .... 28 g	Sugars .... 8 g

Nature's Popsicle: Frozen Grapes

If you haven't experienced frozen grapes yet, you don't know what you're missing!

Take grapes off their vine. (Use red, green, or both).

THOROUGHLY wash the grapes and pat dry on a towel.

Place in a airtight bowl or zip lock bag and freeze.

Serve frozen or partially thawed.

Icy, sweet and delicious!

Super Time Saving Tip

Skip prepping the potatoes and onion by using 4 cups of *Ore Ida® Potatoes O'Brien*. (A frozen hash brown product, I call for frequently). It has no fat, just chopped potatoes, onions and peppers, tastes great, and saves you loads of time!

Chicken and Vegetables in Foil

A super simple dinner that can be cooked indoors or on the outdoor grill.
Your choice, Italian style or barbecue. Best of all, there's no messy cleanup!

SERVES | **MENU:**

4 | BBQ OR ITALIAN CHICKEN

POTATO

BRUSSELS SPROUTS AND CARROTS

WHOLE-GRAIN BREAD

FROZEN GRAPES

Preheat oven to 400°.
Tear off 2 large pieces of foil just larger than the size of a cookie sheet.

1 cup	bottled BBQ sauce *or* ¾ cup lite *or* fat-free Italian dressing

Spread ½ the sauce in the center of the foil.

4	skinless, boneless, chicken breast (halves)
4 medium	potatoes, scrubbed *or* peeled, thinly sliced*
1	onion, sliced into rings*

Layer on the foil in order given. Spread on remaining sauce.

1 box	(10 oz) frozen Brussels sprouts *or* cabbage wedges *or* broccoli/ cauliflower mix
1 box	(10 oz) frozen carrots

Place in a strainer and run hot tap water over them for 1 minute.
Drain and add to foil.

8 grinds	fresh ground pepper

Sprinkle with fresh ground pepper. Place the remaining foil on top.
Seal with double folds. Place in oven and set timer for 75 minutes.

How about a nice long bike ride outdoors? Reserve the last 15 minutes for push-ups and sit-ups. (How many of those are you up to by now?) Stretch!

Serve with rolls (if you choose to) and frozen grapes (see above).

EXCHANGE VALUES

3 Starch	3 Meat	3 Veg.	— Fruit	— Milk	— Fat

* See my Super Time Saving Tip above

Nutrition information for — 1/4 of the recipe			Preparation Time — 15 min.	Oven / Exercise Time — 75 min.
Calories 400	Fat .... 3 g	Fiber .... 10 g	Sodium .... 660 mg	Total Carbohydrate ....58 g
Calories from Fat 6%	Saturated Fat .... < 1 g	Cholesterol .... 68 mg	Protein .... 35 g	Sugars ....16 g

Is your headache a sign of mild dehydration?

Do you ever arrive home with a headache? Did you know that this is often the first sign of dehydration? Hydrating your body may relieve your headache. You'll need to be adequately hydrated in order to feel good and perform well, especially during your workout. **The best habit is drinking fluids all day long.** If you haven't, play catch-up and down a glass of water when you get home.

And be sure to always replace fluids after exercising!

Simple Baked Chicken and Rice

Got 10 minutes? That's all it takes to get this tasty favorite in the oven. Leaving you with 1 whole hour of rejuvenating "all to yourself" exercise time.

SERVES

4

MENU

BAKED CHICKEN & RICE

CALIFORNIA BLEND VEGETABLES

WHOLE-GRAIN BREAD

APRICOT HALVES

Preheat oven to 375°.

1 can	(10.75 oz) **cream of mushroom soup** (*Campbell's® Healthy Request®*)
1 can	(14.5 oz) **reduced-sodium chicken broth**
⅓ cup	**light sour cream** (*or* plain yogurt)

Stir together in a 9" x 13" baking dish.

1 bag	(16 oz) **California blend frozen vegetables**
1 can	(10 oz) **cooked white chicken, rinsed and drained**
1½ cups	**instant whole-grain brown rice**
1 tsp	**dried onion flakes**
10 grinds	**fresh ground pepper**

Add and stir.

Put in oven to bake. Set timer for 1 hour.

Tennis anyone? Remember to end with a thorough stretch session.

Serve with a wedge of crusty whole-grain bread and canned apricots.

EXCHANGE VALUES

2 Starch	2 Meat	3 Veg.	— Fruit	— Milk	— Fat

Nutrition information for — 1/4 of the recipe			Preparation Time — 10 min.	Oven / Exercise Time — 1 hour
Calories 340	Fat .... 5.5 g	Fiber .... 7 g	Sodium .... 800 mg	Total Carbohydrate .... 50 g
Calories from Fat 15%	Saturated Fat .... 2.5 g	Cholesterol .... 38 mg	Protein .... 23 g	Sugars .... 9 g

Still wondering which exercise video to buy?

Call Collage Video at 1-800-433-6769
and ask for their free catalog entitled:
The complete guide to exercise videos.
This includes excellent descriptions of the
346 best videos on the planet. They even
boast that their telephone video consultants
are paid to actually use the tapes so they
can tell you about them. They will even
play the music for you over the phone.
Now that's service!

Chicken and Bean Enchiladas

My thanks to Stacy Rafalko for this neat recipe. Feel free to leave out the chicken or cheese if you prefer. These are easy and tasty!

Preheat oven to 350°.

2 cups	*Benito Bean Dip* (page 57) *or*
1 can	(16 oz) **fat-free refried beans**
1 can	(10 oz) **chunk white chicken, rinsed and drained**

Gently combine in a medium size bowl, break chicken up.

Kids' Favorite

8	**8" flour tortillas**

Place ⅓ cup of bean mixture in a long single row on a tortilla. Roll-up. Place in a 9" x 13" baking dish. Repeat with remaining 7 tortillas.

1 can	(10 oz) **enchilada sauce** (*Old El Paso®*)

Pour over enchiladas.

½ cup	**reduced-fat shredded cheddar cheese**

Sprinkle over all. Place in oven. Set timer for 30 minutes.

Throw on your sweat pants and a T-shirt, and start your favorite exercise video.

When the timer sounds, allow the enchiladas to cool a few minutes while you prepare corn and slice melons. Try to stretch while you work.

½ cup	**light sour cream**
	minced fresh onion (optional)
	chopped green pepper (optional)

Serve enchiladas with 1 T of sour cream over each and optional onion and green pepper.

Buen Appetito!

EXCHANGE VALUES

2 Starch	2 Meat	1 Veg.	1 Fruit	— Milk	— Fat

Nutrition information for — 1 enchilada with 1 T sour cream, 1/2 cup corn, 1 cup watermelon cubes   Preparation Time — 20 min.   Oven / Exercise Time — 30 min.

Calories 360	Fat .... 7 g	Fiber .... 8 g	Sodium .... 600 mg	Total Carbohydrate .... 58 g
Calories from Fat 16%	Saturated Fat .... 2.3 g	Cholesterol .... 23 mg	Protein .... 20 g	Sugars .... 18 g

Do houseguests cramp your exercise routine?

Why not invite them to join you? Make an early morning walk followed by a nutritious breakfast part of a perfect visit. It's amazing what a positive impact you can have on your family and friends!

Creamy Chicken Enchiladas

Creamy, comforting and "to die for" is the best way to describe this. My complete thanks to Diane Petersen for contributing this favorite recipe from her mom, Barb Filler.

Preheat oven to 325°.

6	**skinless, boneless, chicken breast** (halves), **cut into strips**
1 can	(4 oz) **chopped green chilies**

Brown chicken in nonstick skillet with nonstick spray. Add green chilies during last 2 minutes.

1 cup	**light sour cream**
1 can	(10³/4 oz) **cream of chicken soup** (*Campbell's® Healthy Request®*)

Meanwhile… in a medium sauce pan, mix together and heat over medium-low.

Kids' Favorite

1 can	(2.25 oz) **sliced black olives** (optional)
1 cup	**reduced-fat shredded cheddar cheese**

Open olives and cheese and place in assembly line.

Spread ¹/₂ cup of soup mix on bottom of 9" x 13" pan.

10	**8" flour tortillas**

Lay out 5 tortillas on a clean countertop. Put 1 T of sauce in a line down the center of each. Follow with: 2 T of chicken, 1 T of cheese, 1 tsp of olives. Roll up and place in 9" x 13" pan. Repeat with remaining 5 tortillas. Pour remaining sauce over the tortilla rolls. Sprinkle with remaining cheese. Place in oven and set timer for 20 minutes.

1 box	(10 oz) **cut green beans**
1 box	(10 oz) **crinkle cut carrots**

Place in microwave safe bowl. Cover and let set in microwave.

Is the weather nice? How about a nice nature walk? Otherwise, plug in an exercise video.

When oven timer sounds, begin microwaving vegetables 10 minutes on high. (Allow enchiladas to continue baking.) *Do some sit-ups, push-ups and stretches.* When vegetables are done — it's dinner time!

EXCHANGE VALUES

2 Starch	4 Meat	2 Veg.	1 Fruit	— Milk	— Fat

Nutrition information for — 1-1/2 enchiladas, 1 cup vegetables, 1/2 an apple and kiwi

Preparation Time — 30 min.   Oven / Exercise Time — 30 min.

Calories 480	Fat .... 12 g	Fiber .... 7 g	Sodium .... 800 mg	Total Carbohydrate .... 55 g
Calories from Fat 23%	Saturated Fat .... 4.8 g	Cholesterol .... 80 mg	Protein .... 37 g	Sugars .... 17 g

Arriving home starved: What to do

If you arrive home starved, you'll need something to hold you over until dinnertime. For a snack that's great exercise fuel, it's hard to beat a piece of fruit or fruit juice. Or try a few crackers, $1/2$ a bagel or 2 rice cakes. Be sure to chase it with a glass of water. This will give you energy and valuable hydration while holding off hunger throughout your workout until dinnertime.

Encore! Left-over Spanish Rice Roll-up

Spoon leftover *Spanish Red Beans and Rice* (hot or cold) onto a lavash bread.

Add extra salsa, lettuce, tomatoes, and roll it up. Delicious!

Spanish Red Beans & Rice

Every household needs a Spanish red beans and rice dish! Just like mom used to make. Feel free to make this with black beans if you prefer.

Kids' Favorite

Preheat oven to 350°.

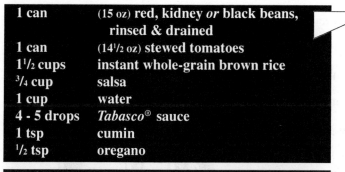

1 can	(15 oz) **red, kidney** *or* **black beans, rinsed & drained**
1 can	(14½ oz) **stewed tomatoes**
1½ cups	**instant whole-grain brown rice**
¾ cup	**salsa**
1 cup	**water**
4 - 5 drops	*Tabasco®* **sauce**
1 tsp	**cumin**
½ tsp	**oregano**

½ cup	**reduced-fat shredded cheddar cheese**

Mix together in a large casserole dish.

Cover and put in oven to bake. Set timer for 55 min.

I don't know about you, but the anticipation of this recipe puts me in the mood for rollerblading. What strikes you?

When the timer sounds, sprinkle cheese on the beans & rice and allow to melt while you set the table.

Serve with a tossed salad and fresh or canned pears.

EXCHANGE VALUES

3 Starch	1 Meat	— Veg.	— Fruit	— Milk	— Fat

Nutrition information for — 1/4 of the recipe — **Preparation Time — 10 min.** — **Oven / Exercise Time — 50 min.**

Calories 280	Fat ...... 3 g	Fiber ...... 8 g	Sodium ...... 900 mg	Total Carbohydrate ...... 50 g
Calories from Fat 10%	Saturated Fat ...... 1.5 g	Cholesterol ...... 5 mg	Protein ...... 15 g	Sugars ...... 1 g

Halloween Survival:
"Boo"tiful Alternatives to Candy

- Stickers

- Hand stamps and removable tattoos

- Dimes or nickels (you can actually "save" money this way)!

- Shoelaces

- Barrettes

- Ponytail holders

- Pencils

- Erasers

- Crayons

- Plastic spiders and other bugs

- Sugar-free gum

- Peanuts
  (small individual packages)

- Cereal
  (small individual boxes)

- Raisins
  (small boxes)

Ratatouille

	SERVES	MENU

An especially excellent dish to make in the fall, or anytime eggplant and zucchini are readily available. This makes a large batch since the flavor improves each day with reheating.

8

RATATOUILLE WITH POTATOES

WHOLE-GRAIN BREAD AND/OR

PUMPKIN SURPRISE PIE

Preheat oven to 350°.

1 medium	eggplant* unpeeled, cut into 1" cubes
8 medium	potatoes, scrubbed clean, cut in ½
1	red pepper, chopped
1	green pepper, chopped
4 small	zucchini (2 can be yellow crooked neck squash, sliced in half lengthwise and then into 1" slices)
2 large	onions, sliced

Prep vegetables and arrange in a large baking dish.

Crockpot option: Cook on high for 3 hours or low for 8 hours. You may need to halve the recipe to make it fit.

2 tsp	minced garlic (4 cloves)
½ cup	fresh minced parsley
1 tsp	dried basil, crushed
¾ tsp	salt
2 cans	(14.5 oz each) stewed tomatoes
2 T	olive oil

Mix together in a medium bowl — then pour over vegetables. Gently toss.

Cover and bake for 2 hours.

This allows ample time for a long fall hike. Aren't the colors beautiful? After exercising, you'll still have time to whip up the Pumpkin Surprise Pie *and get it into the oven for 1 hour.*

*Option: Chicken Ratatouille

Place 8 skinless drumsticks, thighs or breasts under the vegetables before baking.

When timer sounds, remove *Ratatouille* and allow to sit 30 minutes more, still covered. *Meanwhile... do push-ups, sit-ups and stretch.*

Serve with a sprinkle of Parmesan cheese, whole-grain bread or *Pumpkin Surprise Pie* (page 197).

EXCHANGE VALUES

2 Starch	— Meat	3 Veg.	— Fruit	— Milk	1 Fat

Nutrition information for — 1/8 of the recipe (without chicken)		Preparation Time — 20 min.	Oven / Exercise Time — 2 hours
Calories 280	Fat .... 4 g	Fiber .... 9 g Sodium .... 450 mg	Total Carbohydrate .... 58 g
Calories from Fat 12%	Saturated Fat .... .5 g	Cholesterol .... 0 mg Protein .... 7 g	Sugars .... 13 g

Halloween Survival Tips for KIDS

1. Try not to dole candy out piece by piece throughout the day. Repeated exposure to sugar is more likely to cause cavities. Rather, shoot for once a day and have them brush their teeth afterwards.

2. Don't let kids hide their candy underneath their beds. They'll be snacking all night without brushing their teeth.

3. Gently remind kids that candy is not a "grow food." This is why you are asking them to limit themselves to 2 or 3 pieces a day, in order to leave room for plenty of "grow" food.

4. Have them count out 30 (or so) pieces they want to keep and give the rest to families less fortunate.

Jack in the Pumpkin

This delicious and hearty Mexican style dish is baked in a hollowed out pumpkin providing for the ultimate Autumn holiday dish! It's also fun to use small pumpkins for personal single serving bowls for each guest. This dish is equally delicious baked in a casserole dish .

Great Autumn dish! Kids' Favorite!

Preheat oven to 375°.

1 cup	wild/brown rice mixed (¹/₄ wild, ³/₄ brown)
2 cups	water *and/or* broth
1	onion, chopped

Cook for 45 minutes until done.

1 medium	pumpkin (pie pumpkin is best)

Meanwhile… wash and carefully carve open a lid that provides a fairly wide opening. Be sure to carve with your knife at an angle, so that as it cooks, the lid does not slip through the opening. Scoop out all the seeds and pulp using a spoon. Set aside bowl and lid.

1 T	oil (olive *or* canola)
1 tsp	minced garlic (4 cloves)
¹/₂	red, green and yellow bell pepper, chopped
2	onions, chopped

Combine in a large stir-fry pan and sauté.

Recipe continued on next page.

Halloween Survival Tips for ADULTS

1. If you have the tendency to eat most of your Halloween candy before October 31, then refrain from buying until the day before.

2. Buy candy you don't like (if there is such a thing)!

3. Increase your exercise during this period.

4. Use positive self-talk. If you've nibbled a bit more than you wanted to, say "no big deal." Make a decision to end the "haunting" and give the candy away!

³/₄ cup	medium *or* hot salsa (strain so salsa is thick)
2 cups	frozen corn, thawed
2 cans	(16 oz) black beans, drained
¹/₄ cup	chopped fresh parsley
2 tsp	cumin seed
1 tsp	oregano
¹/₈ tsp	cayenne pepper
¹/₄ tsp	salt

Add to sauté along with the cooked rice. Bring to a simmer for a few minutes. There should be minimal liquid.

Carefully spoon mix into the pumpkin. Place the pumpkin on a cookie sheet, with the lid along side.

Bake for 1 hour and 15 minutes. Consider making a colorful *Marinated Vegetable Salad* (page 172).

How about a long fall bike ride? Use the extra time for toning exercises like sit-ups, push-ups and leg lifts, and of course, stretching!

Remove from oven and serve proudly. Meat from inside the pumpkin will be tender and tasty to eat as well.

EXCHANGE VALUES

3 Starch	1 Meat	2 Veg.	— Fruit	— Milk	— Fat

Nutrition information for — approximately 1 cup, without pumpkin			Preparation Time — 1 hour	Oven / Exercise Time — 75 min.
Calories 290	Fat .... 3.5 g	Fiber .... 11 g	Sodium .... 650 mg	Total Carbohydrate .... 60 g
Calories from Fat 9%	Saturated Fat .... < 1 g	Cholesterol .... 0 mg	Protein .... 11 g	Sugars .... 6 g

When is the best time of day to exercise you ask?

The BEST time to exercise is whenever you can and will do it CONSISTENTLY, whether that's morning, noon or night. I recommend mornings, as your energy level is high. Once you are finished, your commitment to fitness has been fulfilled and your self-esteem soars. Take it from a converted "I hate mornings" person, it IS possible to change your habits!

Studies also suggest you will burn a few more calories all day due to an elevated metabolism. Furthermore, fewer interruptions increase the odds of your being consistent.

P.S. So if you can swing it, exercise in the morning. If not, No PROBLEM. This *Oven/Exercise/Eat* chapter was written for you!

Chili Cornbread Pie

SERVES | MENU

A simple one-dish meal that will make your kitchen smell awesome!
Serve with carrot sticks, celery and peppers.

6 | CHILI CORNBREAD PIE
CARROT STICKS
CHOCOLATE CHIP BAR
COOKIE

Preheat oven to 375°.

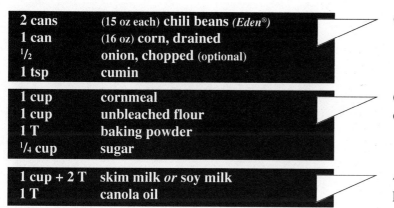

2 cans	(15 oz each) **chili beans** *(Eden®)*
1 can	(16 oz) **corn, drained**
½	**onion, chopped** (optional)
1 tsp	**cumin**

Combine in a 9" x 13" baking dish.

1 cup	**cornmeal**
1 cup	**unbleached flour**
1 T	**baking powder**
¼ cup	**sugar**

Combine in a medium bowl using a fork to be sure baking powder is evenly distributed.

| 1 cup + 2 T | **skim milk** *or* **soy milk** |
| 1 T | **canola oil** |

Add to dry ingredients and stir just until blended.

Pour the batter over the bean mixture.

Place in oven to bake. Set timer for 30 minutes.

*Climb upon your stepper for 20 minutes.
When the timer goes off, you're done
and it's time to eat!*

Note: If you are a cilantro fan, add ¼ cup to the beans and corn.

EXCHANGE VALUES

| 5 Starch | 1 Meat | — Veg. | — Fruit | — Milk | — Fat |

Nutrition information for — 1/6 of the pie | | | **Preparation Time — 15 min.** | **Oven / Exercise Time — 30 min.**

| Calories .... 435 | Fat .... 4 g | Fiber .... 11.5 g | Sodium .... 675 mg | Total Carbohydrate .... 80 g |
| Calories from Fat .... 8% | Saturated Fat .... < 1 g | Cholesterol .... < 1 mg | Protein .... 18.5 g | Sugars .... 14 g |

Pasta

Perhaps known as the health food of the '90's, pasta has been touted *everywhere*. It's the "pre-game" meal of choice for athletes, a favorite among vegetarians, and a new low-fat "diet" food for the weight-conscious. And you thought starchy foods were fattening! What's the deal?

The nutritional plus comes from the fact that if you're eating a big plate of pasta, you're probably NOT eating a 12-ounce steak. This is good. If the pasta is tossed with a low-fat tomato sauce, instead of an artery-clogging Alfredo sauce, then this is really good! And if there are lots of vegetables tossed in the sauce, this is *really really* good!

The overall goal is to decrease the amount of animal sources in our diet, and increase the amount of vegetables and grains. Eating pasta (which is a grain), with a chunky tomato sauce with vegetables and a tossed salad on the side, is a great way to do exactly that.

Combining all of this with the fact that pasta meals are fast and a favorite to both children and adults, makes pasta a definite winner! Do you feel like spaghetti, corkscrews, penne or angel hair? Red or white sauce? How about *Southwest Chili* or *Oriental Noodles* for a change? You'll never get tired of having pasta once a week!

But isn't pasta fattening?

Following these 5 steps, pasta is NOT fattening.

1. Use a low-fat recipe for the sauce (like the ones in this chapter)!

2. Include as many vegetables in the sauce as you can.

3. Choose whole-wheat pasta whenever possible (for added fiber, vitamins and minerals).

4. Eat a tossed salad before the pasta for appetite control.

5. Eat until your stomach says "satisfied" instead of "full." Even pasta becomes fattening when you eat TOO MUCH!

Veggie Sghetti

Occasionally we make this with turkey, but always with lots of vegetables. The vegetables replace the meat beautifully. Use any leftover sauce to top baked potatoes later in the week.

6

VEGGIE SGHETTI
TOSSED SALAD
WHOLE-WHEAT GARLIC CHEESE TOAST

Put a large pot of water on to boil.

4 cups	any of the following:
	carrots, chopped
	green, red *or* yellow pepper, chopped
	zucchini, chopped
	mushrooms, chopped
1 box	(10 oz) frozen chopped broccoli, cauliflower *or* spinach

Clean and chop or use all chopped frozen, to save time and energy.

Delegate Someone to: Make salad and garlic toast.

12 oz	spaghetti *or* any shape pasta — preferably whole-wheat

As soon as water boils, stir in pasta and set timer for 10 minutes.

1 T	olive oil
1	onion, cut into wedges
1 tsp	minced garlic (2 cloves)
1 lb	extra lean ground turkey breast (optional)

Heat oil in a large nonstick sauce pan. Add onion, garlic and above vegetables. Add and brown turkey if using.

1 jar	(26 oz) spaghetti sauce (*Healthy Choice*®)
2 tsp	oregano
2 tsp	basil
dash	red pepper flakes (to taste)

Add to vegetables. Bring to a simmer.

Meanwhile… make a tossed salad and *Whole-Wheat Garlic Cheese Toast* (page 183).

When timer sounds, drain pasta and serve with sauce.

Bón Appetit.

EXCHANGE VALUES

2.5 Starch — Meat 3 Veg. — Fruit — Milk — Fat

Nutrition information for — about 1-1/2 cups of sauce & veggies over 1 cup pasta   Preparation Time — 30 min.

Calories 305	Fat .... 3.5 g	Fiber .... 11.5 g	Sodium .... 416 mg	Total Carbohydrate .... 54 g
Calories from Fat 10%	Saturated Fat .... 1.3 g	Cholesterol .... 0 mg	Protein .... 14 g	Sugars .... 13 g

Vegetable or Turkey Spaghetti

Lickety-Split Meals

When is pasta NOT good for you?

The following are all examples of a "bypass special" wearing the pasta disguise…

1. Restaurant Lasagna, including Spinach Lasagna and Vegetarian Lasagna. (It's the truck load of cheese).

2. Restaurant Fettuccine Alfredo (butter, oil and cream. Enough said).

3. Most white sauces (unless it's a low-fat recipe like the one below)!

Pasta Primavera

You and your guests will never believe that this cream sauce is practically fat-free. Do you feel like chicken, shrimp or vegetables only? I use the shrimp or chicken options when entertaining and vegetables only for every day.

Put a large pot of water on to boil.

10 cups	vegetables — any combination of fresh *or* frozen broccoli carrots cauliflower green, red *or* yellow pepper zucchini yellow squash mushrooms pea pods

Clean & chop the fresh vegetables you happen to have and fill in with frozen vegetables. To save time, use all frozen vegetables. Set aside.

8 oz	pasta (fettuccine *or* linguine)

As soon as water boils, stir in pasta and set timer for 10 minutes. When time sounds, drain and keep warm.

1 T	olive oil
1	onion, cut into wedges
1 - 2 tsp	minced garlic (2 cloves)

Heat oil in a large non-stick fry pan or wok. Add garlic and onion. Cook 1 minute.

Recipe continued on next page.

When is pasta NOT good for you? (Continued)

4. When the pasta is tossed with lots of oil (restaurants commonly do this).

5. When the marinara sauce is made with too much oil to sauté the vegetables.

6. When the "sprinkled" Parmesan cheese exceeds a sprinkle.

7. When the recipe includes sausage and other artery clogging meats.

4	skinless, boneless, chicken breast, (halves) (optional)

Cube chicken and sauté 5 minutes (or skip this step).

When chicken is almost finished cooking, add the vegetables and stir.

1 cup	($\frac{1}{2}$ can) chicken broth, $\frac{1}{3}$ less sodium
$\frac{3}{4}$ cup	($\frac{1}{2}$ can) evaporated skim milk

Meanwhile… in a small bowl, mix the $\frac{1}{2}$ cans of chicken broth & evaporated skim milk. *(Combine the remaining broth and milk in an airtight container, label and freeze for the next time you make this.)*

$\frac{1}{4}$ cup	cornstarch
$\frac{1}{2}$ cup	white wine

Add to broth mixture and stir well.

12 oz	frozen cooked shrimp, peeled & deveined (optional)

Remove tails if necessary. Add to the vegetables (or skip this step).

Add the milk/broth mixture to the vegetables. Simmer until thick and bubbly.

1 tsp	basil
2 tsp	oregano
10 grinds	fresh ground pepper
$\frac{1}{4}$ tsp	salt
$\frac{1}{2}$ cup	Parmesan cheese

Add seasonings and cheese, followed by the cooked, drained pasta. Toss gently.

Serve with *Cranberry Salad* (page 177) and remember to save room for *Flaming Bananas Foster* (page 200).

EXCHANGE VALUES

2 Starch	2 Meat	3 Veg.	— Fruit	— Milk	— Fat

Nutrition information for — about 1-1/2 cups sauce & shrimp (no chicken) over 1 cup pasta   Preparation Time — 45 min.

Calories 370	Fat .... 6 g	Fiber .... 6 g	Sodium .... 520 mg	Total Carbohydrate ....50 g
Calories from Fat 15%	Saturated Fat .... 2 g	Cholesterol .... 117 mg	Protein .... 26 g	Sugars ....8 g

True or False

"Eating 2 cups of regular pasta (not a whole-wheat variety), is like eating 4 slices of white bread."

Depressing, but TRUE.
Most pasta is made from refined wheat. It does not contain the fibrous bran, or the nutrient-dense germ. (Similar to the white flour used for white bread). While eating white bread is better than eating a big steak, we all know it's better to eat WHOLE-WHEAT products. And that includes pasta! (See page 36 for more information about the nutrition lost when whole grain is refined).

Look for whole-wheat pasta products in your grocery store. They may be in the normal pasta section or in the "health food" section.

Southwest Chili Pasta

A delicious and colorful "South of the border" pasta dish. And it is quick!

Delegate someone to: make tossed salad

Put a large pot of water on to boil.

1	green pepper

Chop pepper and set aside.

Open cans that are called for below.
Drain beans reserving liquid.

8 oz	pasta (preferably whole-wheat) any size or shape

As soon as water boils, stir in pasta and set timer for 10 minutes.

1 T	olive oil
2 tsp	minced garlic (4 cloves)

Heat oil, then sauté garlic and chopped pepper for 1 minute.

1½ tsp	whole cumin seeds *or* 1 tsp ground cumin

Add and sauté 10 seconds longer.

1 can	(15 oz) black beans, drained
1 can	(15 oz) kidney beans, drained
1 can	(14.5 oz) stewed tomatoes
2 - 3 tsp	chili powder

Add to pot and simmer for 10 minutes. If chili becomes too thick, thin it slightly with the reserved bean liquid.

When the timer sounds, drain pasta and serve with the chili over top.

Serve with tossed salad.

EXCHANGE VALUES

4 Starch	1 Meat	1 Veg.	— Fruit	— Milk	— Fat

Nutrition information for — about 1-1/4 cups of beans and sauce over 1 cup pasta

Preparation Time — 25 min.

Calories 425	Fat ...... 5.5 g	Fiber ...... 18 g	Sodium ...... 665 mg	Total Carbohydrate ...... 77 g
Calories from Fat 11%	Saturated Fat ...... 2 g	Cholesterol ...... 0 mg	Protein ...... 20 g	Sugars ...... 11 g

Great ideas for first-time whole-wheat pasta users:

1. Serve with lots of chunky tomato sauce.

2. Toss the pasta and sauce in the kitchen so the children will not speculate why the pasta is brown.

3. Try cooking half white and half whole-wheat until you are used to it.

4. Try the 50-50 pastas available from *Eden Foods*®. They offer a wonderful line of pasta that uses $1/2$ "sifted" flour with $1/2$ whole-wheat flour. These products are delicious and you really can't tell they are made with whole-wheat! They of course offer fine 100% whole-wheat pasta as well. Look in your health food store or health food section of your grocery store. If it's not there, ask for it!

Herbed Italian Sausage over Pasta

SERVES | **MENU**

Here's a tasty change from the traditional spaghetti dinner and yet another use for your *Homemade Turkey Sausage* (see Breakfast section).

4

HERBED ITALIAN SAUSAGE OVER PASTA

CRUNCHY TOSSED SALAD

WHOLE-WHEAT GARLIC CHEESE TOAST

SMOOTHIE

Put a large pot of water on to boil, cover and turn on high.

1	onion
1 each	green and yellow pepper
10	baby carrots, chopped (optional)
1 sm	zucchini, cut in half and sliced (optional)

Slice onion into small wedges and vegetables into thin strips or however you'd like.

8 oz	pasta (preferably whole-wheat) any size *or* shape

As soon as water boils, stir in pasta and set timer for 10 minutes.

1 T	oil (olive *or* canola)
4	*Homemade Turkey Sausage** patties (from freezer)

Add oil to a hot nonstick skillet and sauté vegetables for 2 minutes. Add turkey sausage, breaking up into crumbles. Cook until done.

1 jar	(26 oz) spaghetti sauce (*Healthy Choice*®)
1 tsp	Italian seasoning

Add and bring to a simmer.

When timer sounds, drain pasta. Pour sauce over pasta to serve.

Don't forget the tossed salad and *Whole-Wheat Garlic Toast* (page 183).

EXCHANGE VALUES

3 Starch	2 Meat	2 Veg.	— Fruit	— Milk	— Fat

* See *Breakfast* section (page 44).

Nutrition information for — about 1-1/4 cups sauce & veggies over 1 cup pasta   **Preparation Time — 25 min.**

Calories 370	Fat .... 5 g	Fiber .... 12 g	Sodium .... 785 mg	Total Carbohydrate .... 59 g
Calories from Fat 13%	Saturated Fat .... 1.5 g	Cholesterol .... 16 mg	Protein .... 21 g	Sugars .... 17 g

Selecting a spaghetti sauce

The goal is to find a sauce that is 5 or less grams of fat and 800 mg or less of sodium *per cup*. Including lots of chunky vegetables is definitely a plus too. Contrary to what you may be thinking, 5 grams of fat is NOT TOO MUCH. In fact, studies have indicated that the lycopenes (cancer-fighting compounds in tomatoes) are more available to your body cells when the tomatoes ARE cooked with a small amount of oil, vs. no oil. Besides, pour it over 2 cups of pasta and you only have 10% of calories from fat.

I have recommended *Healthy Choice*® in my recipes simply because it meets these recommendations, has a little fat and is readily available. However, I encourage you to shop around for the sauce you like best. Take a look at my selected sampling on page 30, to get an idea of what's out there.

Parmesan Turkey Cutlets over Angel Hair

SERVES	MENU

When you're serving pasta once a week, it's nice to vary the presentation. My thanks to Connie and Rich Bloom for this neat find. If you don't have angel hair, any pasta will do.

6

PARMESAN TURKEY CUTLETS OVER ANGEL HAIR

WHOLE-WHEAT GARLIC CHEESE TOAST

WHERE'S THE LETTUCE? SALAD

Put a large pot of water on to boil.

1 jar	(26 oz) **spaghetti sauce** *(Healthy Choice®)*

Place in a small saucepan and heat over medium-low.

¼ cup	**Parmesan cheese**
¼ tsp	**Italian seasoning**
5 grinds	**fresh ground pepper**

Mix together in a bowl.

12 oz	**angel hair pasta**

As soon as water boils, stir in angel hair and set time for 7 minutes.

1 lb	**fresh turkey breast cutlets**
	(6 slices, ¼" thick each)
1 T	**olive oil**

Heat oil over medium heat. Coat each turkey cutlet with cheese mixture and place in a pan. Cook 2 minutes on each side.

When timer sounds, drain pasta.

To serve, place 1 cup pasta on each plate, top with 1 turkey breast slice and ½ to ¾ cup of sauce over top.

Serve with *Whole Wheat Garlic Cheese Toast* (page 183) and *Where's the Lettuce? Salad* (page 171).

Delegate Someone to: Make Garlic Toast and Where's the Lettuce Salad

EXCHANGE VALUES

3 Starch	3 Meat	1 Veg.	— Fruit	— Milk	— Fat

Nutrition information for — 1 small turkey cutlet, 1 cup pasta, 1/2 cup sauce

Preparation Time — 30 min.

Calories 385	Fat .... 5 g	Fiber .... 3.5 g	Sodium .... 525 mg	Total Carbohydrate .... 54 g
Calories from Fat 11%	Saturated Fat .... 1 g	Cholesterol .... 50 mg	Protein .... 30 g	Sugars .... 10 g

Great ideas from people like you!

"The most important aspect about exercise for me is that it builds a confidence level that carries me through all aspects of my life. I feel exercise is a celebration of life and a blessing on the whole day.

—KAY V. E., 44
2nd grade teacher and
consistent exerciser for 15 years
Once 168 pounds, now 125

White Beans & Penne Pasta

My thanks to neighbors Eric & Anne Tooley for sharing this family favorite. While the drizzling of oil with rosemary over the top before serving seems fattening, the numbers still come out healthy and the taste is exceptional.

6

WHITE BEANS
AND PENNE PASTA

TOSSED SALAD

WHOLE-WHEAT GARLIC
CHEESE TOAST

1 T	olive oil
1 large	onion, cut into wedges
1 tsp	minced garlic (2 cloves)

Sauté 3 or 4 minutes over medium-high heat.

Delegate someone to: Make the tossed salad.

2 cans	(14.5 oz) stewed tomatoes

Add and simmer 10 minutes.
Use this time to put together a tossed salad.

2 cans	(14.5 oz each) chicken broth, $^1/_3$ less sodium
1 jar	(24 oz) Great Northern beans, rinsed and drained

Stir in and bring to a boil.

6 oz	Penne pasta

Stir in and set timer for 10 minutes.

Meanwhile… make *Whole-Wheat Garlic Cheese Toast* (page 183).

2 T	olive oil
1 tsp	dry rosemary (*or* 1 T fresh)

Mix together in small microwave safe bowl. Warm in microwave for 30 seconds.

Prepare the servings of pasta and drizzle rosemary oil over each serving. Top with Parmesan cheese if desired. Don't forget the salad and garlic toast.

EXCHANGE VALUES

3 Starch	1 Meat	2 Veg.	— Fruit	— Milk	1 Fat

SODIUM ALERT! See page 31.

Nutrition information for — about 1-1/2 cups				Preparation Time — 35 min.	
Calories 330	Fat .... 7 g	Fiber .... 10 g	Sodium .... 900 mg	Total Carbohydrate .... 53 g
Calories from Fat 19%	Saturated Fat .... < 1 g	Cholesterol .... 0 mg	Protein .... 13 g	Sugars .... 8 g

White Beans & Penne Pasta

Lickety-Split Meals

What is Tamari?

Tamari (sometimes called Shoyu) is very similar to reduced-sodium soy sauce, but is lighter in color and flavor. Both Tamari and Shoyu are popular in natural food recipes because they are made the more natural and traditional way with long fermentation. Soy sauce, on the other hand, is a general term for the dark-brown flavoring liquids with a soybean base. Soy sauce is prepared unfermented from hydrolyzed vegetable protein, corn syrup, caramel color and salt.

I suggest looking for Tamari or Shoyu for both their "natural product" quality and delightful taste. If you cannot find them, use reduced-sodium soy sauce in their place.

Oriental Noodle Toss with Black Beans

The sesame oil really makes this. Excellent as a main dish or as a side dish to grilled or broiled salmon steak. Serve warm or at room temperature.

ORIENTAL NOODLE TOSS WITH BLACK BEANS

TOSSED SALAD WITH CRUNCHY VEGETABLES

RASPBERRY SORBET

Put a large pot of water on to boil.

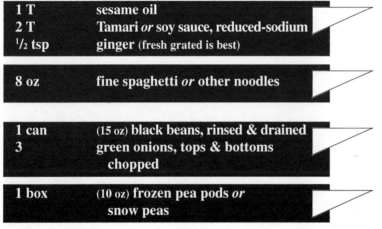

1 T	sesame oil
2 T	Tamari *or* soy sauce, reduced-sodium
1/2 tsp	ginger (fresh grated is best)

Stir together in a medium-large serving bowl.

Delegate someone to: Make tossed salad with crunchy vegetables.

8 oz	fine spaghetti *or* other noodles

As soon as water boils, stir in pasta and set timer for 6 minutes (9 minutes if not using a fine pasta.)

1 can	(15 oz) black beans, rinsed & drained
3	green onions, tops & bottoms chopped

Add to bowl.

1 box	(10 oz) frozen pea pods *or* snow peas

When timer sounds, add pea pods or snow peas to boiling noodles for 1 minute. Drain. Toss with the beans and sauce.

It's meal-time!

EXCHANGE VALUES

3 Starch	1 Meat	1 Veg.	— Fruit	— Milk	— Fat

Nutrition information for — about 1-1/2 cups			Preparation Time — 20 min.	
Calories 345	Fat .... 5 g	Fiber .... 9 g	Sodium .... 530 mg	Total Carbohydrate .... 64 g
Calories from Fat 11%	Saturated Fat .... < 1 g	Cholesterol .... 0 mg	Protein .... 15 g	Sugars .... 3 g

Pizza

What's America's favorite food? Pizza! And what food often gets blamed for being fattening and artery-clogging? Pizza! But NOT anymore!

At first you would think pizza, made healthy and fast at home, would be a complete oxymoron. But thanks to the convenience of pita bread, (which make great individual pizza crusts) or ready-made crusts by *"Boboli®"* or *"Oliveri®"*, ready-made sauces and low-fat cheese, you can make your own healthy pizzas at home. And all in much less time than it takes to get pizza delivered!

The following recipes use ready-made sauces, lean meat (if any), low-fat cheese and ample vegetable toppings, which make the pizzas nutritionally smart. So stock up on your supplies. They're all on the *Lickety-Split* grocery list.

You will notice that some of the recipes instruct you to sauté the vegetable toppings first before placing on the pizza. Other recipes instruct you to place the toppings on raw (leaving them a little "more crunchy" when finished). It will not take long before you decide if more or less crunchy is your family's favorite. Simply add the sauté step if "more tender" is your preference.

I'm sure it's no surprise that the *Lickety-Split Weekly Menu Solution* lists Friday as your pizza night. The family's favorite by far! TGIF!

Pita: The perfect ready-made pizza crust

If you haven't used pita bread for pizzas yet, you haven't lived! Pitas allow everyone to make individual "custom" pizzas with the convenient ready-made "crusts". (Forget about the "pocket" and just lay them flat). Be sure to look through all the recipes in this chapter, because you can adapt any of them to make a pita pizza in seconds.

Another fine benefit of pita's, is that whole-wheat pitas are pretty easy to find, (ask your grocer). This is a nutritional plus over the *Boboli*® or *Oliveri*® pizza crusts (which are unfortunately not available in whole-wheat).

P.S. Buy several packages of pitas for the freezer so you'll always have them on hand.

P.S.S. Be sure to involve the kids! They will love making their own pizzas!

Pita Pizza

A quick and easy meal, that both kids and adults will love.
When you have more time, let the kids assemble their own pizzas.

Turn oven on to broil. Leave the oven door ajar.

2	whole-wheat pita breads	Lay out on a cookie sheet.
6 T	spaghetti sauce *(Healthy Choice®)*	Spread $1/2$ of sauce onto each pita.
$1/4$ tsp	dried oregano	Sprinkle on top of each pita.
$1/4$ tsp	dried basil	
$1 1/2$ cups	bite-size broccoli flowerets	Rinse, drain and place in a microwave safe dish. Cover and cook $1 1/2$ minutes on high.
$1/4$	green pepper	Layer on the pita as desired. Add broccoli.
$1/4$	onion	
3	mushrooms	
$1/2$ cup	reduced-fat shredded mozzarella cheese	Complete the pizza by sprinkling each on top. Broil 6" from heating element for about 2 to 4 minutes, until cheese is melted and beginning to brown.
2 T	Parmesan cheese	
dash	red pepper flakes (as desired)	Serve with tossed salad and fruit for dessert.

EXCHANGE VALUES

2 Starch	1 Meat	2 Veg.	— Fruit	— Milk	— Fat

Nutrition information for — 1 pita pizza

Preparation Time — 15 min.

Calories 275	Fat .... 4 g	Fiber .... 6.5 g	Sodium .... 600 mg	Total Carbohydrate .... 43 g	
Calories from Fat 14%	Saturated Fat .... 2.5 g	Cholesterol .... 14 mg	Protein .... 19 g	Sugars .... 6.5 g	

Pizza AND cookies?
Are you sure this is a *healthy* cookbook?

The only thing better than pizza is pizza and cookies. Limit yourself to 2 slices of pizza, play some frisbee and you can justify heading back to the kitchen for some dessert. *Chocolate No-Bakes* (page 193) are fast and 2 of them really hit the spot!

Garden Vegetable Pizza

"Pre-steaming" the broccoli flowerets turns them bright green and keeps them from drying out. If you prefer your onion and peppers soft versus a little crunchy, microwave them along with the broccoli, adding 1 minute.

Preheat oven to 425°.

1	ready-made pizza crust (*Boboli®*)
1 cup	(or more) **spaghetti sauce** (*Healthy Choice®*)

Spread sauce evenly onto crust.

1½ cups	**fresh broccoli flowerets** (cut into bite-size flowerets)

Rinse, drain and place in a microwave safe dish.
Cover and cook 1 minute on high.

1 small	**onion, thinly sliced into rings**
5	**fresh mushrooms, sliced** *or* 1 small can sliced mushrooms, drained
½	**red pepper, sliced into strips**
½	**green pepper, sliced into strips**
1	**fresh tomato, thinly sliced**

Prep vegetables and neatly arrange on pizza.
Top with broccoli flowerets.

2 T	**Parmesan cheese**
1 cup	**reduced-fat shredded mozzarella cheese**
4 dashes	(or more) **hot pepper flakes**
4 sprinkles	**Italian seasoning**

Sprinkle evenly on pizza in order given.

Bake 10 to 12 minutes.

Meanwhile… make *Where's the Lettuce? Salad* (page 171).

Cut into 8 slices and serve.

EXCHANGE VALUES

3.5 Starch	2 Meat	2 Veg.	— Fruit	— Milk	— Fat

SODIUM ALERT! See page 31.

Nutrition information for — 2 slices   **Preparation Time — 25 min.**

Calories 425	Fat .... 10 g	Fiber .... 4.3 g	Sodium .... 1050 mg	Total Carbohydrate .... 62 g
Calories from Fat 19%	Saturated Fat .... 4 g	Cholesterol .... 16 mg	Protein .... 26 g	Sugars .... 9 g

Solution to typical pizza problem #1:

CHEESE and LOTS of it.

Making pizza at home means you can select part-skim mozzarella mixed 50-50 with the fat-free variety, for 3 grams of fat per ounce and use just 4 ounces (1 cup) of cheese for an entire pizza. This makes an incredibly low-fat pizza!

Hot & Spicy Pizza with Sausage

Here's another reason for making the "Homemade Turkey Sausage" from the Breakfast section. The sausage offers great flavor and convenience. Note vegetarians: Even without the sausage, this recipe is **very** delicious!

Preheat oven to 425°.
Spray nonstick pan with nonstick spray.

2	(4 oz) *Homemade Turkey Sausage** **patties**
1	**onion, thinly sliced**
½	**red pepper, sliced into strips**
½	**green pepper, sliced into strips**

Sauté until sausage is done,
break up and crumble the patties.

1	**ready-made pizza crust** (*Boboli®*)
1 cup	(or more) **spaghetti sauce** (*Healthy Choice®*)

Meanwhile… spread sauce evenly onto crust.
Spread sausage mixture over sauce.

8 - 12	**pickled hot pepper rings** (optional)

Evenly place onto pizza.

4 dashes	(or more) **hot pepper flakes**
1 T	**Parmesan cheese**
1 cup	**reduced-fat shredded mozzarella cheese**

Add to pizza.

Bake 10 to 12 minutes.

Meanwhile… make *Where's the Lettuce? Salad* (page 171).

Cut into 8 slices and serve.

SODIUM ALERT! See page 31.

* See *Breakfast* section (page 50)

EXCHANGE VALUES

3.5 Starch	3 Meat	2 Veg.	— Fruit	— Milk	— Fat

Nutrition information for — 2 slices (without hot pepper rings) — **Preparation Time — 30 min.**

Calories 433	Fat .... 9 g	Fiber .... 3.2 g	Sodium .... 1150 mg	Total Carbohydrate .... 60 g
Calories from Fat 18%	Saturated Fat .... 3.8 g	Cholesterol .... 25 g	Protein .... 30 g	Sugars .... 8 g

What is chutney?

Chutney is the relish that traditionally accompanies Indian food, made of chopped fruits and spices like ginger, allspice, cinnamon, garlic, vinegar and hot pepper. Look for it in the specialty section of your grocery store. Trust me: it's a delicious spicy-sweet dynamo.

Chicken Chutney Pizza

My husband ordered this in a restaurant once. I said, "What? Are you crazy?"
And yes, crazy we both are now for Chutney Pizza! This stuff is *really* great!

Preheat oven to 425°.
Spray nonstick pan with nonstick spray.

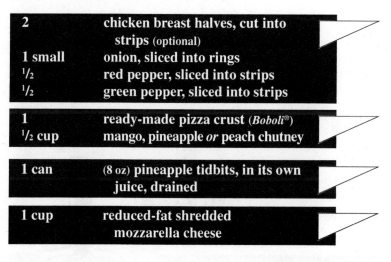

2	chicken breast halves, cut into strips (optional)
1 small	onion, sliced into rings
½	red pepper, sliced into strips
½	green pepper, sliced into strips

Sauté all together until chicken is no longer pink.

| 1 | ready-made pizza crust (*Boboli*®) |
| ½ cup | mango, pineapple *or* peach chutney |

Meanwhile… spread sauce evenly onto crust. When chicken is done spread chicken mixture over sauce.

| 1 can | (8 oz) pineapple tidbits, in its own juice, drained |

Place on pizza.

| 1 cup | reduced-fat shredded mozzarella cheese |

Sprinkle on pizza.

Bake 10 to 12 minutes.

Meanwhile… make tossed salad.

Cut into 8 slices and serve.

EXCHANGE VALUES

| 4 Starch | 3 Meat | — Veg. | 1 Fruit | — Milk | — Fat |

Nutrition information for — 2 slices

Preparation Time — 30 min.

| Calories .... 530 | Fat .... 9 g | Fiber .... 3 g | Sodium .... 850 mg | Total Carbohydrate .... 78 g |
| Calories from Fat .... 16% | Saturated Fat .... 3.7 g | Cholesterol .... 48 mg | Protein .... 37 g | Sugars .... 27 g |

Solution to typical pizza problem #2: Fatty toppings

I probably don't have to tell you how bad pizza toppings like pepperoni (a.k.a. pig fat puddles) are for you. Saturated fat, sodium, preservatives….YUK!!! You'll also notice that I've included a meat topping that will surprise you: sautéed chicken breast strips. I have to admit, it sounded weird at first, but give it a try! In the meantime, for the true "hard-core pizza traditionalists" try this:

1. Opt for just 1 meat topping.

2. Choose leaner meat toppings like ham or Canadian bacon.

3. Select as many vegetable toppings as possible.

Other pizza ordering tips….

4. Ask for the regular or thin crusts (more "dry") instead of deep dish which are often more greasy…notice the shine on your fingers?

5. Refrain from double cheese (you can do it!) and request "half the cheese you usually put on, please."

Southwest Chicken Pizza

Since we like to have pizza once a week, this gives us some nice variety. Enjoy!

Preheat oven to 425°.
Spray a nonstick skillet with nonstick spray.

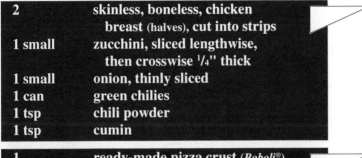

2	skinless, boneless, chicken breast (halves), cut into strips
1 small	zucchini, sliced lengthwise, then crosswise ¼" thick
1 small	onion, thinly sliced
1 can	green chilies
1 tsp	chili powder
1 tsp	cumin

Sauté all together until chicken is no longer pink.

1	ready-made pizza crust (*Boboli®*)
1 cup	thick salsa*

Meanwhile… spread salsa evenly on crust.

Spread cooked chicken mixture on pizza.

1 cup	reduced-fat shredded cheddar cheese
5	black olives, sliced

Add to pizza in order given.

Bake 8 to 10 minutes.

Meanwhile… prepare tossed salad and fresh orange sections.

Cut into 8 slices and serve.

SODIUM ALERT! See page 31.

* If your salsa is thin, use a slotted spoon to lift out the thick parts.

EXCHANGE VALUES

3.5 Starch	3 Meat	2 Veg.	— Fruit	— Milk	— Fat

Nutrition information for — 2 slices — **Preparation Time — 30 min.**

Calories 490	Fat .... 12 g	Fiber .... 3 g	Sodium .... 1350 mg	Total Carbohydrate .... 59 g
Calories from Fat 22%	Saturated Fat .... 4.3 g	Cholesterol .... 47 mg	Protein .... 36 g	Sugars .... 5 g

Solution to typical pizza problem #3

Pizza is usually the only food choice served at the meal. I know what you're thinking. Pizza contains all of the necessary food groups right? But NOT in the right proportions to provide enough fiber and cancer-fighting nutrients to balance out all of the cheese fat. I remind you in each recipe that a serving of pizza is 2 slices; (3 or 4 slices for *very* active people). In addition to this, you should serve it with salad or vegetables and fruit. With this strategy, you can include pizza into a healthy diet every single week! TGIF!

Polynesian Pizza

This pizza features the unexpected, BBQ sauce! Now I know what you're thinking, but be brave. Try it!

Preheat oven to 425°.

1	ready-made pizza crust (*Boboli*®)
⅓ cup	BBQ sauce (*Open Pit*®)

Spread sauce evenly onto crust.

1	onion, thinly sliced into rings
½	red pepper, sliced into strips
½	green pepper, sliced into strips
1 can	(8 oz) pineapple tidbits, in it's own juice, well drained

Layer on pizza. Reserve pineapple juice for another use.

1 cup	reduced-fat shredded mozzarella cheese

Sprinkle evenly across pizza.

Bake 10 to 12 minutes.

Meanwhile… make *Crunchy Apple Salad* (page 174).

Cut into 8 slices and serve.

EXCHANGE VALUES

3 Starch	2 Meat	1 Veg.	1 Fruit	— Milk	— Fat

SODIUM ALERT! Use pita bread instead of *Boboli*® crust and save about 250 mg of sodium.

Nutrition information for — 2 slices   **Preparation Time — 25 min.**

Calories 425	Fat .... 8.5 g	Fiber .... 2.5 g	Sodium .... 1130 mg	Total Carbohydrate .... 66 g
Calories from Fat 18%	Saturated Fat .... 3.5 g	Cholesterol .... 14 mg	Protein .... 23 g	Sugars .... 13 g

Is shrimp high in cholesterol or not?

Contrary to what you may have heard, shrimp, scallops, lobster and crab (as long as they are not fried or sautéed in lots of fat) can definitely be part of a healthy diet. Here's what you need to know about seafood:

1. Seafood is naturally very low in total fat, including saturated fat.

2. Ounce for ounce, seafood has about the same amount of cholesterol as chicken.

3. Seafood contains the beneficial Omega III fatty acids (see page 102 for more information).

4. Stick with MODERATE portions (3 ounces or 7 medium shrimp) and avoid those "all you can eat" buffets.

5. Dip lobster in lemon not butter.

6. Avoid fried shrimp or broiled scampi or scallops that are swimming in butter!

7. Ask for "dry broiled" or steamed.

8. Of course, include lots of vegetables with your meal.

Shrimp Pizza

Yet another delicious way to enjoy pizza at home. The cocktail sauce provides a nice change.

SHRIMP PIZZA

SUNSHINE CARROT-RAISIN SALAD

Appeteaser idea: Use mini pitas (like 2" round) to build tasty single serving appetizers, with one shrimp on each.

Preheat oven to 425°.

1	ready made pizza crust (*Boboli®*)
¹/₂ cup	seafood cocktail sauce

Spread sauce evenly onto crust.

¹/₂	green pepper, sliced into strips
1 sm can	sliced mushrooms, drained

Arrange evenly across sauce.

1 cup	reduced-fat shredded mozzarella cheese

Sprinkle evenly across vegetables.

4 oz	(about 18 medium) **cooked shrimp** (frozen works well)

Arrange shrimp over cheese. (If using frozen, cooked shrimp, run warm water over them to quick thaw, then drain. Remove tails, if necessary.)

Bake 8 to 10 minutes.

Meanwhile… make *Sunshine Carrot-Raisin Salad* (page 173).

Cut into 8 slices and serve.

EXCHANGE VALUES

4 Starch	2 Meat	— Veg.	— Fruit	— Milk	— Fat

SODIUM ALERT! Use pita bread instead of *Boboli®* crust and save about 250 mg of sodium.

Nutrition information for — 2 slices

Preparation Time — 25 min.

Calories 420	Fat .... 9 g	Fiber .... 2 g	Sodium .... 1200 mg	Total Carbohydrate .... 59 g
Calories from Fat 18%	Saturated Fat .... 3.6 g	Cholesterol .... 70 mg	Protein .... 29 g	Sugars .... 7.5 g

Stir-Fry

"I highly recommend woking once a week. Not to be confused with walking of course, which should be done much more often!"

There are 3 complaints I hear quite often from clients:

- "4 ounces of meat looks SO tiny on my plate!"
- "Vegetables are boring without butter and salt."
- "If you want me to eat rice, I want a nice sauce to go over it."

Well, there's an easy way to end all 3 complaints in a hurry, and that's with a stir-fry!

But doesn't that sound like a lot of work? Don't you need special equipment? How do you make a nice flavorful sauce? Aren't commercially prepared sauces high in sodium? Can't you walk to China in the time it takes to chop all those vegetables?

As you're about to find out, stir-frying is a fast and simple way to get a delicious, vegetable packed meal on the table. You'll love how just a small amount of beef, chicken or pork (or no meat at all!) can flavor the entire dish. (Even meat lovers are fooled by the small meat portions)!

You can use your largest nonstick fry pan, or pick up a nonstick wok. (Whether it's electric or stove-top, I suggest a nonstick coating). You can vary the vegetables you use according to what's in season and what your family likes. You can use frozen vegetables to eliminate time consuming chopping. And *yes*, you can shop for commercially-made sauces that don't break the sodium rules. (See page 38.)

Perhaps the best part is, you can select a different type of stir-fry each week, so "Saturday night stir-fry nights" are never boring. Happy woking!

The four secrets to long-term weight loss

Being overweight is like having a big weed in your yard. Going on a diet is like taking your weed wacker and nipping away at it. And sticking to the diet long enough, you can nip that weed right down to the ground.

But what happens after that? The weed grows back. Why? Because all weeds have **roots**.

The secret to permanent weight loss means succeeding within four critical habits. Not just "diet and exercise" mind you, but four! You can visualize the importance of these four areas similarly to the four wheels on a car. Without all four, it's impossible to drive anywhere and likewise impossible to navigate yourself to permanent weight loss.

Wheel #1 — The habit of eating healthy

The goal here is to achieve a healthful eating style that's natural to you, or second nature. Which means you habitually gravitate to foods low in fat and high in fiber, at least 80% of the time. Whether you are eating out, at a party, buying groceries or just snacking, it's a natural habit for you to choose plenty of fruits, vegetables and low-fat, high fiber foods. (Note: Acquire this habit slowly over time and keep in mind that 2 out of 10 meals or snacks do not have to be perfect)!

Wheel #2 — A consistent and dedicated exercise routine

It is imperative to have a regular exercise routine that you enjoy. The time you spend exercising should be a time of "peace" in your life with high priority. This is generally 30-60 minutes, 3-6 times per week. (The higher numbers yield the most weight loss of course). Incorporating resistance muscle training (for a further enhanced metabolism) and stretching (for needed flexibility and injury prevention) is ideal.

Wheel #3 — Emotional well-being

Learn to identify habits like stress eating, boredom eating or emotional eating, and replace them with a more healthful coping response. Learn to listen and respond correctly to your internal appestat which tells you when you are hungry and when you are satisfied (versus just eating things because they are "there"). Plan menus which are completely satisfying to you.

Wheel #4 — A support system

You must create a support system that will help you hang on to and continue to establish healthy habits. This can be sharing weekly fitness goals with a spouse, friend, counselor, personal trainer or coach. Being accountable to someone pays off with big rewards. It's also excellent to have an exercise buddy. Even simple encouragers like people at work who cover for you while you walk are important contributors to your support wheel. Any way you look at it, the support system is as important as any other!

The Easiest Stir-Fry Ever!

Looking for a "Stir-Fry for Dummies?" Here you go! Absolutely **no** chopping and **no** sauce making.   Make it with chicken or without.

SERVES | MENU

6

THE EASIEST STIR-FRY EVER!
BROWN RICE
2 CHOCOLATE GRAHAM CRACKERS OR FORTUNE COOKIES

| 2 cups | instant whole-grain brown rice |
| 1¾ cup | water (adjust according to package directions, brands vary) |

Place rice and water on stove. Cover, bring to a boil and reduce heat to medium low. Set timer for 5 minutes. When timer sounds, remove from heat and allow to sit, covered.

| 1 small | onion |
| 3 | skinless, boneless, chicken breast (halves) (optional)* |

Meanwhile… cut onion into wedges and chicken into strips.

| 1 T | oil (canola or sesame) |

Heat in a nonstick wok. Add onion and chicken. Cook until chicken is browned.

| 2 bags | (16 oz each) frozen mixed stir-fry vegetables (Freshlike Oriental Blend, Sugar-Snap Stir-Fry, Pepper Stir-Fry) |

Add to wok. No need to thaw. Cook 11 to 13 minutes to desired tenderness. (It's ready when the water from the vegetables evaporate.)

| 1 jar | (10 oz) La Choy® Sweet & Sour Sauce |
| ½ cup | slivered almonds or chopped walnuts or cashews |

Stir in. Let cook for 2 more minutes, then serve over the brown rice.

Save room for dessert.

EXCHANGE VALUES
3 Starch   1 Meat   2 Veg.   — Fruit   — Milk   — Fat

* As another option, a cube (12 oz.) of firm tofu cut into strips works great instead of chicken.

Nutrition information for — 1/6 of the recipe over rice

Preparation Time — 20 min.

Calories 390	Fat .... 10 g	Fiber .... 7 g	Sodium .... 220 mg	Total Carbohydrate .... 54 g
Calories from Fat 22%	Saturated Fat .... 1 g	Cholesterol .... 34 mg	Protein .... 2 g	Sugars .... 24 g

Isn't 800 mg of sodium too much???

For a cup of soup, or a ¹/₂ cup of *Rice-a-Roni®,* yes.

For a complete entrée, no. Keep in mind these sodium facts:

- 2,000 to 3,000 mg are allowed each day.

- While 800 mg sounds like a lot, as an entire *entrée,* it fits into your day quite easily.

- Even 2 slices of bread contains 400 mg of sodium!

Sweet & Sour Stir-Fry

Chicken, pork tenderloin or tofu—it's up to you! The pineapple and nuts really make this dish.

MENU

SWEET & SOUR STIRFRY
BROWN RICE
1-2 FIG NEWTONS OR
FORTUNE COOKIES

2 cups	instant whole-grain brown rice
1¾ cup	water (adjust according to package directions, brands vary)

Combine in a microwave safe dish. Cover and cook on high 7 minutes.

8 oz	pork tenderloin or 2 skinless boneless chicken breasts (halves) or 12 oz tofu (or try ½ meat, ½ tofu)

Meanwhile… trim meat. Slice into strips or cube tofu. Set aside.

1	onion
1 bunch	broccoli

On a clean cutting board, cut vegetables into small pieces, keeping piles separate.

2 cans	(8 oz each) pineapple tidbits, in its own juice, drained

Drain the juice in a 2 cup measuring cup. Add orange juice or water to equal ¾ cup of liquid.

1 T	corn starch
2 T	soy sauce, reduced-sodium
1 T	oil (canola or sesame)
1 tsp	minced garlic (2 cloves)
1 tsp	ginger (grated tastes best)

Stir into the pineapple juice. Set mix aside.

Heat a large skillet or wok. Add oil and spices. Then add meat and onions. Stir-fry 4 minutes, or until meat is cooked.

Stir pineapple juice mix and add to wok.

3 T	slivered almonds or chopped almonds or cashews

Add the pineapple, broccoli and almond slivers.

Cover and let simmer on medium low heat for 3 to 4 minutes.

Serve immediately over rice, while broccoli is still bright green.

EXCHANGE VALUES

2 Starch	2 Meat	2 Veg.	1 Fruit	— Milk	— Fat

Nutrition information for — 1/4 of the recipe using pork over rice   **Preparation Time — 40 min.**

Calories 420	Fat .... 11 g	Fiber .... 6.3 g	Sodium .... 335 mg	Total Carbohydrate .... 60 g
Calories from Fat 22%	Saturated Fat .... 1.5 g	Cholesterol .... 45 mg	Protein .... 25 g	Sugars .... 19 g

Stir-Fry
145

Sweet & Sour Stir-Fry

Lickety-Split Meals

As a 23 year veteran of the Michigan State Police, who passes the annual physical fitness test always at the highest (gold) level, how do you do it?

"I receive added motivation from reading books like Personal Best *by George Sheehan. He refers to the Latin term* `Arete, *which is 'functioning as one should.' His analogy of being fit is 'being a good animal.' My training run is an exercise for my body, but even more an exercise for my mind. I find it an unequalled haven for concentration, creativity and problem solving.'"*

—My brother,
CLIFF EDWARDS, 42
23 year veteran of the
Michigan State Police
Never lost a race
that really counts,
(chasing criminals)

Easy Pepper Steak Stir-Fry

A great way to pacify hard-core meat eaters with a small 3 oz. serving of steak.

SERVES

4

MENU

EASY PEPPER STEAK STIR-FRY
BROWN RICE
ZUCCHINI & YELLOW SQUASH
RASPBERRY SORBET

2 cups	instant whole-grain brown rice
1¾ cups	water (adjust according to package directions, brands vary)
1	zucchini, sliced into ½" rounds
1	yellow crooked neck squash, sliced into ½" rounds

Combine in a microwave safe dish. Cover and cook on high 9-10 minutes. (Steam the squash separately if you prefer.)

1 lb	top sirloin steak, well trimmed

Slice "across the grain" into very thin strips. Set aside.

1 can	(14½ oz) beef broth
3 T	cornstarch
1 T	soy sauce, reduced-sodium

Mix together in medium-size bowl. Stir and set aside.

1 T	oil (sesame)
1 tsp	minced garlic (2 cloves)
1	onion, cut into wedges
1	red pepper, cut into strips
1	green pepper, cut into strips
1	yellow pepper, cut into strips

After slicing onion and peppers, heat the oil in a large non-stick fry pan or wok. Add vegetables and stir-fry 2 minutes. Add beef and cook 2 minutes or until done.

Re-stir the broth and add to wok. Stir until thick and bubbly.

Serve over rice. Clean your palate with a scoop of rasberry sorbet.

EXCHANGE VALUES

2 Starch	4 Meat	3 Veg.	— Fruit	— Milk	— Fat

Nutrition information for — 1/4 of the recipe over rice　　　　**Preparation Time — 35 min.**

Calories 455	Fat .... 11.5 g	Fiber .... 5.3 g	Sodium .... 570 mg	Total Carbohydrate .... 48 g
Calories from Fat 22%	Saturated Fat .... 3 g	Cholesterol .... 83 mg	Protein .... 42 g	Sugars .... 6 g

Dining out tips for a Chinese restaurant

1. Order the plain steamed rice vs. the fried rice and you will save about 13 grams of fat!

2. For a 15 gram fat savings, skip the egg roll. Ask for double the rice instead.

3. Eat just half the order, save the rest for tomorrow. (The extra rice allows you to do this easily).

4. Say: "Steam the chicken and vegetables please and add no sesame oil at the end."

5. Be brave and try a tofu dish. The Chinese know how to do tofu!

6. Ask that your meal be made without MSG.

Saucy Almond Chicken Stir-Fry

You'll love all the extra sauce which thoroughly smothers the rice. The crunch of the almonds and water chestnuts makes for a delightful contrast.

6

SAUCY ALMOND CHICKEN OVER BROWN RICE

SLICED APPLES, KIWI, AND ORANGES

Delegate Someone to: Chop red pepper and slice fruit.

3 cups	instant whole-grain brown rice
2²/₃ cups	water (adjust according to package directions, brands vary)

Combine in a microwave safe dish. Cover and cook on high 9 to 10 minutes.

1 can	(14¹/₂ oz) chicken broth, ¹/₃ less sodium
1 T	sugar
2 T	vinegar (cider)
¹/₄ cup	cornstarch
¹/₄ cup	soy sauce, reduced-sodium

Stir together in a medium-size bowl. Set aside.

1 T	sesame oil
1 tsp	minced garlic (2 cloves)
¹/₂ cup	slivered almonds
4	skinless, boneless, chicken breast (halves), cut into ¹/₂" pieces

Heat oil and garlic in a large nonstick skillet or wok. Add chicken and almonds. Cook 5 minutes or until chicken is done and almonds are golden brown.

1	red pepper, cut into ³/₄" pieces
2	boxes (10 oz each) frozen pea pods *or* whole green beans
1 can	(8 oz) sliced water chestnuts, drained

Meanwhile… chop pepper and open containers. Add to stir-fry when chicken is done. Cook 3 to 4 minutes.

Re-stir the broth cornstarch mixture and pour in. Cook and stir until thick and bubbly.

Serve over rice with fruit on the side.

EXCHANGE VALUES

3 Starch	3 Meat	2 Veg.	— Fruit	— Milk	— Fat

Nutrition information for — 1/6 of the recipe over rice   **Preparation Time — 35 min.**

Calories 430	Fat .... 10 g	Fiber .... 8 g	Sodium .... 620 mg	Total Carbohydrate .... 58 g
Calories from Fat 20%	Saturated Fat .... 1 g	Cholesterol .... 46 mg	Protein .... 30 g	Sugars .... 7 g

Electric Rice

You may want to consider buying an electric rice cooker. You'll no longer need to buy instant rice, and with very little effort you will have perfectly cooked rice that's held warm and ready whenever you arrive home. Leftover rice can be stored in the refrigerator and used all week. (Be sure you have the storage space since it's a fairly large contraption).

"Unfried" Rice Dinner

Although initially you may want to serve this as a side dish, you will soon discover that this is a satisfying one dish meal. Perfect for a light supper.

4

"UNFRIED" RICE

ORANGE & KIWI SLICES

APPLESAUCE DUMPLINGS

Note: If you don't have leftover cooked rice on hand, put 2 cups of instant whole-grain brown rice in microwave safe dish with 1³/4 cups of water. Cover and microwave 7 minutes on high while you prep vegetables.

Great use for left-over cooked rice.

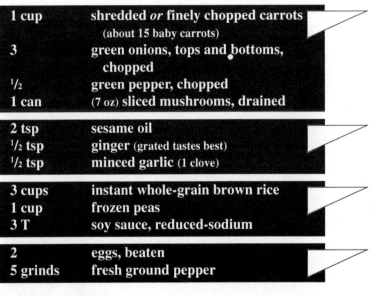

1 cup	shredded *or* finely chopped carrots
	(about 15 baby carrots)
3	green onions, tops and bottoms, chopped
¹/₂	green pepper, chopped
1 can	(7 oz) sliced mushrooms, drained

Prep vegetables. For speed, use the food processor to coarsely shred or finely chop the carrots.

2 tsp	sesame oil
¹/₂ tsp	ginger (grated tastes best)
¹/₂ tsp	minced garlic (1 clove)

Heat in a nonstick skillet over medium-high. Add above vegetables, and stir-fry 1 to 2 minutes.

3 cups	instant whole-grain brown rice
1 cup	frozen peas
3 T	soy sauce, reduced-sodium

Stir in and cook 5 minutes.

2	eggs, beaten
5 grinds	fresh ground pepper

In a small cup, beat eggs with a fork. Push rice mixture to side of skillet, add eggs and pepper to the open side. Allow eggs to thoroughly set. Cut the cooked eggs into rectangular bites.

Gently combine eggs with rice and serve with orange and kiwi slices. Consider *Applesauce Dumplings* (page 202) for dessert.

EXCHANGE VALUES

3 Starch	1 Meat	1 Veg.	— Fruit	— Milk	— Fat

Nutrition information for —

Preparation Time — 30 min.

Calories 280	Fat .... 6 g	Fiber .... 6.5 g	Sodium .... 675 mg	Total Carbohydrate .... 47 g
Calories from Fat 19%	Saturated Fat .... 1 g	Cholesterol .... 106 mg	Protein .... 12 g	Sugars .... 8 g

Soups

No doubt about it, winter or summer, rain or shine, soup satisfies. The 30 or so minutes required to make a steamy pot of soup can yield high rewards. Just take a look at all the benefits of making soup at home:

- A tasty way to eat lots of healthy vegetables and beans.
- *You* control the sodium and fat content.
- Weight loss aide (soup before dinner can suppress your appetite).
- A pot can be stored in the refrigerator and single servings reheated all week.
- Individual servings can be frozen for another day.

So just when you thought you didn't have time to make soup from scratch, take a peek through this chapter. The time spent on a Saturday or Sunday afternoon will be well worth it!

Weight loss tip: Eat negative calorie foods

Think "cooked and raw vegetables" every day. There's no science to this recommendation, it's just a reminder to eat 2 healthy doses of vegetables every day. When it comes to losing weight, you will want to have lots of these "negative calorie foods" (foods that require more calories to digest than they yield) at each meal. Each serving of *Miracle Soup* will take care of the "cooked" vegetable goal. Remember, almost all vegetables are negative calorie foods, so enjoy, enjoy, enjoy!

Miracle Soup

Ever heard of a negative calorie food? That's a food that burns more calories to digest than it yields. Hence the name "Miracle." This soup is a great for weight loss. Enjoy a bowl with lunch *and* dinner! A pot lasts several days.

6 cups	water
1 quart	low-sodium vegetable juice

Place in a large soup pot, over medium-high heat.

3 large	onions
1	green pepper
6	celery stalks
10	carrots
2 cans	(14.5 oz each) stewed tomatoes
4 cups	shredded cabbage*
1/2 cup	salsa
1/4 tsp	garlic powder
1/4 tsp	pepper
1/2 tsp	red pepper flakes (optional)
1 tsp	basil
2 tsp	oregano
1 envelope	dry onion *or* vegetable soup mix *or* 2 tsp low-sodium chicken boullion

Meanwhile... chop vegetables into bite sized pieces. Toss vegetables and other ingredients into pot. Boil for 20 minutes, or until the vegetables are done how you like them.

Serve hot off the stove with low-fat whole-wheat crackers or a sandwich and fruit.

Miracle Soup keeps in the refrigerator for up to 5 days and also freezes well.

EXCHANGE VALUES

— Starch	— Meat	4 Veg.	— Fruit	— Milk	— Fat

* Use your food processor or buy pre-shredded.

Nutrition information for — about 1-1/2 cups		Preparation Time — 35 min.	
Calories 85	Fat .... 0 g	Fiber .... 4.5 g	Sodium .... 425 mg	Total Carbohydrate .... 19 g
Calories from Fat .... 0 %	Saturated Fat .... 0 g	Cholesterol .... 0 mg	Protein .... 3 g	Sugars .... 11 g

Have a cold?

"The main objective of natural remedies is to stimulate a person's inherent ability to heal themselves."

—My homeopath,
CAROLINE SMOYER, DHom
Salt Lake City, Utah

I keep the following items in my medicine cabinet, in case a cold strikes…

1. Studies have shown that **zinc gluconate lozenges** (containing 13.3 mg of zinc) taken every 2 hours at the onset of a cold help decrease the duration from 7 days down to 4. The brand which the studies used was "Cold-Ease." (Since zinc can interfere with copper absorption, do not exceed 6 days of use).

2. **Herbal remedy, ECHINACEA** has also been determined to help boost immune functioning which in turn reduces the severity of a cold. (Do not take Echinacea routinely as it loses it's effectiveness). Medical experts recommend buying the extract for purity.

3. Taking **vitamin C** during a cold may also help alleviate the severity and symptoms. I keep 500 mg tablets on hand and take 1 or 2, twice a day, until the cold is gone.

Lentil Spinach Soup

If lentils aren't a favorite of yours yet, just give it some time, they will be! I love this refreshing, easy-to-make soup any time of the year, including summer. It keeps in the refrigerator for 5 days and freezes well.

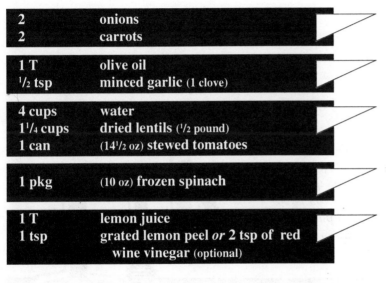

2	onions
2	carrots

Chop into bite-size pieces.

1 T	olive oil
1/2 tsp	minced garlic (1 clove)

Sauté with vegetables, in a medium soup pot for 2 minutes.

4 cups	water
1 1/4 cups	dried lentils (1/2 pound)
1 can	(14 1/2 oz) stewed tomatoes

Add water and lentils to pot. Cover and bring to a boil, then simmer for 45 minutes. (Feel free to make some cornbread and a salad now!)

1 pkg	(10 oz) frozen spinach

Take out of freezer to thaw. Add to the soup after the 45 minute simmer.

1 T	lemon juice
1 tsp	grated lemon peel *or* 2 tsp of red wine vinegar (optional)

Add to soup and simmer 5 minutes longer.

Serve with cornbread, crackers or popcorn.

EXCHANGE VALUES

2 Starch	1 Meat	1 Veg.	— Fruit	— Milk	— Fat

Nutrition information for — about 1-1/2 cups

Preparation Time — 1 hour

Calories 215	Fat .... 3 g	Fiber .... 8 g	Sodium .... 200 mg	Total Carbohydrate ....35 g
Calories from Fat 11%	Saturated Fat .... < 1 g	Cholesterol .... 0 mg	Protein .... 12 g	Sugars ....7 g

Secrets from a long-term weight maintainer ...

"Every morning I weigh myself. I have a 4 pound window in which I vary. The day I go one pound over that window, a switch goes on in my brain that says 'cut back on what you're eating, and put in a longer run.'"

— My mom,
GRACE EDWARDS, 60,
maintaining 123 lbs.
for 32 years

Creamy Cauliflower Soup

SERVES	MENU

A great way to enjoy cancer-fighting cauliflower. This creamy low-fat soup is delicious. (Please note that the marjoram and savory make this soup, and substitutions are not recommended.)

SERVES 6

MENU

CREAMY CAULIFLOWER SOUP
SALTINES OR FRENCH BREAD
TOSSED SALAD

2 cans	(14.5 oz each) **chicken broth,** $^1/_3$ **less sodium**

Bring to a boil.

2 large	potatoes

Peel and cut into chunks. Add and simmer for 20 minutes.

2 ribs	celery
1 head	cauliflower
1 tsp	dried marjoram
1 tsp	dried savory
$^1/_2$ tsp	salt

After 20 minutes, slice and add to soup. Simmer 30 more minutes.

1 T	olive oil
1 medium	onion
$^1/_2$ tsp	minced garlic (1 clove)

Chop onion. Sauté all for 2 minutes, then add to simmering soup.

Pureé soup in a food processor or blender (in small batches if required).

Serve with whole-wheat saltines or French bread and tossed salad.

EXCHANGE VALUES

1 Starch	— Meat	1 Veg.	— Fruit	— Milk	— Fat

Nutrition information for — about 1-1/2 cups

Preparation Time — 1 hour

Calories 125	Fat .... 3 g	Fiber .... 5 g	Sodium .... 430 mg	Total Carbohydrate .... 21 g
Calories from Fat 17%	Saturated Fat .... < 1 g	Cholesterol .... 0 mg	Protein .... 6 g	Sugars .... 4 g

Creamy Cauliflower Soup

Lickety-Split Meals

True or False?

"As long as you don't add butter to popcorn, it's generally low-fat."

Answer: FALSE!

Truck-loads of fat are often used to pop the popcorn, as is the case with:

- Movie popcorn

- Microwave popcorn (the regular varieties as well as some of the "lite" ones)!

- Home-made, where you use $1/4$ cup or more of oil in the pan or popper

Even without adding butter, the fat's already at near MAXIMUM CAPACITY!

3-Bean Turkey or Vegetarian Chili

This very fresh and light chili is a wonderful change from the heavy flavor of traditional chili loaded with fat.

Great for football parties!

2	onions
1	red pepper
1	green pepper
4	whole carrots *or* 1 cup shredded carrots

Chop vegetables into small wedges.

1 T	olive oil
1 tsp	minced garlic (2 cloves)
1 lb	extra-lean ground turkey breast (optional)

Heat oil in your largest kettle. Add garlic, chopped vegetables and turkey. Sauté 5 minutes.

1 can	(15 oz) **kidney beans**
1 can	(15 oz) **garbanzo** *or* **pinto beans**
2 cans	(15 oz each) **black beans**

While the vegetables are sautéing, open all the beans. Toss them in a colander, rinse, drain and add to sauté.

2 T	cumin seed *or* 1 T ground cumin
1 T	chili powder
1 tsp	oregano
1/4 tsp	red pepper flakes (optional)
3 shakes	cayenne pepper (optional)
1/4 cup	hot pepper rings from a jar (optional)

Add all spices to sauté.

2 jars	(32 oz each) **low-sodium V-8® juice**
1 can	(14.5 oz) **stewed tomatoes**

Add to the pot and bring to a simmer for 10 to 20 minutes.

Serve with whole-wheat crackers or cornbread and raw vegetables.

EXCHANGE VALUES

2 Starch	2 Meat	1 Veg.	— Fruit	— Milk	— Fat

Nutrition information for — about 1-1/2 cups including ground turkey   Preparation Time — 35 min.

Calories	250	Fat	3 g	Fiber	9.5 g	Sodium	575 mg	Total Carbohydrate	36 g
Calories from Fat	11%	Saturated Fat	< 1 g	Cholesterol	22 mg	Protein	19 g	Sugars	15 g

Popcorn Facts — True or False?

"Popcorn should be reserved as a snack and a snack only. It would be unhealthy to serve popcorn as the grain in your meal."

Answer: FALSE!

Popcorn is corn, and corn is a healthy contribution to a meal, right? Corn is actually a grain (sorry, not a vegetable) and a grain or starch should be a major part of every meal. Who says potatoes, rice, pasta and bread are the only grains allowed at mealtime? As long as your popcorn is healthfully prepared, (including the truly low-fat versions of microwave), it's fine to include popcorn in a meal. My personal combination favorites are beans and popcorn, and soup and popcorn!

Speedy Minestrone with Rice

No idea what to have for dinner? How about this 10 minute soup?
It's as close to a homemade soup as a busy person gets. Enjoy!

Remember—
You want your
evening meal to be
the smallest meal
of the day!

2 cans	(14½ oz each) **chicken broth,** **⅓ less sodium**
1 cup	**water**
2 cans	(14.5 oz) **stewed tomatoes**

In a large saucepan,
bring to a boil on medium-high heat.

1 cup	**instant whole-grain brown rice,** **uncooked**
1 can	(15½ oz) **kidney beans, rinsed** **and drained**
1 pkg	(10 oz) **frozen mixed vegetables**
½ tsp	**dried oregano leaves**
¼ tsp	**pepper**

Stir in remaining ingredients. Return to boil.

Reduce heat to low, cover and simmer 5 minutes.

Remove from heat and let stand 3 minutes while you set the table.

1 tsp	**Parmesan cheese** (per serving)

Sprinkle servings with cheese if desired.

Serve with popcorn or whole-wheat crackers and frozen yogurt
for dessert.

EXCHANGE VALUES

2 Starch — Meat 2 Veg. — Fruit — Milk — Fat

Nutrition information for — about 2 cups

Preparation Time — 10 min.

Calories 212	Fat .... 2 g	Fiber .... 7 g	Sodium .... 870 mg	Total Carbohydrate ....40 g
Calories from Fat 7%	Saturated Fat .... .8 g	Cholesterol .... 2 mg	Protein .... 10 g	Sugars ....12 g

True or False?

"Air popping your popcorn is always better than oil popping."

TRUE, with one exception. What do you put on top? Do you add melted butter or margarine to go on top? How much do you use? I bet you didn't know that if you're using 2 T or more of margarine to put on top, you'd be better off popping your corn in 1 T of OIL. (Because yes, oil is better for you than margarine). And, 1 T of oil in popping goes a lot further than does 1 T of margarine dribbled on top.

The solution: Air-pop and use a product like *"I can't Believe It's Not Butter"* spray, lightly on top, or oil pop $^{1}/_{4}$ cup of kernels in 1 T of canola or olive oil. (Serves 2 or more).

Quick Creamy Tomato Soup

For those of you especially keen on the health benefits of soy, here's a surprisingly delicious way to sneak it in.

4

MENU

CREAMY TOMATO SOUP

TOSSED SALAD

POPCORN OR WHOLE-WHEAT GARLIC CHEESE TOAST

3 GINGERSNAP COOKIES

Makes a great sauce over pasta or mashed potatoes.

1 jar	(26 oz) **spaghetti sauce** (*Healthy Choice®*)
6 oz	**silken soft tofu**
½ tsp	**oregano, basil *or* Italian seasoning**

Combine in a food processor or blender and blend until creamy.

| 1 can | (14½ oz) **chicken broth, ⅓ less sosdium** |

Add and blend again to thin the consistency.

Heat the desired amount in the microwave or over medium heat.

Serve with a salad & crackers or whole-wheat toast. Treat yourself to 3 gingersnap cookies for dessert.

EXCHANGE VALUES

— Starch   — Meat   3 Veg.   — Fruit   — Milk   — Fat

Nutrition information for — about 1-1/2 cups   **Preparation Time — 10 min.**

Calories 110	Fat .... 2 g	Fiber .... 3.5 g	Sodium .... 620 mg	Total Carbohydrate .... 18 g
Calories from Fat 15%	Saturated Fat .... < 1 g	Cholesterol .... 2 mg	Protein .... 6 g	Sugars .... 12 g

Book Review—Make the Connection by Bob Greene and Oprah Winfrey

For an inspirational book on exercising and eating right, I highly recommend the book *Make the Connection* by Oprah Winfrey and Bob Greene, (Oprah's personal trainer). You'll enjoy reading Oprah's personal journal entries about her years of battling weight and getting it right this time by "making the connection." This refers to the connection about changing your whole life to include regular exercise, eating right, and overcoming the use of food for comfort and stress. Bob Greene describes all the components of his program that have worked for Oprah to keep her weight off permanently.

Also of tremendous encouragement, the video, *Oprah: Make the Connection*. It will touch your heart and inspire you to new heights!

Hearty Bean & Pasta Stew

Have you always thought beans required some sort of meat for flavoring? Well this recipe is a good example of how beans can taste great without meat. You must try this!

2 medium	onions
1	green pepper

Chop into pieces.

2 T	olive oil
1 tsp	minced garlic (2 cloves)

Heat, in a large nonstick pot. Add onion and pepper. Sauté for 3 minutes on medium.

1 can	(14.5 oz) stewed tomatoes
1	(14.5 oz) chicken broth, $\frac{1}{3}$ less sodium
1 qt	low-sodium V-8® Juice
2 cups	water

Meanwhile… open cans and V-8® jar. Add to the pot.

This dish will keep in the frig. for up to 5 days and also freezes well.

1 can	(15 oz) each pinto beans, garbanzo beans, and kidney beans

Open cans. Rinse and drain in colander. Add to the pot.

2 T	low-sodium chicken bouillon
1 T	oregano
2 tsp	basil
$\frac{1}{4}$ tsp	red pepper flakes (optional)
25 grinds	fresh ground pepper

Add and mix thoroughly.

4 cups	small pasta shells, macaroni *or* corkscrew (preferably whole-wheat)

Bring pot to a boil, then add. Set timer for 12 minutes. Make a salad and slice whole-grain bread. At the sound of the timer—it's time to eat!

8 T	reduced-fat shredded mozzarella cheese
8 tsp	Parmesan cheese

Sprinkle 1 T of mozzarella and 1 tsp of Parmesan cheese on top of individual servings.

EXCHANGE VALUES

3 Starch	1 Meat	1 Veg.	— Fruit	— Milk	— Fat

Nutrition information for — 1 cup serving with mozzarella and Parmesan — Preparation Time — 35 min.

Calories 300	Fat .... 4.5 g	Fiber .... 11 g	Sodium .... 510 mg	Total Carbohydrate .... 52 g
Calories from Fat 13%	Saturated Fat .... 1 g	Cholesterol .... 3 g	Protein .... 14 g	Sugars .... 10 g

A slow-cooker, (or crockery-cooker or *Crock-Pot®*) is simply a *must* for a busy family. You know that high stress, *just home from work, what's for dinner* chaos? Well, coming home to a house filled with a delicious aroma **completely** takes care of that!

The question is, where is your slow-cooker right now? Is it where it can be easily used each week? Or is it way back in some forgotten cupboard, with an inch of dust on it?

Well get ready to unearth it, because low-fat, easy-to-load recipes are all right here. Just when you thought, slow-cooking "all tastes the same," or only has high-fat recipes," this section comes to the rescue. And if you don't own one yet, then check out the buying tips located within the chapter.

Since coming home to a nice stuffed slow-cooker makes for a completely stress-free easy dinner, I suggest Monday as your slow-cooker day. You can do the loading the night before (store it in the refrigerator) and simply plug it in on Monday morning for a complete "no cook" day!

It's time to get slow-cookin'. You're going to absolutely love coming home to the delicious aroma of dinner awaiting you!

Note: These recipes are designed for a 2-quart cooker.

Slow-Cooking

Secrets to successful slow-cooked meat and vegetables

Some slow-cooker recipes recommend adding meat frozen to the crock, to help vegetables get a head start on cooking. This assures that the meat is tender but not overcooked when the vegetables are done.

Dense vegetables such as carrots, potatoes, and rutabagas take longer to cook than many meats. When combining ingredients in a slow-cooker, place root vegetables on the bottom of the pot; then add meats, seasonings, other vegetables and liquid. This keeps vegetables moist during cooking, and cooks them more evenly.

Turkey Vegetable Stew

Here's my favorite way to serve stew. Look for turkey tenderloins in the fresh poultry section of your grocery store. Freeze them when you get home. Add them frozen to the crockpot to prevent the meat from becoming overcooked before the vegetables are done.

6 - 8 med	potatoes
6	carrots
2	onions
2	skinless, boneless, turkey tenderloins, frozen (about 1¹/₂ lbs)*
1 cup	each of frozen peas and corn
1 tsp	oregano
¹/₂ tsp	hot pepper flakes
¹/₂ jar	(about 13 oz) spaghetti sauce (*Healthy Choice*®)
2 cups	water

7 to 11 hours before serving:

Thoroughly wash and scrub, or peel if commercial potatoes. Quarter them. Place into slow-cooker.

Peel and slice into chunks. Add to potatoes.

Place in slow-cooker while still frozen.

Place ingredients in slow-cooker using the order listed. Mix slightly.

Cook on HIGH for 7 hours, or on LOW for 10 to 11 hours.

8 minutes before serving:

Whip up a quick *Crunchy Apple Salad* (page174) and serve with whole-wheat rolls.

EXCHANGE VALUES

2 Starch	2 Meat	2 Veg.	— Fruit	— Milk	— Fat

* Chicken breasts can be substituted.

Nutrition information for — about 1-1/2 cups   **Preparation Time — a.m. 12 min.**

Calories 270	Fat .... 1.4 g	Fiber 6.5	Sodium .... 255 mg	Total Carbohydrate .... 40 g
Calories from Fat 4%	Saturated Fat .... 0 g	Cholesterol .... 40 mg	Protein .... 26 g	Sugars .... 8.5 g

Who has time in the morning to load the slow-cooker?

If this is your attitude, try this 1-minute super-easy recipe. If that still seems like too much work, keep in mind that you can load the slow-cooker the night before. (Simply store in the refrigerator overnight). And remember, a 1-minute investment now, means a GREAT reward later.

Come on! You can find 1 minute!

Ravioli Stew

You can load the crockpot in less than a minute with this recipe! Popular with small kids, although, you may want to serve the green beans on the side.

Kids' Favorite

1 bag	(25 oz) **frozen cheese ravioli**
1 bag	(16 oz) **frozen cut green beans**
1 jar	(26 oz) **spaghetti sauce** (*Healthy Choice*®)
½ jar	(13 oz) **water**

5 to 9 hours before serving:

Place ingredients in slow-cooker using the order listed. Mix slightly.

Cook on HIGH for 5 to 6 hours or on LOW for 8 to 9 hours.

5 minutes before serving:

Serve with canned peaches and *Whole-Wheat Garlic Cheese Toast* (page 183).

EXCHANGE VALUES

2.5 Starch	1 Meat	2 Veg.	— Fruit	— Milk	— Fat

Nutrition information for — 8 ravioli   **Preparation Time — a.m. 1 min.**

Calories 290	Fat .... 6.5 g	Fiber .... 5 g	Sodium .... 735 mg	Total Carbohydrate ....47 g
Calories from Fat 19%	Saturated Fat .... 4 g	Cholesterol .... 13 mg	Protein .... 13 g	Sugars ....17 g

Slow-cooker buying tips

Size: Slow-cookers range in size from 1 to 6 quarts, with the most common being the mid-range. It's up to you and depends on the size of your family and whether or not you enjoy leftovers. These recipes are designed for a 2-quart cooker.

Removable inside crock: I like this because it's easier to clean, prettier to serve and when you load it the night before, it fits in the refrigerator much more easily.

Side versus bottom heating elements: Most slow-cooking cookbooks, use an appliance with the side element. In this design, the heat element stays on continuously while the designs with a bottom element "cycle" on and off. My recipes have been tested with the side element type.

Buffet Bonus

Slow-cookers are handy for buffets. Simply keep the pot on LOW and the food will be just as warm for the last guest as it was for the first.

Mexican 5-Bean Soup

Here's a delicious bean soup. I know what you're thinking—
"Can I just drink the beer with the soup instead?"

1 can	(15 oz) **red kidney beans**
1 can	(15 oz) **garbanzo beans**
1 can	(15 oz) **navy beans**
1 can	(15 oz) **black beans**

1 large	**onion**
1 can	(4 oz) **green chilies**

1 package	(9 oz) **frozen cut green beans**
4 tsp	**chili powder**
1 1/2 tsp	**dried basil**
1/2 tsp	**dried oregano**
1/4 tsp	**tabasco sauce**
3 cups	**water**
2 cans	(14.5 oz each) **chicken broth,** 1/3 **less sodium**
1 can	(12 oz) **beer,** *or* **12 oz water**

2 T	(per soup bowl) **reduced-fat shredded cheddar cheese** *or* **mozzarella cheese**

5 to 10 hours before serving:

Place a strainer in the sink.
Rinse and drain the beans thoroughly.
Place in slow-cooker.

Dice and place in slow-cooker.

Place in slow-cooker and stir.

Cook on HIGH for 5 to 6 hours or on LOW for 9 to 10 hours.

Just before serving:

Ladle into serving bowls.

Place on top of soup.

Serve with whole-wheat saltines or cornbread and tossed salad.

EXCHANGE VALUES

2 Starch	1 Meat	1 Veg.	— Fruit	— Milk	— Fat

Nutrition information for — about 1 cup   **Preparation Time — a.m. 20 min.**

Calories 110	Fat .... 2 g	Fiber .... 10 g	Sodium .... 735 mg	Total Carbohydrate .... 35 g
Calories from Fat 9%	Saturated Fat .... < 1 g	Cholesterol .... 2 mg	Protein .... 12 g	Sugars .... 6 g

Beat the heat and save electricity!

A slow-cooker:

Does not heat the kitchen like your oven does—a real bonus during summer months.

Saves energy by using very little electricity since the wattage is low.

You may also like to know…

The low-heat setting cooks foods in 8 to 10 hours, while the high-heat setting cooks foods in 5 to 6 hours.

Exact timing with slow-cooking is not critical. If you are working a little late or delayed in traffic, another hour of extra cooking time won't make a big difference to most recipes that are cooking on LOW.

Split Pea Soup

Why is it that some people do not like split pea soup? This soup thickens as it cools and I love it thick. Tasty, quick and a good money saving recipe as well.

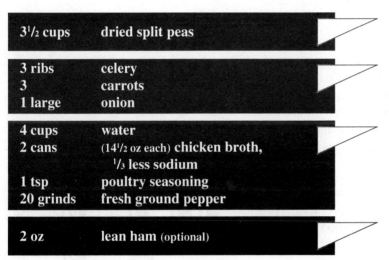

3¹/₂ cups	dried split peas

3 ribs	celery
3	carrots
1 large	onion

4 cups	water
2 cans	(14¹/₂ oz each) chicken broth, ¹/₃ less sodium
1 tsp	poultry seasoning
20 grinds	fresh ground pepper

2 oz	lean ham (optional)

8 to 11 hours before serving:

Rinse in a colander and place in slow-cooker.

Chop and place in slow-cooker.

Place in slow-cooker and mix.

Cook on HIGH for 8 to 9 hours or on LOW for 10 to 11 hours.

30 minutes before or just before serving:

Cut ham into small cubes. Add in the last hour of cooking.

Serve with crackers or cornbread, tossed salad and low-fat frozen yogurt for dessert.

EXCHANGE VALUES

3 Starch	2 Meat	— Veg.	— Fruit	— Milk	— Fat

Nutrition information for — about 1 cup   **Preparation Time — a.m. 15 min.**

Calories 270	Fat .... 1.5 g	Fiber .... 19 g	Sodium .... 325 mg	Total Carbohydrate .... 46 g
Calories from Fat 4%	Saturated Fat .... 0 g	Cholesterol .... 3 mg	Protein .... 20 g	Sugars .... 8 g

No peeking allowed!

A slow-cooker makes foods moist and flavorful. Meat and vegetable juices blend together, creating a delicious combination of flavors.

Resist the temptation to lift the lid to take a quick peek or stir frequently. Slow-cooking depends on the heat that builds up in the crock itself and takes quite a bit of time to reheat. Stirring is not required unless noted in the recipe.

Beef Barley Soup

Did you know barley has even more cholesterol lowering powers than does oatbran? Yes, we should eat more of it. And this soup, made with lean beef, is a great place to start.

1½ pounds	sirloin steak, well trimmed

1 cup	thinly sliced carrots
1 cup	sliced celery
1 medium	onion, chopped
1	green pepper, chopped

2 cans	(14½ oz each) beef broth
1 can	(14.5 oz) stewed tomatoes
1 cup	spaghetti sauce (*Healthy Choice®*)
½ cup	quick-cooking or pearl barley
1½ tsp	dried basil
¼ cup	fresh parsley, chopped
dash	pepper

4 to 12 hours before serving:

Cut meat into 1" cubes. Place in slow-cooker.

Prep and place in slow-cooker.

Add to slow-cooker.

Cover and cook on low for 10 to 12 hours or on high 4 to 5 hours.

Just before serving:

Skim off any fat.

Serve with crackers and lite fruit cocktail.

EXCHANGE VALUES

1 Starch	4 Meat	1 Veg.	— Fruit	— Milk	— Fat

Nutrition information for — about 1-1/2 cups

Preparation Time — a.m. 25 min.

Calories 265	Fat ..... 7 g	Fiber ..... 4.5 g	Sodium ..... 640 mg	Total Carbohydrate ..... 20 g
Calories from Fat 24%	Saturated Fat ..... 2.7 g	Cholesterol ..... 77 mg	Protein ..... 30 g	Sugars ..... 7 g

Slow-cooker tips for dried beans

- They cook very well in the slow-cooker.

- Pre-soaking is usually not necessary.

- They cook best on the high-setting, and will require 4 to 6 hours of cooking.

- These are a great way to save money over buying canned beans.

Gypsy Stew

A delicious way to cook dried beans in the crockpot. Choose from chicken, pork or go meatless.
The sweet potatoes and Spanish flavors are terrific together.

8

CHICKEN & BEAN FLORENTINE

BROCCOLI SALAD WITH DRIED
CHERRIES

FRENCH BREAD

1¹/₂ cups	dried garbanzo *or* navy beans

5 to 11 hours before serving:

Sort and rinse beans, place
in a 3¹/₂ quart slow-cooker.

1 box	(10 oz) frozen spinach

Place in a microwave safe dish and defrost in microwave 3 minutes.

¹/₄ lb	pork tenderloin *or* skinless, boneless, chicken breast (optional)
2 cans	(14¹/₂ oz each) chicken broth, ¹/₃ less sodium
1 cup	water
1 can	(14¹/₂ oz) stewed tomatoes
1 large	sweet potato (peeled and cubed)
1	onion
1	red *or* yellow bell pepper
2 tsp	paprika
2 tsp	cumin
¹/₄ tsp	cinnamon
1 tsp	dried basil
¹/₂ tsp	salt
8 grinds	fresh ground pepper
8 dashes	cayenne (optional)

Cut meat into ¹/₂" cubes. Cut vegetables into wedges. Add all
ingredients into slow-cooker.

Add thawed spinach to slow-cooker.

Cover and cook on LOW for 10 to 11 hours or on HIGH for 5 to 6
hours until beans are tender.

Just before serving:

For a delicious side dish, consider making *Broccoli Salad with Dried
Cherries* (page 176).

Serve with whole-wheat french bread and applesauce for dessert.

Note: Add 1 to 2 tsp of sugar to smooth the flavors, if desired.

EXCHANGE VALUES

2 Starch	1 Meat	1 Veg.	— Fruit	— Milk	— Fat

Nutrition information for — about 1-1/2 cup serving with pork | **Preparation Time — a.m. 20 min.**

Calories 230	Fat .... 3 g	Fiber .... 9 g	Sodium .... 585 mg	Total Carbohydrate .... 38 g
Calories from Fat 12%	Saturated Fat .... < 1 g	Cholesterol .... 11 mg	Protein .... 15 g	Sugars .... 11 g

**Slow-Cooking
163**   Gypsy Stew

Lickety-Split Meals

Lessons learned from friends

It's amazing what you learn while living with friends. My husband and I had this opportunity for 6 weeks when the completion of our new home was taking longer than expected. In our friends' refrigerator, I couldn't help but notice on the upper shelf was this 8 x 4 inch glass relish plate. It would mysteriously be replenished daily with sliced peppers (green and red), carrots, cucumbers, (or whatever was on hand). The plate would join the table during the preparation of every lunch and dinner, (and sometimes breakfast too)! Everyone was invited to munch until the meal was served, in addition to throughout the meal. Talk about a super way to increase the family's vegetable consumption. It *really* worked!

—Lesson learned from
my friend, JAY JOHNSON, 33
(mother of 2 girls who **adore**
sliced red and green peppers)
practicing what she learned from
her mother Carita Rick, 72

Crockpot® Fajitas

You want chicken fajitas—use chicken. You want beef fajitas—use beef!
Vegetarian? Got that covered too. These fajitas are a family favorite. OLÉ!

1 lb	beef flank steak *or* skinless, boneless, chicken breast *or* pork tenderloin *or* 2 cubes (12 oz each) tofu

4 to 8 hours before serving:

Trim meat well and cut into 6 portions. Crumble or cube tofu. Place in slow-cooker.

1	onion
1	green bell pepper
1	red bell pepper
1	yellow pepper

Cut vegetables into strips and place in slow-cooker.

10	jalepeno pepper rings from a jar
1 tsp	minced garlic (2 cloves)
1 tsp	ground cumin
1 can	(15 oz) kidney *or* pinto *or* black beans, drained and rinsed
1 pkt	(1.27 oz) fajita seasoning mix *(Lawry's®)*

Add and mix well.

Cook on LOW for 7 to 8 hours or on HIGH for 4 to 5 hours.

Just before serving:

Remove meat from slow-cooker and shred. Return the shredded meat to the pot and mix well.

12	8" flour tortillas
3	fresh tomatoes
1 cup	lettuce
12 T	light sour cream (1 T per fajita)

Warm tortillas in the microwave. Chop tomatoes and lettuce. (Use a slotted spoon when removing contents from slow-cooker.) Assemble fajitas with the toppings of your choice.

Serve 2 fajitas per person with raw veggies and fruit for dessert.

EXCHANGE VALUES

4 Starch	2 Meat	1 Veg.	— Fruit	— Milk	— Fat

Nutrition information for — 2 fajitas using beef, with tomatoes, lettuce and sour cream   **Preparation Time — a.m. 20 min.**

Calories 505	Fat .... 14 g	Fiber .... 9 g	Sodium .... 1040 mg	Total Carbohydrate .... 64 g
Calories from Fat 25%	Saturated Fat .... 5.5 g	Cholesterol .... 40 g	Protein .... 30 g	Sugars .... 10 g

Gourmet Taste Tip for Cumin Seed

Try "toasting" the cumin seed to intensify its flavor. Place cumin seed in a small dry saucepan over medium-high heat until toasty and the seeds begin to pop. Then add to the beans. This will take you less than 2 minutes to do and really boosts the flavor!

Encore! For Mexican Black Beans

Serve heated leftovers over rice or over a baked potato. Also superb as "nachos."

Pour hot beans over baked tortilla chips and top with low-fat cheese. Mmmm!

Mexican Black Beans

SERVES | MENU

Thick, hearty and awesome! By minimizing the liquid, the flavor is intensified. My thanks to fellow nutritionist Lynne DeMoor, M.S., R.D. for discovering this winner.

8

MEXICAN BLACK BEANS

CORNBREAD, CRACKERS OR BAKED TOSTITOS®

RAW VEGETABLES & DIP

SLICED BANANAS W/ CHOCOLATE SYRUP & NUTS

1 lb	dried black beans *or* 2½ cups
6 cups	water

4 to 13 hours before serving:

Place beans in a strainer 1 handful at a time, sorting out rocks. Rinse well. Put drained beans in slow-cooker with the 6 cups of water.

Cook on HIGH for 4 hours, or LOW for 12 to 13 hours.

Note: Recipe can be made on top of the stove in 2½ hours. Can also be doubled and freezes well.

½	green pepper, chopped
½	yellow pepper, chopped
½	red pepper, chopped
1 large	onion, chopped
1 T	olive oil
1 tsp	minced garlic (2 cloves)

1 hour before serving:

Towards the end of the cooking time, prep these vegetables and sauté about 5 minutes.

While veggies are sautéing, place a strainer over a bowl. Pour entire slow-cooker full of beans into strainer. Return beans to slow-cooker along with 1 cup only of bean water. (Discard remaining bean water or save for another use.)

Add sautéed vegetables to slow-cooker.

1 T	cumin seed (*or* 2 tsp ground cumin)
1 T	oregano
½ tsp	salt
2 tsp	paprika
¼ tsp	cayenne pepper (optional)
10	hot pepper rings (from a jar), chopped
1 can	(14.5 oz) stewed tomatoes

Add and mix well. Allow to cook on high 30 minutes to 1 hour longer. Use this time to make cornbread if you'd like.

Serve with crackers, *Baked Tostitos*® or cornbread and crunchy raw veggies on the side.

EXCHANGE VALUES

2 Starch   1 Meat   2 Veg.   — Fruit   — Milk   — Fat

Nutrition information for — about 1-1/2 cups | Preparation Time — a.m. 2 min. — p.m. 20 min.

Calories ... 240	Fat ... 2.5 g	Fiber ... 10 g	Sodium ... 525 mg	Total Carbohydrate ... 43 g
Calories from Fat ... 9%	Saturated Fat ... < 1 g	Cholesterol ... 0 mg	Protein ... 13 g	Sugars ... 7 g

Slow-Cooking 165   Mexican Black Beans   *Lickety-Split Meals*

After Dinner Exercisers — True or False

"It is OK to exercise soon after eating dinner."

TRUE!

You should be able to do mild exercise like walking without discomfort. If not, that "full stomach feeling" is telling you, you have eaten TOO MUCH. The difference lies in finishing your meal NOT when you are "full," but when you are "satisfied." This simple habit will do wonders for your evening energy level and for weight control! Remember that your EVENING meal should be your SMALLEST MEAL of the day!

Low-Fat Slow-Cooking

When using meat in a slow-cooker, stick to the exceptionally lean choices such as skinless chicken and turkey, beef sirloin or round steak, pork tenderloin and lean ham, AND trim well. Otherwise, all the fat that cooks out of the meat ends up in the surrounding food and then on you!

Beef Stroganoff over Noodles

Delicious down home creamy taste. Hard to believe this finds a place on a healthy menu!

1 can	(10.75 oz) **cream of mushroom soup**	
	(*Campbell's® Healthy Request®*)	
1 can	(14½ oz) **beef broth**	
1 can	(4 oz) **sliced mushrooms, drained**	
2 T	**quick-cooking tapioca**	
¾ tsp	**dried thyme**	
¼ tsp	**garlic powder**	

4½ to 10 hours before serving:

Combine all together in slow-cooker.

Make up the Chocolate Amaretto Cheesecake the night before for a truly decadent meal!

1 large	**onion, thinly sliced**
2 lbs	**lean sirloin steak, trimmed of all fat**

Add and slightly mix to cover meat in sauce.

Cover and cook on LOW for 9 to 10 hours or on HIGH for 4½ to 5 hours.

22 minutes before serving:

1½ cups	**light sour cream**

Place a large pot of water on to boil. Stir sour cream into slow-cooker mixture. Beef should easily break apart.

12 oz	**egg noodles**

Add to boiling water. Set timer for 9 minutes. Meanwhile… see if you can find some raw salad fixings and set the table.

1½ lb bag	**frozen peas and carrots**

When timer goes off, add to the bubbling noodles. Set timer for 1 more minute.

Drain the noodles and vegetables. Serve the beef and mushroom sauce over top, with a tossed salad on the side.

EXCHANGE VALUES

3 Starch   4 Meat   1 Veg.   — Fruit   — Milk   — Fat

Nutrition information for — 1 cup beef and sauce, 1-1/2 cups noodles & vegetables   Preparation Time — a.m. 15 min. — p.m. 22 min.

Calories 485	Fat .... 13 g	Fiber .... 5 g
Calories from Fat 24%	Saturated Fat .... 6 g	Cholesterol .... 131 mg

Sodium .... 550 mg	Total Carbohydrate .... 49 g
Protein .... 39 g	Sugars .... 11 g

Pork. "The Other White Meat®"

Chicken. Chicken. Fish.

Chicken. Chicken. Fish.

Many of you may feel you are about to grow feathers and gills. But did you know today's pork averages 31% less fat than it did 10 years ago? We can thank farmers for raising leaner hogs and butchers for trimming leaner cuts. The following cuts of pork have a slightly higher fat content than skinless chicken breast.

- Pork tenderloin
- Pork boneless sirloin chop or top loin chop
- Pork boneless loin roast or sirloin roast
- Pork loin chop
- Canadian bacon

As always trim well, and keep serving size to 3 - 4 ounces (the size of a deck of cards).

Cranberry Pork Roast over Noodles

Guests will rave about this unique and tender roast. You'll love it because it's so simple.

2 lb	pork tenderloin, frozen (one long roast *or* cut into thick slices)

8 hours before serving:

Place in slow-cooker.

1 can	(16 oz) **jellied cranberry sauce**
½ cup	sugar
½ cup	cranberry juice
1 tsp	dry mustard
¼ tsp	ground cloves

In a medium bowl, mix together (mashing cranberry sauce). Pour over roast.

Cook on low for 8 hours.

25 minutes before serving:

1 bag	(16 oz) **egg noodles** (*or* 8 potatoes)

Put a large pot of water on to boil. If you have the energy, peel potatoes for mashed potatoes or just boil noodles.

1 bunch	broccoli (2 *or* 3 stalks), **cut into flowerets**
1 bag	(1 lb) **baby carrots**

Put broccoli and carrots in microwaveable dish, cover and cook on high 7 minutes.

Drain 2 cups of juice from the roast. Skim off any fat (if there is any, pork tenderloin is so lean). Add water, to make 2 cups if necessary. Pour into a sauce pan. Bring to a boil over medium heat.

2 T	cornstarch
2 T	water

In a small cup, mix together and pour into boiling juice while whisking. Cook 1 minute until thick and bubbly. Serve sauce over the sliced pork, potatoes or noodles with vegetables on the side.

EXCHANGE VALUES

4 Starch	4 Meat	2 Veg.	1 Fruit	— Milk	— Fat

Nutrition information for — 4 oz. pork, 1 cup noodles, 1/4 cup gravy, 1 cup broccoli & carrots | Preparation Time — a.m. 5 min. — p.m. 25 min.

Calories 580	Fat .... 8 g	Fiber .... 4.7 g	Sodium .... 120 mg	Total Carbohydrate .... 85 g
Calories from Fat 13%	Saturated Fat .... 25 g	Cholesterol .... 143 mg	Protein .... 42 g	Sugars .... 35 g

The Top 10 Sources of Calories in the U.S. Diet

1. White bread, rolls, crackers

2. Doughnuts, cookies, cakes

3. Alcoholic beverages

4. Whole milk

5. Hamburger, cheeseburgers

6. Beef steaks, roasts

7. Soft drinks

8. Hot dogs, ham, lunch meat

9. Eggs

10. French fries, potato chips

Source: The Food and Health of Western Man,
J.L. Mount, 1975

Chicken Cacciatore

Once again "Chicken Tonight®" comes to the rescue.

SERVES | MENU

6 | CHICKEN CACCIATORE
CORKSCREW PASTA
TOSSED SALAD
APPLESAUCE DUMPLINGS
OR
HOT FUDGE BROWNIE
CAKE

6	chicken leg quarters (thigh & drumsticks), **skin removed**
	or
6	**skinless, boneless, chicken breast** (halves) (still frozen is fine)

4 to 11 hours before serving:

Place in slow-cooker.

4	zucchinis *or* yellow-crooked neck squash, cut in 1/2 lengthwise and sliced into 1" pieces
1	onion cut into wedges

Add to slow-cooker.

1 jar	(24 oz) **cacciatore sauce** (*Chicken Tonight®*)

Pour over all.

Cook on HIGH 4 to 5 hours or on LOW 9 to 11 hours.

15 minutes before serving:

8 oz	corkscrew (or any shape) **pasta** (preferably whole-wheat)

Put a large pot of water on to boil. Cook pasta 10 minutes.

Meanwhile… put together a salad.

Serve over pasta with salad on the side.

Note: Stick with light portions and after an evening walk, enjoy *Applesauce Dumplings* (page 202) or *Hot Fudge Brownie Cake* (page 201).

EXCHANGE VALUES

2 Starch   3 Meat   3 Veg.   — Fruit   — Milk   — Fat

Nutrition information for — 1/6 of the recipe using chicken leg quarters over 2/3 cup pasta | **Preparation Time — a.m. 15 min. — p.m. 15 min.**

Calories 410	Fat .... 10 g	Fiber .... 6.5 g	Sodium .... 565 mg	Total Carbohydrate .... 45 g
Calories from Fat 22%	Saturated Fat .... 2.4 g	Cholesterol .... 91 mg	Protein .... 36 g	Sugars .... 12 g

Tip

Do YOU have high blood pressure?

6 Keys to Your Lowest Blood Pressure Ever!

1. **If you're at all overweight, lose weight**. Even losing just 5 or 10 pounds can have a very positive effect on your blood pressure.

2. **Enjoy regular exercise!** A lifestyle with regular exercise definitely helps lower your blood pressure. (As always, check with your doctor first!) See page 108 for suggestions.

3. **EAT MORE** foods high in potassium, calcium and magnesium. These work in opposition of sodium in the body, therefore lowering blood pressure. Include your 5 to 9 (or more!) fruits and vegetables per day, plus non-fat and low-fat dairy foods, whole-grains and dried beans.

4. **Limit** your sodium intake to 2,000 mg or less per day. Keep in mind that the salt shaker is only $^1/_4$ of the problem. The major culprit is processed foods—and not just the ones that taste salty. See pages 31 & 145 for more information.

5. **Avoid or limit alcohol.** There is increasing evidence of a link between high blood pressure and alcohol consumption.

6. **Find ways to relax and release stress** from your body. How about yoga? Also, always make time for your favorite hobbies that are relaxing.

Sweet & Sour Chicken

You're gonna love this "Chicken Tonight®" sauce. Sometimes I omit the potatoes and make quick cooking rice, just before dinner time, to serve with it instead.

5 to 9 hours before serving:

6 medium	potatoes, cut into wedges
24	baby carrots, left whole
1 large	green pepper, cut into 1" pieces
1 medium	onion, cut into wedges

Add to slow-cooker in order given.

6	skinless, boneless, chicken breasts
	(halves) (still frozen is fine)

Stack on top.

1 jar	(24 oz) sweet & sour simmer sauce
	(*Chicken Tonight*®)

Pour over all.

Cook on LOW 8 to 9 hours or on HIGH 5 to 6 hours.

Just before serving:

Slice apples and kiwi.

Serve with whole-grain rolls.

EXCHANGE VALUES

2 Starch	3 Meat	2 Veg.	1 Fruit	— Milk	— Fat

Nutrition information for — 1/6 of the recipe | Preparation Time — a.m. 10 min.

Calories 375	Fat .... 2 g	Fiber .... 5 g	Sodium .... 390 mg	Total Carbohydrate .... 57 g
Calories from Fat 5%	Saturated Fat .... < 1 g	Cholesterol .... 70 mg	Protein .... 32 g	Sugars .... 26 g

Salad Bar

Salads & Sides

I've forgotten to mention…be SURE to eat LOTS and LOTS of isothiocyanates, indoles, dithiolthiones, limonene, allyl sulfides and saponins. Oh, and don't forget the caffeic acid, ellagic acid, ferulic acid and phytic acid.

What in the *world* am I talking about? I'm talking about just a few of the hundreds (perhaps thousands) of phytochemicals. (And you thought chemicals were bad)? While these sound like chemicals made in a lab, they are as natural as natural can be. They happen to be manufac- tured within the walls of plants, hence their name phyto (plant) chemicals. So what's the big deal about plant chemicals? They're big cancer fighters, that's what! New studies indicate that these compounds seem to play an important role in the production of enzymes that help dispose of potential carcinogens. For the past 20 years, scientists all over the world have consistently found that **people who eat greater amounts of fruits and vegetables have lower rates of most cancers.** Of course fruits and vegetables are already rich in life-saving folacin, vitamin C and beta carotene, but these newly discovered compounds now add even more gold to the pot.

This chapter is full of tasty ways to enjoy more fruits and vegetables! Many of these salads can be made ahead (like on the weekend) and enjoyed over the next several hectic weekdays.

The Leafy Facts

Many people eat an iceberg salad with a tomato fragment and think, "I got my fiber in for the day!"

But just how nutritious is iceberg lettuce, compared to darker greens like romaine or spinach? Just as its color indicates, it **pales in comparison** with less than half the fiber and valuable nutrients. To get more from your salads, try these suggestions:

1. Choose darker greens like romaine and spinach. Mix them 50-50 with iceberg until your family adjusts.

2. Buy the ready-to-eat dark green salad mixes for a real timesaver.

3. If you choose to buy the "fresh" lettuce and clean it yourself, buy a salad spinner. This allows you to quickly wash and spin your lettuce dry.

4. Always chop as many vegetables as you can to go on top of the salad. The vegetables pack more nutrition and fiber than the greens do.

5. Or, just skip the lettuce altogether and hit the veggies hard, like *Where's the Lettuce? Salad* (page 171).

Where's the Lettuce? Salad

Out of lettuce? No problem! All you need are vegetables and any combination of what you find in your refrigerator will do.

2pts 6

Scrounge through the refrigerator for whatever vegetables you can find.

4 cups	**any of the following:**
	• green, red *or* yellow peppers, chopped
	• celery, chopped
	• tomatoes, chopped
	• onions, chopped
	• fresh parsley, chopped fine
	• carrots, sliced
	• cauliflower, chopped
	• broccoli, chopped

Place in a medium-size bowl.

1 can	**(15 oz) Garbanzo beans, drained** (optional)
1 can	**(15 oz) beets, drained** (optional)

Add to bowl.

⅓ cup	**low-fat dressing** (*Henri's® Private Blend TAS-TEE®*) *or* **light Thousand Island dressing**

Toss with dressing and serve, or let guests dress their own.

This is a convenient recipe for later in the week, that "cleans" out your fridge.

EXCHANGE VALUES

1 Starch	— Meat	3 Veg.	— Fruit	— Milk	.5 Fat

Nutrition information for — about 1-1/3 cups, including the Garbanzo beans and beets   **Preparation Time** — 10 min.

Calories 145	Fat .... 2.5 g	Fiber .... 7 g	Sodium .... 440 mg	Total Carbohydrate .... 27 g
Calories from Fat 14%	Saturated Fat .... < 1 g	Cholesterol .... 0 mg	Protein .... 5 g	Sugars .... 14 g

Tip

Fruits & vegetables: Zon's favorite way to get 10 to 11-a-day

Breakfast	Cereal with 2 T raisins and 1 orange	2
Snack	4 oz. of juice diluted in 8 ounces of water and ice (sparkling water is great!)	1
Lunch	¹/₄ of a cantaloupe	1
	1 whole tomato (2 slices on my sandwich and I eat the rest)	1
	6 baby carrots	1
Snack	1 kiwi	1
	4 more ounces of juice diluted in 8 ounces of water and ice	1
Dinner	1¹/₂ cups of mixed vegetables or stir-fry, or a huge green salad with lots of vegetables on top, or 1¹/₂ cups of *Marinated Vegetable Salad*	<u>2-3</u>

10-11 servings!

Marinated Vegetable Salad

A colorful dish to bring to potlucks and picnics.

3	raw carrots, sliced diagonally
2 cups	broccoli flowerettes
2 cups	cauliflower flowerettes

Clean and prep vegetables, and place in a microwave cooking dish with 2 tsp of water. Cover and microwave for 4 minutes, or until vegetables just begin to get tender. Transfer to a colander and rinse with cold water to halt the cooking process.

$\frac{1}{2}$ each	green, red and yellow pepper
2	green onions
$\frac{1}{2}$ cup	light *or* fat-free Italian dressing
1 tsp	dried oregano

Cut peppers into 1" slices and chop onions. Combine everything with cooked vegetables and toss.

Allow to marinate for 1 to 3 hours and serve.

Note: This salad does not keep longer than 1 day. The vegetables begin to wilt, due to the salt in the dressing.

Canned sliced beets, drained, are also nice in this salad.

EXCHANGE VALUES

— Starch   — Meat   2 Veg.   — Fruit   — Milk   .5 Fat

Nutrition information for — about 1 cup			Preparation Time — 10 min.	
Calories 60	Fat .... 2 g	Fiber .... 3.6 g	Sodium .... 190 mg	Total Carbohydrate .... 9 g
Calories from Fat 30%	Saturated Fat .... < 1 g	Cholesterol .... 1 mg	Protein .... 2 g	Sugars .... 5 g

Food Coloring

Let's talk food colorings: reds, oranges, yellows, purples and greens. And I'm not talking about the kind made in a lab, but the kind made within the walls of plants. How colorful is your diet? In addition to the fine vitamins and minerals present in vegetables and fruits, the colors alone (called carotenoids) of peppers, carrots, sweet potatoes, etc., nourish your cells with powerful agents to fight disease.

How often do you serve carrot- raisin salad? I'm warning you that once you make this, your family will want it on the menu 30 times a year!

Sunshine Carrot-Raisin Salad

This salad is a great way to get loads of beta-carotene and tastes like candy!
Toss this together 30 minutes before your main dish is done.

Kids' Favorite

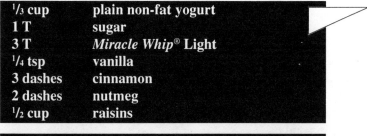

⅓ cup	plain non-fat yogurt
1 T	sugar
3 T	*Miracle Whip®* **Light**
¼ tsp	vanilla
3 dashes	cinnamon
2 dashes	nutmeg
½ cup	raisins

In a medium-size bowl,
mix together to form the dressing.

1 can	(8 oz) **pineapple tidbits, in its own juice, drained**

Reserve juice for another use. Mix pineapple into dressing.

3 cups	**finely shredded carrots** (about 5 medium *or* 45 baby carrots)

Use a food processor to shred carrots. Stir into dressing. Chill salad until ready to serve.

Optional Additions:

2 T	**shredded coconut** (remains less than 2.2 grams of fat per serving)
	or
1 T	**peanut butter**

For a nice variation, add 1 of these as an option.

EXCHANGE VALUES

— Starch — Meat 2 Veg. 1 Fruit — Milk — Fat

Nutrition information for — about 2/3 cup without optional additions   **Preparation Time — 10 min.**

Calories 110	Fat .... 1.7 g	Fiber .... 2.5 g	Sodium .... 91 mg	Total Carbohydrate .... 23 g
Calories from Fat 13%	Saturated Fat .... 0 g	Cholesterol .... 0 mg	Protein .... 2 g	Sugars .... 18 g

Did you know that pineapple juice works just as well as lemon juice to keep sliced apples from turning brown? Remember this the next time you make a fresh fruit salad with sliced apples or pears. (We call this a *Fruit Explosion*). Simply stir in a can of pineapple chunks, along with the juice to prevent browning (and also to avoid that tart lemon taste)!

Crunchy Apple Salad

Do you have apples in your fruit bowl that are, well, shall we say, "past their prime?" Let this recipe resuscitate them back to life. It only takes about 8 minutes to put this together.

Kids' Favorite

⅓ cup	plain non-fat yogurt
1 T	sugar
1 T	*Miracle Whip*® Light
¼ tsp	vanilla
3 sprinkles	cinnamon (*or* Chinese Five Spice)
2 T	walnuts *or* raisins *or* both

Mix ingredients together in a medium size bowl.

2 large	apples, preferably one red and one green

Slice, core and cut into chunks. Add to bowl.

1 can	(8 oz) pineapple tidbits, in its own juice, drained

Drain pineapple, reserving juice for another use. Add to the bowl and toss gently.

Chill salad until ready to serve.

EXCHANGE VALUES

— Starch   — Meat   — Veg.   2 Fruit   — Milk   .5 Fat

Nutrition information for — about 1 cup   **Preparation Time — 8 min.**

Calories 160	Fat ....3.5 g	Fiber ....4.5 g	Sodium ....45 mg	Total Carbohydrate ....32 g
Calories from Fat 19%	Saturated Fat ....< 1 g	Cholesterol ....0 mg	Protein ....2.5 g	Sugars ....27 g

5-a-day (at least!) for better health

So, how does your plate rate? Americans in general average 2.1 servings per day of fruits and vegetables *combined*. The Center for Science in the Public Interest recommends 5-9 servings per day. The American Cancer Institute is so convinced about the cancer-fighting abilities of fruits and vegetables, that it is considering raising the recommendation to 9-11 servings each day! And you thought 5-a-day was a lot!

So what about the "5-a-day" campaign? I recommend aiming for 5-a-day *without* counting juice servings, since juice does not contain important fiber. Also, if you can achieve 5-a-day and then drink 8 ounces of juice a day, (2 fruit servings) this will get you up to 7 servings. Double your "token" portion of vegetables at dinner and you're up again. Think of fruit at every snack time. While it may seem tough at first, just take it one meal and one snack at a time. You'll get better and better at remembering to include fruit and or vegetables with every meal!

Veggie Pasta Salad

This recipe relies on my favorite dressing, Henri's® Private Blend TAS-TEE® low fat dressing. It not only makes this taste great, but makes it easy too. Keep in mind for lunch, dinner and potlucks! *Please Note:* This is an intentionally large batch, as it will keep for 3 days for quick meals throughout the week.

1 box	(16 oz) **dry pasta of your choice**

Begin boiling water for pasta. While you wait for water to boil, begin steps below. As soon as water is ready, add pasta and follow directions on box.

2 cups	**carrots**
1 large	**bunch broccoli**
1 each	**red, yellow and green pepper**
¾ cup	*Henri's® Private Blend TAS-TEE®* **low-fat dressing (or a light coleslaw dressing)**

Cut carrots diaganolly. Cut broccoli into bite-sized flowerettes. Seed and cut peppers into small chunks.

At the sound of the timer, quickly toss carrots and broccoli into boiling water with pasta. Set timer for 1 minute. When timer goes off again, quickly drain and rinse in cold water to halt the cooking process. (This step brightens the vegetables while taking the edge off their rawness.)

Transfer pasta into a large bowl that has a tight-fitting lid. Add peppers and dressing. Mix.

2	**tomatoes***

Chop tomatoes. Prepare dishes for immediate serving. Add chopped tomato and serve.

EXCHANGE VALUES

3 Starch	— Meat	3 Veg.	— Fruit	— Milk	1 Fat

* **Adding chopped tomato to the large batch in this recipe will not allow it to be kept for 3 days. Each time you are ready to serve the dish, just add more freshly chopped tomato.**

Nutrition information for — about 2 cups

Preparation Time — 30 min.

Calories 305	Fat .... 3 g	Fiber .... 5.3 g	Sodium .... 200 mg	Total Carbohydrate .... 62 g
Calories from Fat 8%	Saturated Fat .... < 1 g	Cholesterol .... 0 mg	Protein .... 10 g	Sugars .... 15 g

Try this "golden rule" for eating 7-9 servings of fruit and vegetables a day

Eat at least one fruit and/or vegetable with every meal and every snack (without counting juices).

Once you do this, THEN add in the juice servings you drink, you will hit the mark with little effort. This really works!"

Broccoli Salad with Dried Cherries

I bet you're surprised to see such a high fat salad in my book. I figure the price of the pecans and dried cherries will assure that you make it on special occasions only. As I always say, "With moderation and balance, all foods can fit!"

8

SLOW-COOKED DISHES LIKE:
RAVIOLI STEW OR
GYPSY STEW

1 bunch	broccoli, cut into bite sized pieces
1/2	red onion, thinly sliced, then chopped
1/2 cup	chopped pecans
1 cup	dried cherries

Combine in a large attractive serving bowl .

1/2 cup	*Miracle Whip*® Light
1/2 cup	plain non-fat yogurt
1/4 cup	Parmesan cheese
1 T	sugar
1 T	vinegar (cider *or* any variety)
1/2 tsp	cinnamon

Combine in a small bowl.
Pour over broccoli mixture, toss gently and serve.

EXCHANGE VALUES

— Starch   — Meat   2 Veg.   1 Fruit   — Milk   2 Fat

Nutrition information for — 1/8 of the recipe			Preparation Time — 8 min.	
Calories 185	Fat .... 9 g	Fiber .... 3 g	Sodium .... 190 mg	Total Carbohydrate .... 24 g
Calories from Fat 40%	Saturated Fat .... < 1 g	Cholesterol .... 2 mg	Protein .... 4.5 g	Sugars .... 15 g

Hunger versus thirst

Many people mistake feelings of mild thirst for hunger. (Confusing these feelings is especially common, if you are fatigued). Eating when you are thirsty can put on unwanted pounds. If weight control is important to you, drink a glass of water first before nibbling.

Cranberry Salad

A festive and popular holiday and potluck favorite. Simple, low calorie and delicious.

TASTES GREAT WITH:

THANKSGIVING DINNER OR EVERYDAY SANDWICHES

Make 4 to 12 hours ahead

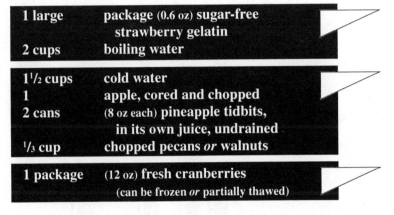

1 large	package (0.6 oz) **sugar-free strawberry gelatin**
2 cups	**boiling water**

Place gelatin into a decorative serving bowl. Dissolve with water.

1½ cups	**cold water**
1	**apple, cored and chopped**
2 cans	(8 oz each) **pineapple tidbits, in its own juice, undrained**
⅓ cup	**chopped pecans** *or* **walnuts**

Add and stir.

1 package	(12 oz) **fresh cranberries** (can be frozen *or* partially thawed)

Place in a food processor and process until partly chunky, mostly smooth. Add to salad and stir well.

Refrigerate at least 4 hours before serving.

EXCHANGE VALUES

— Starch   — Meat   — Veg.   1 Fruit   — Milk   .5 Fat

Nutrition information for — 1/8 of the recipe			Preparation Time — 8 min.	
Calories 90	Fat .... 2.6 g	Fiber .... 3 g	Sodium .... 4 mg	Total Carbohydrate .... 16 g
Calories from Fat 24%	Saturated Fat .... < 1 g	Cholesterol .... 0 mg	Protein .... 2 g	Sugars .... 9 g

Which picnic would your heart rather have?

Typical Picnic "A"

1 oz potato chips

1 charbroiled bratwurst on a bun

1/2 cup traditional coleslaw

1 cup traditional potato salad

Another 1 oz. of potato chips

2 chocolate brownies

This meal contains 1,485 calories and 90 grams of fat!

That's equal to 6 tablespoons of shortening or lard!

Or ...

Picnic "B"

4 carrot sticks

1/2 skinless chicken breast

2 T BBQ sauce

Whole-wheat bun

1/2 cup reduced-fat coleslaw

1 cup *5-Bean Salad*

Fresh fruit for dessert

This meal contains 700 calories, and 12.5 grams of fat! What a BIG FAT DIFFERENCE!!

The choice is yours!

Potato Salad

Here's that delicious Henri's® Private Blend TAS-TEE® low-fat dressing again, that's the secret ingredient. Traditional tasting potato salad with a nice twist.

Put both a large and small pot of water on to boil.

8 medium	redskin potatoes, scrubbed clean and cubed

Add to large pot of boiling water.

4	eggs

Add to small pot of boiling water. Set timer for 10 minutes.

1 small	red or yellow onion, minced
3 ribs	celery, diced (optional)

Meanwhile… chop. Place in a large serving bowl.

When timer sounds, drain eggs and rinse with cold water. Set timer for 20 additional minutes (to finish potatoes). Crack and peel eggs. Chop and add to bowl.

When timer sounds, drain potatoes and cool slightly before adding to bowl.

½ cup	*Henri's® Private Blend TAS-TEE® low-fat dressing®* (or light coleslaw dressing)
¼ cup	*Miracle Whip® Light*
10 grinds	fresh ground pepper
¼ tsp	salt (optional)
2 T	mustard (plain or Dijon)

Gently mix with potatoes.

2	fresh tomatoes (optional)

Garnish with tomato wedges.

EXCHANGE VALUES

1 Starch — Meat — Veg. — Fruit — Milk .5 Fat

Nutrition information for — about 1/2 cup with 1 tomato wedge   Preparation Time — 45 min.

Calories 105	Fat .... 3 g	Fiber .... 1.6 g	Sodium .... 174 mg	Total Carbohydrate .... 17 g
Calories from Fat 23%	Saturated Fat .... < 1 g	Cholesterol .... 53 mg	Protein .... 3.5 g	Sugars ....3 g

Trying to lower your cholesterol?

In addition to making the low-fat, high fiber recipes in this book, be sure to:

1. Choose several (2 to 4) bean recipes each week.

2. Eat oatmeal or oat bran cereal and muffins as often as possible.

3. Limit saturated fats even more by selecting cheeses that are fat-free instead of low-fat.

4. Cook with as much garlic as possible and or consider a garlic supplement.

5. Include soy products as much as possible.

6. Choose fish 2 to 3 times per week.

Following these steps will lead to your absolute best cholesterol level ever!

5-Bean Salad

Why stop at 3 bean salad? This has triple the cholesterol lowering power of 3-bean salad, and a lot less oil. This makes a big batch so plan on enjoying it **all** week long.

If you wish to make only 1/2 this batch, simply reserve 1/2 the beans for an upcoming batch of chili.

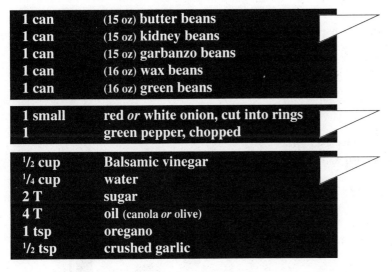

1 can	(15 oz) **butter beans**	
1 can	(15 oz) **kidney beans**	
1 can	(15 oz) **garbanzo beans**	
1 can	(16 oz) **wax beans**	
1 can	(16 oz) **green beans**	

Open cans and rinse and drain thoroughly. Transfer to a large bowl with a tight fitting lid.

1 small	**red** *or* **white onion, cut into rings**
1	**green pepper, chopped**

Add to beans.

¹/₂ cup	**Balsamic vinegar**
¹/₄ cup	**water**
2 T	**sugar**
4 T	**oil** (canola *or* olive)
1 tsp	**oregano**
¹/₂ tsp	**crushed garlic**

Mix together in a 2 cup measuring cup. Pour over beans and toss to coat.

Best if allowed to marinate 4 or more hours.

EXCHANGE VALUES

1 Starch	— Meat	2 Veg.	— Fruit	— Milk	1 Fat

Nutrition information for — about 1 cup

Preparation Time — 10 min.

Calories 195	Fat .... 6.5 g	Fiber .... 7 g	Sodium .... 672 mg	Total Carbohydrate .... 30 g
Calories from Fat 29%	Saturated Fat .... < 1 g	Cholesterol .... 0 mg	Protein .... 7 g	Sugars .... 12 g

Attention ladies:
Exercise helps prevent breast cancer

Researchers at the University of Southern California* found that **1 to 3 hours of exercise** per week during the reproductive years cuts breast cancer risk **by 30%.**

4 or more hours of exercise each week **cuts risk by 60%!**

How many hours have you gotten in so far this week?

* Bernstein L, Henderson BE, Hanisch R, Sullivan-Halley J, Ross RK. *Physical exercise and reduced risk of breast cancer in young women.* J Natl Cancer Inst 1994;86:1403-08.

Creamy Tuna Twist

Tired of sandwiches in your lunch box? Try this! A batch of this will provide a family with lunches for 3 days. Great for picnics and potlucks.

SERVES	TASTES GREAT WITH:
12 AS A SIDE DISH	A BOWL OF VEGETABLE SOUP
6 AS A MAIN DISH	AND FRUIT

Put a medium pot full of water on to boil.

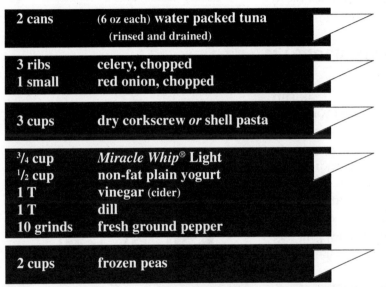

2 cans	(6 oz each) **water packed tuna** (rinsed and drained)

Open cans and place in a large bowl which has a tight fitting lid.

3 ribs	**celery, chopped**
1 small	**red onion, chopped**

Chop onions and celery and mix with the tuna.

3 cups	**dry corkscrew *or* shell pasta**

When water is boiling add pasta. Set timer for 8 minutes.

¾ cup	*Miracle Whip*® **Light**
½ cup	**non-fat plain yogurt**
1 T	**vinegar** (cider)
1 T	**dill**
10 grinds	**fresh ground pepper**

Mix together in a 2 cup measuring cup. Mix with tuna.

2 cups	**frozen peas**

When timer sounds, add peas to boiling pasta. Set timer for 2 minutes.

When timer sounds, quickly drain and rinse. Toss with the tuna mixture.

EXCHANGE VALUES

1 Starch	1 Meat	1 Veg.	— Fruit	— Milk	1 Fat

Nutrition information for — about 2/3 cup **Preparation Time — 25 min.**

Calories 175	Fat .... 4 g	Fiber .... 2 g	Sodium .... 255 mg	Total Carbohydrate .... 22 g
Calories from Fat 20%	Saturated Fat .... 0 g	Cholesterol .... 9 mg	Protein .... 12 g	Sugars .... 5 g

The wonder of cruciferous vegetables

How often do you eat cabbage? Brussels Sprouts? Kale? Important studies show cruciferous vegetables (the cabbage family) appear to protect you against colorectal, stomach and respiratory cancers. Cruciferous vegetables are **broccoli, Brussels sprouts, cabbage, cauliflower, collards, kale, kohlrabi, mustard greens, bok choy, rutabaga, turnip greens and turnips.**

Please take a hard look at this list. How many of these cabbage family vegetables do you eat in a week? How can you increase that number? You guessed it! Pasta slaw comes to the rescue. It's both low calorie and full of cancer fighters. Enjoy!

Produce Shopping the European Way

The Europeans make it an afterwork ritual to stop at a corner produce market so they can enjoy the freshest of ingredients for dinner. Have you ever considered this habit for your family? Or do you find huge grocery stores too overwhelming? Maybe it's time to break out of your grocery store rut and find a more intimate place to shop.

If you live in or near Ann Arbor, you're in luck! Stop in at *Coleman's Four Seasons* on Liberty and say hi to the owners Lynda and Ben. It's a really neat place! Simply stop in after work, you'll be in and out in a flash. And be sure to take the coupon (in the back) for up to $10 off!

Pasta Slaw

You know how salads are great for helping you lose weight? Well, so is this. I make this up whenever my clothes are fitting snug. I then include a serving with lunch and dinner. Just think of it as a negative calorie food!

8 | GRILLED CHICKEN OR FISH

Put a medium size pot full of water on to boil.

2 cups	shredded cabbage
2 cups	shredded carrots

Buy already shredded, or shred using a food processor. Place in a large serving bowl.

2 oz	dry spaghetti pasta (1 cup cooked)

When water is boiling, add pasta. Set timer for 10 minutes.

1	green pepper, chopped
1	red pepper, chopped
½	red onion, *or* 4 green onions, chopped

Add to cabbage and carrots.

1 T	lemon juice (preferably fresh squeezed)
2 T	Balsamic vinegar (*or* red wine)
½ tsp	salt
½ tsp	oregano
1 T	oil (olive *or* canola)
½ tsp	crushed garlic
dash	pepper (to taste)

Mix together in a small bowl.

At sound of timer, drain pasta and add to vegetables while still hot.

Toss all together with dressing. Serve warm or chilled.

EXCHANGE VALUES

.5 Starch	— Meat	2 Veg.	— Fruit	— Milk	.5 Fat

Nutrition information for — about 1 cup   **Preparation Time — 20 min.**

Calories 100	Fat .... 2 g	Fiber .... 3 g	Sodium .... 220 mg	Total Carbohydrate .... 18 g
Calories from Fat 18%	Saturated Fat .... < 1 g	Cholesterol .... 0 mg	Protein .... 3 g	Sugars .... 6 g

Anti-oxidants

You've been hearing this word a lot lately. What is it again? The best example is to slice an apple and watch what happens. In only a few minutes the milky white flesh turns brown. This is "oxidation." Every good cook knows that lemon juice will slow the browning process. The vitamin C in the lemon juice is the "anti-oxidant." Here are some examples of oxidation in the human body:

Cataracts: Eye fluids normally contain large amounts of vitamin C, but with aging, these levels decline. As that happens, proteins in the lens oxidize, making the lens more susceptible to clouding and the development of cataracts.

Cancer: Many scientists believe that some cancers result from oxidative damage to cells, therefore reducing their resistance to carcinogens.

Heart disease: Scientists are now concerned not only with the presence of "bad" LDL (low density lipoprotein) cholesterol in the blood stream, but at what rate it oxidizes with the artery wall to create plaque.

Therefore, eating a diet high in antioxidants becomes increasingly important to fight the onset of common diseases.

Cinnamon Butternut Squash is LOADED with the powerful anti-oxidant, beta carotene, as well as tons of phytochemicals. Make it often!

Cinnamon Butternut Squash

Train yourself to make this delicious side dish frequently. Winter squash is one of the best anti-aging foods around!

Preheat oven to 375°.

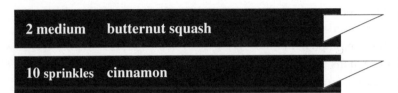

2 medium butternut squash

10 sprinkles cinnamon

Slice squash in $^1/_2$ lengthwise, scoop out the seeds.

Sprinkle cinnamon into the squash.

Place **cut side down** on a cookie sheet and add about $^1/_2$ cup of water to the pan. (This helps keep it moist without having to add butter to the squash.)

Bake 1 hour.

Scoop squash out and into a bowl. Mash with a fork. Sprinkle with additional cinnamon if desired.

(Brown sugar can be added, but taste it first. Sometimes the squash is so naturally sweet it doesn't need it!)

EXCHANGE VALUES

— Starch   — Meat   2 Veg.   — Fruit   — Milk   — Fat

Nutrition information for — about 1/2 cup mashed squash			Preparation Time — 5 min.	Oven Time — 1 hour
Calories 50	Fat .... 0 g	Fiber .... 1 g	Sodium .... 10 mg	Total Carbohydrate .... 10 g
Calories from Fat 0%	Saturated Fat .... 0 g	Cholesterol .... 0 mg	Protein .... 0 g	Sugars .... 3 g

When to serve bread, garlic toast or rolls at your meal

Why is it that some meals get bread and some don't? While it often just depends "what goes good together," each meal really should have 2 or 3 servings of starch (high complex carbohydrate).

A slice of bread, garlic toast or roll is best included when the meal has just one starch serving, such as: broiled fish, broccoli and a baked potato, or a pasta dish. Examples of meals containing 2 starch servings are: potatoes and corn, or rice and beans. It's up to you if you'd like a third starch. Active individuals who burn a great deal of calories and most men, need the third serving of carbohydrate calories. So let them eat bread at every meal!

Remember, if a substantial dessert is planned, weight conscious individuals and people with diabetes will want to forego the bread or some of the potatoes or rice, to "save up" for a small serving of dessert.

Whole-Wheat Garlic Cheese Toast

	SERVES	TASTES GREAT WITH:

Throughout my recipes, I call for serving dishes with garlic toast. Here's what I make that's healthy and fast.

4

SOUPS

ANY PASTA DISH INCLUDING LAZONYA

Turn oven on to broil. Remember to leave the door ajar.

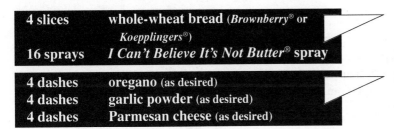

| 4 slices | whole-wheat bread (*Brownberry®* or *Koepplingers®*) |
| 16 sprays | *I Can't Believe It's Not Butter®* spray |

Place bread on a cookie sheet. Spray bread with 4 sprays each slice.

4 dashes	oregano (as desired)
4 dashes	garlic powder (as desired)
4 dashes	Parmesan cheese (as desired)

Sprinkle on bread.

Broil 1 to 2 minutes. Set the timer, they can burn quickly! I usually just broil one side, but flip the bread and toast another minute if desired.

For serving, cut toast diagonally in each direction to make 4 triangles per slice.

EXCHANGE VALUES

1 Starch	— Meat	— Veg.	— Fruit	— Milk	— Fat

Nutrition information for — 4 triangles (1 slice of bread)

Preparation Time — 5 min.

| Calories .... 75 | Fat .... 1.5 g | Fiber .... 2 g | Sodium .... 171 mg | Total Carbohydrate .... 13 g |
| Calories from Fat .... 18% | Saturated Fat .... .5 g | Cholesterol .... 0 mg | Protein .... 3 g | Sugars .... 1 g |

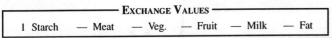

Whole-Wheat Garlic Cheese Toast

Lickety-Split Meals

Margarine vs. butter, the slippery debate

Thinking butter is "natural" and therefore better for you than margarine? Think again. Butter is more saturated than LARD. You are better off putting lard on your bread than butter!

Margarine on the other hand, is not picture perfect either. It's "hydrogenated" (which makes it thick and spreadable) and contains troublesome "trans-fatty acids."

What should you do?

1. At breakfast, opt for low-sugar jams, jellies, apple butter, honey and/or natural peanut butter, instead of habitually spreading on margarine.

2. When sautéing use nonstick spray or 1 T of oil, instead of butter or margarine.

3. When making grilled cheese sandwiches or garlic toast, lightly brush on oil instead of spreading on margarine.

4. In baking, use applesauce or other mashed fruit, and use small amounts of oil when necessary.

5. Use a product like *I Can't Believe It's Not Butter*® spray for popcorn and baked potatoes.

6. Buy a small tub of light margarine. Store it in the back of your refrigerator and use it rarely. (Following steps 1-5, you should not need to use it more than twice a week.)

P.S. Try honey on this cornbread instead of the "habitual" margarine!

Cornbread

Even as a child, I've loved cornbread. I can mix this up in 5 minutes and pop it in the oven for 20 minutes. This gives me time to whip up a main dish. Remember to make a double batch while you're at it! This recipe uses oil instead of shortening and less of it.

Preheat oven to 425°.
Thoroughly spray a 9" pie plate or an 8" x 8" pan with nonstick cooking spray.

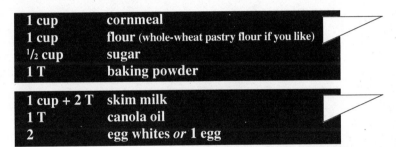

1 cup	cornmeal
1 cup	flour (whole-wheat pastry flour if you like)
½ cup	sugar
1 T	baking powder

Mix together in a bowl using a fork. Be sure baking powder is well distributed.

1 cup + 2 T	skim milk
1 T	canola oil
2	egg whites *or* 1 egg

Add to dry ingredients and mix until blended.

Pour into the sprayed baking pan. If you prefer muffins, spray 8 muffin cups with nonstick cooking spray and pour in the batter.

Bake for 20 minutes or until a toothpick comes out clean. Bake muffins 16 to 17 minutes.

EXCHANGE VALUES

2 Starch — Meat — Veg. — Fruit — Milk — Fat

Nutrition information for — 1/10 of a piece			Preparation Time — 10 min.	Oven Time — 20 min.
Calories 155	Fat .... 2 g	Fiber .... 2.5 g	Sodium .... 145 mg	Total Carbohydrate .... 31 g
Calories from Fat 11%	Saturated Fat .... < 1 g	Cholesterol .... 0 mg	Protein .... 4 g	Sugars .... 11 g

Sweet Treats

Dessert before dinner anyone?

Have you ever wished that a scrumptious dessert could be so good for you that you could actually justify eating it before dinner? How about eating it for breakfast? Well look no further. Desserts from a well-devised recipe, like the ones in this chapter, can actually provide as much nutrition as a healthy snack or breakfast!

Sure, you can save time and buy commercially made fat-free cookies and cakes, but they are generally loaded with sugar and made with few, *if any*, whole grains. Of course consuming these is fine *in moderation*. But if you'd like to have dessert more often, (and who doesn't?) then check out the recipes in this chapter!

A low-fat, high-fiber diet is much easier to stick with when there are frequent desserts on the menu. And these desserts are truly "crime without punishment." Enjoy!

Do you suffer from sweet cravings?

How much fruit have you been eating? Chances are, you've been missing the mark. Your brain requires simple carbohydrates for its functioning. Fruit is very high in simple carbohydrates. When you don't get enough, your body sends you a fruit craving. The problem is you *misinterpret* the signal as "sweets" or "chocolate" cravings!

Solution: Eat 3 to 4 pieces of fruit every day and notice the difference!

P.S. A slice of this scrumptious pie counts as 1 fruit serving!

Simple Summer Fresh Fruit Pie

Here's a simply gorgeous dessert. One summer weekend at the lake, my husband suggested we eat the pie first, since it looked so good. Everyone agreed. It was so light and delicious, we all had another piece afterwards!

MAKES 2 PIES
8 SERVINGS EACH

1 large pkg	**(0.6 oz) sugar-free strawberry gelatin**
2 cups	**boiling water** (as called for on box)

Place gelatin in a medium bowl, add boiling water and stir to dissolve. (You *will not* be adding the cold water step.)

1 large pkg	**(5.1 oz) instant vanilla pudding**
1½ cups	**skim milk** (instead of 3 cups called for on package)

In a large bowl, mix together with an electric mixer. It will be thicker than usual. Add the dissolved gelatin and mix until smooth.

2	**graham cracker crusts, regular** *or* **chocolate** (I use the 9 oz. crust for the larger 10 serving pie)
1 quart	**fresh strawberries, cleaned and left whole**
2	**bananas, sliced**
4	**fresh peaches** *or* **nectarines, sliced into wedges**
1 pint	**fresh blueberries, washed and drained**

Place the fruit attractively filling the crust, using the order listed.

Pour ½ of the jello/pudding mix over each pie. The jello/pudding mix will seep between each piece of fruit.

Refrigerate until firm, about 2 hours.

Serve proudly and prepare for rave reviews.

EXCHANGE VALUES

1 Starch	— Meat	— Veg.	1 Fruit	— Milk	1 Fat

Nutrition information for — 1/8 of one pie			Preparation Time — 25 min.	
Calories 170	Fat .... 4 g	Fiber .... 2.5 g	Sodium .... 250 mg	Total Carbohydrate .... 31 g
Calories from Fat 21%	Saturated Fat .... 1 g	Cholesterol .... < 1 mg	Protein .... 3 g	Sugars .... 13 g

A tasty whole-grain secret

In many of the recipes, you will see that I've called for "whole-wheat pastry flour." This flour is different from the "whole-wheat flour" you commonly find in grocery stores. "Whole-wheat pastry flour" or sometimes called "whole-grain pastry flour" is very nutritious because it is a "whole grain" flour, yet is very light and cakey in texture, similar to that of white flour. It can be used in equal amounts to replace all-purpose flour in any "non-yeast" recipe. It makes wonderfully light cookies, cakes, muffins and quick breads, and the best part is; only you will know that you used "healthy" flour!

Yeast recipes, on the other hand, require gluten for structure and whole-wheat pastry flour has very little. This is where the common "whole-wheat flour" referred to as "bread" flour (that you find commonly in stores) is required. Just remember, if the recipe calls for baking powder or baking soda, it will work fine with whole-wheat pastry flour. If it uses yeast, it will not.

Now, where do you find it? Be aware, that you will probably not find it in the standard flour section of your grocery store. It is considered specialty flour and may be found in the health food section among special brands like *Arrowhead Mills* or *Bob's Red Mill*. If you do not find it, request it from your grocer. I buy it in bulk quantities at natural food stores or co-ops. Please look for it. It really is worth the effort. Until you find it, you can substitute for each cup of whole-wheat pastry flour: $1/2$ cup all-purpose and $1/2$ cup whole-wheat flour or (as a last resort) use 1 cup of all-purpose flour.

Blueberry Buckle

This recipe, amazingly, contains no fat. It's super easy to make and delicious. Don't
feel guilty eating it for breakfast either. It's just as nutritious as toast with jam and fruit!

8

Preheat oven to 375°.
Spray a 9" x13" pan with nonstick cooking spray.

2 bags	(12 oz each) **frozen blueberries** *or* **2 pints fresh blueberries**
3 T	**sugar**
½ cup	**orange juice**

Berry Bottom

Place blueberries in baking dish. Sprinkle sugar on top, then add juice.

1 cup	**whole-wheat pastry flour***
½ cup	**sugar**
1 tsp	**baking powder**
3	**egg whites**
¼ tsp	**lemon, orange** *or* **almond extract** (optional)

Cake Topping

Mix together in a medium-sized bowl. Drop 8 equal spoonfuls of dough on top of the blueberries in 2 rows of 4 .

1 T	**sugar**

Sprinkle sugar over the dough. Bake for 35 minutes or until cake is lightly browned.

Take out of oven. Serve warm with a scoop of fat-free vanilla ice cream or yogurt. Yummm!

EXCHANGE VALUES

| 1.5 Starch | — Meat | — Veg. | 1 Fruit | — Milk | — Fat |

* If you don't have whole-wheat pastry flour, you can substitute with ½ cup whole-wheat flour and ½ cup all-purpose flour.

Nutrition information for — 1/8 of the recipe, without ice cream				Preparation Time — 15 min.	Oven Time — 35 min.
Calories 165	Fat .... < 1 g	Fiber .... 4 g	Sodium .... 72 mg	Total Carbohydrate .... 39 g
Calories from Fat 4%	Saturated Fat .... 0 g	Cholesterol .... 0 mg	Protein .... 3 g	Sugars .... 26 g

Sweet Treats
187
Lickety-Split Meals

Tip

What's it like being married to a nutritionist?

"Most awesome."

—My husband,
SCOTT FOCO, 34
Maintaining a
20 pound weight loss,
since 3 months after we met.

Chocolate-Amaretto Cheesecake

When invited over to friends for dinner, I love bringing this dessert. They can't believe a "dietitian" could bring anything so good. This is truly "Crime without Punishment!"

Preheat oven to 300°.

12	chocolate wafers *or* 6 graham cracker squares

8 hours or day before serving:

Finely crush and sprinkle into bottom of 8" springform pan.† Set aside.

Note: This recipe requires 8 hours of chilling. Make this the day before or morning of the day you plan to serve it.

1 cup	light cream cheese
1 cup	sugar
1½ cup	low-fat cottage cheese
6 T	unsweetened baking cocoa
¼ cup	all purpose flour
¼ cup	Amaretto*
1 tsp	vanilla extract

Position knife blade in food processor bowl. Add ingredients, processing until smooth.

1	egg

Add and process just until blended.

Pour mixture over crumbs in pan.

2 T	semi-sweet chocolate mini-morsels

Sprinkle on top of mixture.

Bake for 45 to 50 minutes or until cheesecake is set. Let cool in pan on wire rack. Once cheesecake is cool, cover and chill at least 8 hours. Remove sides of pan and serve.

1 - 2 cups	clean whole raspberries *or* sliced strawberries

Place in a bowl and serve alongside the cheesecake platter. Invite guests to top their cake as desired.

EXCHANGE VALUES

2 Starch	1 Meat	— Veg.	— Fruit	— Milk	— Fat

* **Chocolate-mint Cheesecake:** Substitute ¼ cup Creme de Menthe for the Amaretto.
† An 8-inch round pan can be used, but it's more difficult to remove a slice neatly.

Nutrition information for — 1/2 slice topped with 3 to 6 berries			Preparation Time — 25 min.	Oven Time — 45-50 min.
Calories 215	Fat .... 6 g	Fiber .... 2 g	Sodium .... 256 mg	Total Carbohydrate .... 30 g
Calories from Fat 26%	Saturated Fat .... 3 g	Cholesterol .... 29 mg	Protein .... 8 g	Sugars .... 24 g

An argument FOR desserts

Many nutrition professionals suggest NOT getting in the habit of dessert every night. I certainly work with many clients who blame their "dessert after every meal" upbringing for their weight problems. On the other hand, clients who grew up never being allowed dessert, now have the strong tendency to overeat them. Many studies clearly suggest that deprivation is a major contributor to overeating forbidden foods. **The solution is to include something satisfyingly sweet in moderation.**

Super Time Saving Tip:

Buy shredded carrots from your grocer. I tested the matchstick cut carrots and they turned out very tender in this recipe.

Creamy Frosted Carrot Cake

Did you know traditional carrot cake uses 1 cup of oil? Add the cream cheese frosting and you're looking at 50 to 60 grams of fat per slice! Well, throw out that old recipe and replace it with this delicious treat. No one will know, I promise.

Preheat oven to 350°.

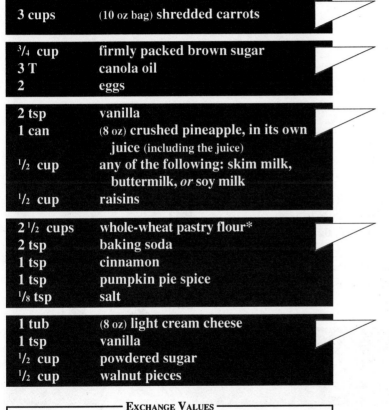

3 cups	(10 oz bag) **shredded carrots**

Buy pre-shredded carrots or use a food processor to shred. Set aside 3 cups for this recipe. Use any leftovers in your next salad.

³/₄ cup	**firmly packed brown sugar**
3 T	**canola oil**
2	**eggs**

Using a large bowl, mix well with a wire whisk.

2 tsp	**vanilla**
1 can	(8 oz) **crushed pineapple, in its own juice** (including the juice)
¹/₂ cup	**any of the following: skim milk, buttermilk,** *or* **soy milk**
¹/₂ cup	**raisins**

Stir in the large bowl.

2¹/₂ cups	**whole-wheat pastry flour***
2 tsp	**baking soda**
1 tsp	**cinnamon**
1 tsp	**pumpkin pie spice**
¹/₈ tsp	**salt**

Mix in a medium-size bowl. Add mix, a little at a time into the large bowl and mix well. Add carrots to mix.

Spray a 9" x 13" pan or (2) 8" round pans with nonstick cooking spray. Pour batter into pan(s). Bake 28 to 30 minutes.

1 tub	(8 oz) **light cream cheese**
1 tsp	**vanilla**
¹/₂ cup	**powdered sugar**
¹/₂ cup	**walnut pieces**

Allow the cream cheese to soften on the counter while the cake is baking. When the cake comes out of the oven, mix ingredients together in a bowl. Once cake has cooled, frost it. (If using round pans, frosting will only cover tops of cakes, not the sides.)

* If you don't have whole-wheat pastry flour, you can substitute with 1¹/₄ cups whole-wheat flour and 1¹/₄ cups all-purpose flour.

Exchange Values

2 Starch	— Meat	— Veg.	— Fruit	— Milk	1 Fat

Nutrition information for — 1/8 slice with frosting

Preparation Time — 25 min.   **Oven Time — 28-30 min.**

Calories 195	Fat .... 7 g	Fiber .... 2 g	Sodium .... 235 mg	Total Carbohydrate .... 30 g
Calories from Fat 31%	Saturated Fat .... 1.9 g	Cholesterol .... 30 mg	Protein .... 5 g	Sugars .... 18 g

How much dessert is TOO much?

First, take a look at the recommended serving size. Use this as a guide, but most importantly, listen to your body. It will tell you when you've had enough. Never eat dessert when you are "full." Always SAVE ROOM FOR DESSERT.

Chewy Multi-Grain Bars

These mock *Kellogg*® *NutriGrain Bars* make a fabulous snack, dessert or lunchbox treat. They're even nutritious enough for breakfast along with a glass of milk or yogurt and a piece of fruit. You can freeze half of the bars in *Ziplock*® bags for future use.

Preheat oven to 350°.

1 cup	raisins	Measure raisins into a glass measuring cup. Add water and microwave for 1 minute on high. Allow to soak.
1 T	water	

¾ cup	firmly packed brown sugar
2 T	canola oil
1 cup	applesauce
4	egg whites
2 T	skim milk *or* soy milk
2 tsp	vanilla

Place in large bowl and mix thoroughly.

Purée the soaking raisins in a food processor. Add to the large bowl, unsweetened, and mix thoroughly. (People who don't care for raisins will tolerate them better puréed. Puréeing increases sweetness and moisture. Raisins can be added without puréeing if you prefer.)

1½ cups	whole-wheat pastry flour*
1 tsp	baking soda
1½ tsp	cinnamon

Measure and sift into the large bowl (or combine in another bowl using a fork to evenly distribute soda and cinnamon).

3 cups	Multi-Grain Oats by Quaker
	(*or* quick *or* old fashion oatmeal)
⅓ cup	walnuts, coarsely chopped

Add and mix. Spread dough into an ungreased 9" x 13" baking pan. Bake for 23 minutes. Cool and cut into 32 bars.

Icing

½ cup	powdered sugar
¼ tsp	vanilla
1 T	skim milk

Mix together in a small bowl. Drizzle over cooled bars before or after cutting.

EXCHANGE VALUES

| 1 Starch | — Meat | — Veg. | — Fruit | — Milk | — Fat |

* If you don't have whole-wheat pastry flour, you can substitute with ¾ cup whole-wheat flour and ¾ cup all-purpose flour.

Nutrition information for — 1 bar with icing			Preparation Time — 30 min.	Oven Time — 23 min.
Calories 100	Fat .... 2 g	Fiber .... 1.5 g	Sodium .... 50 mg	Total Carbohydrate .... 19 g
Calories from Fat 18%	Saturated Fat .... < 1 g	Cholesterol .... 0 mg	Protein .... 3 g	Sugars .... 9 g

Tip

Who has time to bake anymore?

Even the busiest people can find themselves in the middle of a rainy weekend, hankering for some fun in the kitchen. Besides, the stress-reducing power of tinkering in the kitchen, sending heavenly aroma throughout the house, is excellent therapy. The fact that these recipes are simple to put together, makes this "therapy session" easy. And to double the benefits of your efforts, make a double batch and freeze.

Chocolate Chip Bar Cookies

Fellow Registered Dietitian Lori Hunt adapted this recipe from a Mrs. Fields oatmeal chocolate chip cookie recipe. The instant pudding and applesauce replaces the shortening entirely. Use chocolate pudding for chocolate chocolate chip cookies. Since these cookies are so moist, I suggest storing them in the refrigerator or freezer. They freeze wonderfully.

2 Doz.	4 Doz.	Preheat oven to 350°.
1 c	2 c	applesauce, unsweetened
³/₄ c	1¹/₂ c	firmly packed brown sugar
2 tsp	1T+1tsp	vanilla
4	8	egg whites

Mix together well in a large bowl using a fork.

2 Doz.	4 Doz.	
1 lg pkg	2 lg pkg	(5.1 oz) instant vanilla or chocolate pudding
1 tsp	2 tsp	baking soda
1 tsp	2 tsp	baking powder
2 c	4 c	whole-wheat pastry flour*

In a medium sized bowl, mix together with a fork. Then add to the liquid ingredients. Using a large wooden spoon, stir well.

2 Doz.	4 Doz.	
1 c	2 c	dry oats (quick-cooking or old fashioned)

Add and mix.

2 Doz.	4 Doz.	
¹/₂ pkg	1 pkg	(12 oz) semi-sweet chocolate chips

Add and mix. Let dough sit about 10 minutes. Spray (1 or 2) 9" x 13" pans with nonstick spray. Place dough in pan(s). Lay a sheet of wax paper on top. Press dough out. Remove wax paper.

Bake 25 minutes. When you take the cookies out of the oven, they will look lightly browned on top and soft to the touch. They will firm up as they cool. Then cut into bars. If keeping past 2 days, store cookies in refrigerator or freezer.

* If you don't have whole-wheat pastry flour, you can substitute with 1 cup whole-wheat flour and 1 cup all-purpose flour, or for the large recipe, 2 cups whole-wheat flour and 2 cups all-purpose flour.

EXCHANGE VALUES

2 Starch	— Meat	— Veg.	— Fruit	— Milk	— Fat

Nutrition information for — 1 cookie | Preparation Time — 35 min. | Oven Time —15 min.

Calories 125	Fat .... 2 g	Fiber .... 1.5 g	Sodium .... 170 mg	Total Carbohydrate .... 26 g
Calories from Fat 14%	Saturated Fat .... 1 g	Cholesterol .... 0 mg	Protein .... 3 g	Sugars .... 10 g

EXERCISE: A new way to get your quota

Long gone are the days that you MUST exercise 30-40 minutes NON-STOP to receive the benefits. Studies show that breaking your 30 to 40 minute exercise into 3 or 4 separate 10-minute segments, has the same cardiovascular AND weight-loss benefits.

Now there is additional good news from the University of Pittsburgh about improved "stick-to-it" ness. Researchers determined that at the end of 6 months, women on the short-bout program exercised 30 more minutes per week. That's an extra day's worth! They also lost 2 pounds more, on average, than the long-bout exercisers. Obviously 10 minutes here and there is easier to stick to!

Also keep in mind:

- 10 minutes doesn't work up enough of a sweat to require a shower

- The frequent 10 minute breaks will do wonders for alleviating stress!

Is short-bout exercise the answer for you?

Oatmeal Cookies

This recipe was inspired by one of Evelyn Tribole's recipe makeovers in Shape magazine. I found that the sugar could come down further. The cream cheese works nicely for both flavor and moistness. As I love to say, 3 of these with milk and an orange are nutritious enough for breakfast!

Preheat oven to 350°.

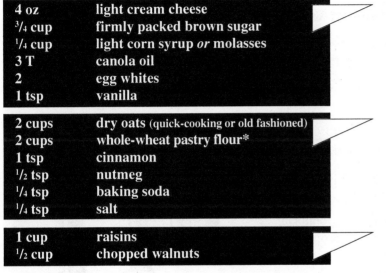

4 oz	light cream cheese
3/4 cup	firmly packed brown sugar
1/4 cup	light corn syrup *or* molasses
3 T	canola oil
2	egg whites
1 tsp	vanilla

In a large mixing bowl, use an electric mixer to beat together. Set aside.

2 cups	dry oats (quick-cooking or old fashioned)
2 cups	whole-wheat pastry flour*
1 tsp	cinnamon
1/2 tsp	nutmeg
1/4 tsp	baking soda
1/4 tsp	salt

In a medium size bowl, mix together until soda and salt are well distributed. Add to liquid mixture and mix well.

1 cup	raisins
1/2 cup	chopped walnuts

Mix in.

With a knife, cut dough into 3 equal sections. (Use this as a guide to make 3 dozen cookies.) Drop by slightly heaping tablespoons. Flatten each cookie with the back of your spoon.

Bake for 10 minutes.

* If you don't have whole-wheat pastry flour, you can substitute with 1 cup whole-wheat flour and 1 cup all-purpose flour.

Exchange Values

1 Starch	— Meat	— Veg.	— Fruit	— Milk	— Fat

Nutrition information for — 1 cookie		Preparation Time — 30 min.	Oven Time —10 min.
Calories 100	Fat ...... 3 g	Fiber ...... 1 g	Sodium ...... 50 mg	Total Carbohydrate ...... 16 g
Calories from Fat 26%	Saturated Fat ...... .6 g	Cholesterol ...... 1 mg	Protein ...... 2.5 g	Sugars ...... 8 g

Chocoholics unite!

The following are a few of my favorite "healthier" ways to lick a chocolate craving:

- Cup of hot cocoa

- Glass of chocolate milk (bottle of chocolate syrup comes in handy)

- Sliced banana drizzled with chocolate syrup

- Frozen cherries (defrosted slightly) drizzled with chocolate syrup

- Low-fat chocolate chip granola bar

- *Chocolate No-Bakes* (this page!)

- *Cocoa Lava Kisses* (page 194)

- *Chocolate Chip Cookie Bars* (page 191)

Chocolate No-Bakes

The same wonderful cookie from my childhood with only ½ the fat!

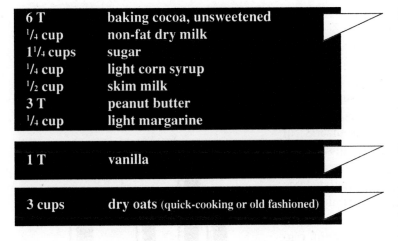

6 T	baking cocoa, unsweetened
¼ cup	non-fat dry milk
1¼ cups	sugar
¼ cup	light corn syrup
½ cup	skim milk
3 T	peanut butter
¼ cup	light margarine

In a medium saucepan, bring to a boil and continue to boil 1 to 2 minutes. Remove from heat.

1 T	vanilla

Stir in.

3 cups	dry oats (quick-cooking or old fashioned)

Measure into a medium sized bowl.
Pour hot mixture over oats and mix well.

Drop by spoonfuls onto waxed paper and allow to cool. Be sure to make 36 cookies if you want the nutrition information to be accurate.

Transfer to a *Tupperware*® container and refrigerate. (Because these have less saturated fat, they do not set up "solid" at room temperature like the traditional No-Bakes. Expect them to be gooey and good.)

EXCHANGE VALUES

1 Starch	— Meat	— Veg.	— Fruit	— Milk	— Fat

Nutrition information for — 1 cookie   Preparation Time — 20 min.

Calories 80	Fat .... 2 g	Fiber .... 1 g	Sodium .... 20 mg	Total Carbohydrate ....14 g
Calories from Fat 20%	Saturated Fat .... .5 g	Cholesterol .... < 1 mg	Protein ....2 g	Sugars ....8 g

Chocolate facts: Did you know?

Chocolate is basically a creamy mixture of 3 ingredients: cocoa, sugar and fat. Studies have shown that it is this combination of ingredients that creates the impulsive, addictive "lack of control" behavior, with fat being the key culprit. The fat provides the creamy smoothness, dulling the sweetness slightly, so you don't tire of the teaspoons upon teaspoons of sugar that you are consuming. The fat combined with the sugar makes the calories soar.

But say you get smart and use the cocoa and sugar, but not the fat? Could you gain chocolate satisfaction with fewer calories and more control to stop at a few? Try this strategy in these *Cocoa Lava Kisses*. You'll be surprised at the satisfaction you'll feel, with fewer bites.

Cocoa Lava Kisses

These heavenly clouds of sweet chocolate work great to take care of a chocolate craving. Unbelievably, they're fat-free! They are intensely sweet which will make it easier to stop at 3, which is only 75 calories!

Preheat oven to 250°.
Line 2 cookie sheets with wax paper.

These freeze well, making them convenient for future chocolate cravings!

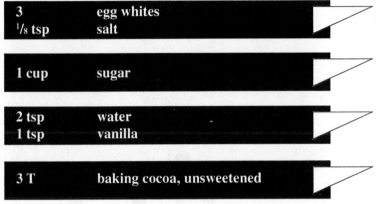

3	egg whites
1/8 tsp	salt

Place in medium size bowl. Whip with an electric mixer until soft peaks form.

1 cup	sugar

Gradually add 1/2 cup of the sugar to egg whites while constantly whipping.

2 tsp	water
1 tsp	vanilla

Combine in a cup. Add to mix, a few drops at a time alternating with the remaining 1/2 cup sugar while constantly whipping.

3 T	baking cocoa, unsweetened

Flake cocoa with a fork to break clumps. Sift if necessary. Fold into mix.

Place bite-size rounded **teaspoons** (*not* tablespoons) of mix onto the wax paper on a cookie sheet.

Bake approximately 30 minutes. They will be dry on the outside, but moist and lava like on the inside. They will retain their shape. (If they become completely dry like styrofoam, they are overbaked.)

While kisses are still hot, remove from wax paper and place on a wire rack so they will not stick.

After cooling, store kisses in an airtight container.

EXCHANGE VALUES

.5 Starch	— Meat	— Veg.	— Fruit	— Milk	— Fat

Nutrition information for — 1 cookie		Preparation Time — 30 min.	Oven Time — 30 min.
Calories 25	Fat .... 0 g	Fiber .... 0 g	Sodium .... 16 mg	Total Carbohydrate .... 6 g
Calories from Fat 0%	Saturated Fat .... 0 g	Cholesterol .... 0 g	Protein .... 0 g	Sugars .... 5 g

Banana buying and ripening tips

1. Buy a few yellow and a few green, for "just in time" bananas all week.

2. Once your bananas reach their desired ripeness, place them in the refrigerator to halt the ripening process for a few days. Don't be alarmed when the skins turn black. They will still be perfect on the inside.

3. If your bananas have reached the banana bread stage, but you don't have the 30 minutes to mix this up, simply peel them and slip them into *Ziplock®* bags for the freezer. They can be thawed and used another time for *'Nana bread,* page 195; *Banana Nut Cake,* page 199; or *Smoothies,* page 49.

'Nana Bread

Who doesn't love banana bread? Every household needs a banana bread recipe for those bananas that peter out before the family can get around to eating them all. And the recipe needs to be without all the fat, yet so moist that each slice can be eaten as is! Ask no more, it's all right here!

MAKES 2 LOAVES
12 SERVINGS EACH

Preheat oven to 350°.

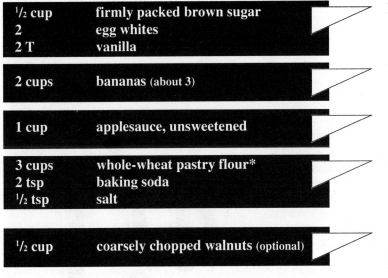

In this recipe, applesauce completely replaces the shortening or margarine!

½ cup	firmly packed brown sugar
2	egg whites
2 T	vanilla

Mix together in a large mixing bowl.

2 cups	bananas (about 3)

Mash. (I use a food processsor). Stir into mix.

1 cup	applesauce, unsweetened

Add to mix and stir.

3 cups	whole-wheat pastry flour*
2 tsp	baking soda
½ tsp	salt

Place in a sifter and sift into the mix (or place in a separate bowl and use a fork to equally distribute the salt and soda). Stir together with the wet ingredients thoroughly.

½ cup	coarsely chopped walnuts (optional)

Add to mix.

Spray loaf pans with nonstick cooking spray.

Divide batter evenly into each pan (loafs will not be high).

Bake for 45 minutes, or until a toothpick comes out with no batter sticking to it.

EXCHANGE VALUES

1 Starch	— Meat	— Veg.	— Fruit	— Milk	— Fat

* If you don't have whole-wheat pastry flour, you can substitute with 1½ cups whole-wheat and 1½ cups all-purpose flour.

Nutrition information for — 1 slice (1/12 of one loaf)			Preparation Time — 15 min.	Oven Time — 45 min.
Calories 90	Fat .... 2 g	Fiber .... 2 g	Sodium .... 160 mg	Total Carbohydrate .... 17 g
Calories from Fat 16%	Saturated Fat .... < 1 g	Cholesterol .... 0 mg	Protein .... 2.6 g	Sugars .... 6 g

What's moderation?

I am often asked, "Zon, do you ever eat full-fat foods?" And my answer is, "Sure! But not real often." Of course the next question is "How often is often?"

My answer is the "80-20 rule." All foods can fit *when* your base diet is healthfully selected 80% of the time. That's 80% of all your breakfasts, lunches, dinners and snacks being healthy low-fat choices. The remaining 20% leaves room for the special occasions, holidays and "treats." The sweet treats in this chapter can be considered more like the "80%" instead of the "20%", since they are low in fat and offer good nutritional value.

Enlightened Zucchini Bread

Toss out that old recipe that called for 1 cup of oil, because now you have a much healthier alternative, without sacrificing taste! My thanks to Ann Jones, MS, RD and her daughter for this great find.

1 loaf	2 loaves	Preheat oven at 350°.	
1 1/2 c	3 c	whole-wheat pastry flour*	Mix together in a small bowl.
1/2 tsp	1 tsp	baking soda	
1/4 tsp	1/2 tsp	baking powder	
1 tsp	2 tsp	cinnamon	
1/4 tsp	1/2 tsp	each, cloves and nutmeg	
3/4 c	1 1/2 c	sugar	Beat together in a separate medium size bowl.
2	4	egg whites	
1/4 c	1/2 c	skim milk *or* non-fat plain yogurt	
1 tsp	2 tsp	vanilla	
1 T	2 T	lemon juice	
1/4 tsp	1/2 tsp	lemon extract	
1 c	2 c	shredded zucchini, unpeeled	Stir into liquid mix in the medium bowl.
1/2 c	1 c	nuts *or* raisins	Stir flour mix into zucchini mix. Add optional nuts and/or raisins and mix.

Spray loaf pan(s) with nonstick cooking spray. Pour batter into pan(s). Bake 45 to 55 minutes.

* If you don't have whole-wheat pastry flour, you can substitute with 3/4 cup whole-wheat flour and 3/4 cup all-purpose flour, OR for the large recipe, 1 1/2 cup whole-wheat flour and 1 1/2 cup all-purpose flour.

EXCHANGE VALUES

1.5 Starch	— Meat	1 Veg.	— Fruit	— Milk	.5 Fat

Nutrition information for — 1 slice (1/12 of one loaf)		Preparation Time — 30 min.	Oven Time — 45-55 min.
Calories 125	Fat .... 3 g	Fiber .... 1.5 g Sodium .... 73 mg	Total Carbohydrate .... 22 g
Calories from Fat 22%	Saturated Fat .... 0 g	Cholesterol .... 0 mg Protein .... 3.5 g	Sugars .... 13 g

True or False?

"People with diabetes cannot eat foods containing sugar"

Answer: FALSE.

People with diabetes need to control how many carbohydrates they are consuming at every meal and snack. Eating foods high in sugar makes this very difficult to do, since high sugar foods contain high amounts of carbohydrates. On the other hand, they *can* include foods containing sugar when done in the following way:

1. Know how many carbohydrates the serving of food contains (by reading the nutrition facts).

2. Choose recipes using less sugar and more whole grains (like the ones in this book). The less sugar a dessert contains, the more generous the portion can be.

3. "Make room" for the dessert by equally cutting back on other carbohydrate containing foods like bread, rice, potatoes or pasta. Cutting back exactly 30 grams of carbohydrate to enjoy a 30 gram carbohydrate dessert, means a controlled blood sugar level.

People with diabetes must remember that eating a diet that is low in fat and high in fiber is also of **KEY** importance for success in the control of their health.

Surprise Pumpkin Pie

"Surprise" because it makes its own crust. What a time and fat saver! This pie is so fast that you can have it in the oven in less than 10 minutes. It's delicious **and** beta-carotene rich. Why not serve all year round?

8

9" DEEP DISH PIE*

Preheat the oven to 350°.

2	eggs *or* 4 egg whites *or* ¹/₂ cup egg beaters
³/₄ cup	sugar
¹/₂ cup	reduced-fat *Bisquick®* mix
1¹/₂ cups	pumpkin
2 tsp	pumpkin pie spice (*or* 1 tsp cinnamon, ¹/₂ tsp ginger, ¹/₄ tsp cloves, and ¹/₄ tsp nutmeg)
¹/₄ tsp	salt
1 can	(13 oz) evaporated skim milk

Mix all ingredients in a blender or food processor for 2 minutes.

Spray a 9" pie plate (preferably glass) with nonstick cooking spray. Pour in the batter.

Bake at 350º for 50 to 60 minutes, or until firm.

Cool completely before cutting. Serve with fat-free ice cream or yogurt, if desired.

* This recipe makes either (1) 9" deep dish (4 cup volume) or (2) shallow dish (2 cup volume) pies. If making the (2) shallow pies, adjust baking time to 35 to 45 minutes. Nutrition information per slice will be ¹/₂ of what is listed below.

— EXCHANGE VALUES —

2 Starch	— Meat	1 Veg.	— Fruit	— Milk	— Fat

Nutrition information for — 1/8 slice			Preparation Time — 10 min.	Oven Time — 50-60 min.
Calories 175	Fat .... 2 g	Fiber .... 1.4 g	Sodium .... 240 mg	Total Carbohydrate .... 34 g
Calories from Fat 9%	Saturated Fat .... < 1 g	Cholesterol .... 55 mg	Protein .... 6.5 g	Sugars .... 20 g

Coffee: the diuretic

Did you know that chances are, you wake up in the morning dehydrated? You haven't consumed any liquids for 8 hours or longer. Charging off to work with 2 cups of coffee makes matters worse. A cup of caffeinated coffee works like a diuretic. For every cup, you excrete a cup and a half. No wonder so many people get headaches by mid-afternoon, which is a classic sign of dehydration. Coupled with fatigue, this means you're definitely not operating at your optimal level.

Solution:

Make it a goal to drink a glass of water or diluted juice FIRST THING in the morning. In fact, you may find it convenient to just open up in the shower! (Think about it! There isn't anything weird about using your showerhead as a drinking fountain. *Try it*!)

Pumpkin Oatbran Bread or Muffins

A super way to eat beta carotene loaded pumpkin. This makes a large batch so freeze the muffins for another busy time, especially breakfast!

Preheat oven to 350°.

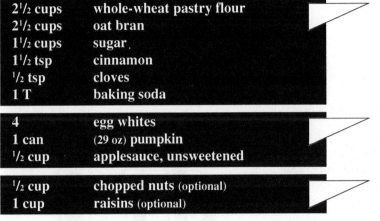

2½ cups	whole-wheat pastry flour
2½ cups	oat bran
1½ cups	sugar
1½ tsp	cinnamon
½ tsp	cloves
1 T	baking soda

Mix dry ingredients in a large bowl.

Make a well in the center of the mix.

4	egg whites
1 can	(29 oz) pumpkin
½ cup	applesauce, unsweetened

Add to the well in the dry mix. Stir just until moistened.

½ cup	chopped nuts (optional)
1 cup	raisins (optional)

Stir in.

Spray loaf pans or muffin tins with nonstick cooking spray.

Pour in batter.

Bake loaf 45 minutes; muffins 30–35 minutes or until toothpick inserted in center comes out clean.

EXCHANGE VALUES

1 Starch	— Meat	— Veg.	.5 Fruit	— Milk	— Fat

* If you don't have whole-wheat pastry flour, you can substitute with 1¼ cups whole-wheat flour and 1¼ cups all-purpose flour.

Nutrition information for — 1 slice (1/12 of one loaf) or 1 muffin		Preparation Time — 15 min.	Oven Time — 30-45 min.
Calories 120	Fat .... 2 g	Fiber .... 3 g	Sodium .... 110 mg	Total Carbohydrate .... 23 g
Calories from Fat 13%	Saturated Fat .... < 1 g	Cholesterol .... 0 mg	Protein .... 4 g	Sugars .... 12 g

"I'd like the non-adhesive muffin papers please."

Have you ever noticed how low-fat or fat-free muffin recipes tend to make muffin papers stick to the muffin? Peeling the paper down takes half the muffin with it. Well until they invent edible muffin papers, try this:

Lightly spray the inside of each muffin paper with nonstick cooking spray. Your muffin papers will now peel off easily, leaving the muffin unscathed!

Banana Nut Cake or Muffins

This recipe is somewhat similar to the Nana Bread recipe. It's whole-grain, no added fats, and delicious.

Preheat oven to 350°.
Spray pan(s)† with nonstick spray.

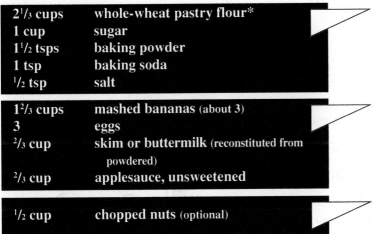

2¹/₃ cups	whole-wheat pastry flour*
1 cup	sugar
1¹/₂ tsps	baking powder
1 tsp	baking soda
¹/₂ tsp	salt

Mix dry ingredients in a large bowl using a fork.
Be certain the baking powder and soda are well distributed.

1²/₃ cups	mashed bananas (about 3)
3	eggs
²/₃ cup	skim or buttermilk (reconstituted from powdered)
²/₃ cup	applesauce, unsweetened

Mash bananas in a food processor or in a separate bowl by hand. Add liquids and bananas to dry ingredients and mix.

¹/₂ cup	chopped nuts (optional)

Mix in.

Pour batter into prepared pan(s). Bake until wooden pick inserted in center comes out clean; rectangle 40 minutes, rounds 35 minutes.

Cool and cut into 18 squares and serve as a snacking cake.

Note: If it's someone's birthday, I'll frost with Snackwell's frosting.

† **Attention muffin lovers: Makes great muffins. Adjust baking time to 22 to 25 minutes.**
* **If you don't have whole-wheat pastry flour, you can substitute with 1 cup whole-wheat flour and 1¹/₃ cups all-purpose flour.**

EXCHANGE VALUES

1 Starch	— Meat	— Veg.	1 Fruit	— Milk	.5 Fat

Nutrition information for — 1 piece (1/18 slice of the cake)		Preparation Time — 25 min.	Oven Time — 40 min.
Calories 140	Fat .... 3 g	Fiber .... 2 g	Sodium .... 185 mg	Total Carbohydrate ....26 g
Calories from Fat 19%	Saturated Fat .... .4 g	Cholesterol .... 35 mg	Protein .... 4 g	Sugars .... 14 g

Flaming tips:

- Turn lights down to enjoy the flame.

- This recipe can be done outdoors, using your grill as your heat source.

- Especially nice after dark.

- Use caution. The flames may rise 2 feet.

- Be aware that flaming does not remove all the alcohol.

Flaming Bananas Foster

I learned to make this when I was 15 years old, after dining at "Brennans" in New Orleans.
It's my absolute favorite dessert for entertaining. Talk about fun, fast, tasty and impressive!

Delegate
Someone to:
Find the matches
and scoop ice cream
(1/2 cup each
serving)

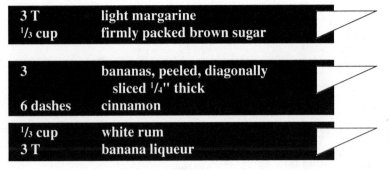

3 T	light margarine
1/3 cup	firmly packed brown sugar

Melt brown sugar and margarine
in a nonstick sauté pan over medium heat.

3	bananas, peeled, diagonally sliced 1/4" thick
6 dashes	cinnamon

Add bananas and cinnamon, and sauté until tender,
turning once. (Use this time to find your matches!)

1/3 cup	white rum
3 T	banana liqueur

Combine in a cup. With matches ready, pour over bananas, stand back
and attempt to "touch" the liquid with your lit match. Be sure to yell
"everybody now… OOMPA!" as it lights. (The louder the OOMPA's,
the better it will taste!)

Continue to simmer dish over medium heat throughout flaming process
(about 20 seconds).

6 scoops	(1/2 cup each) vanilla fat-free ice cream *or* yogurt

Once flame goes out on its own, serve immediately over ice cream.

EXCHANGE VALUES

2 Starch	— Meat	— Veg.	1 Fruit	.5 Milk	— Fat

Nutrition information for — 1/6 of the recipe over 1/2 cup frozen yogurt		Preparation Time — 15 min.	
Calories 270	Fat .... 3 g	Fiber .... 1 g	Sodium .... 100 mg	Total Carbohydrate .... 48 g
Calories from Fat 10%	Saturated Fat .... < 1 g	Cholesterol .... 0 mg	Protein .... 4.5 g	Sugars .... 35 g

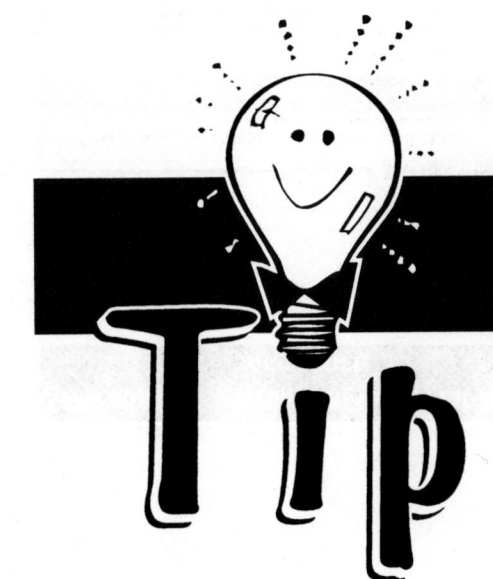

Save room for dessert

It is customary in this country to eat until full and **then** eat dessert. This makes the dessert COMPLETELY fattening! Yes, even if it is fat free! Thin people eat dessert, but they "save room" for it. When you know you'll be having dessert, plan ahead by eating $\frac{1}{2}$ of your potato or skip the bread.

Hot Fudge Brownie Cake

A quick way to bake up a super chocolate treat. The hot water poured over the top will turn into a yummy hot fudge.

Preheat oven to 350°.

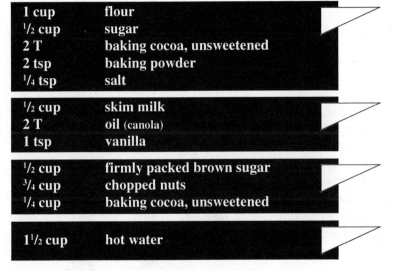

1 cup	flour
1/2 cup	sugar
2 T	baking cocoa, unsweetened
2 tsp	baking powder
1/4 tsp	salt

In a medium bowl, combine well with a fork until well distributed.

1/2 cup	skim milk
2 T	oil (canola)
1 tsp	vanilla

Stir in until smooth. Spread into an ungreased 9" square baking pan.

1/2 cup	firmly packed brown sugar
3/4 cup	chopped nuts
1/4 cup	baking cocoa, unsweetened

Sprinkle each over batter.

1 1/2 cup	hot water

Pour over all and do not stir. (This is not a mistake!) Bake for 35 to 40 minutes. Allow to stand for 10 minutes. Serve warm with a scoop of low-fat frozen yogurt.

EXCHANGE VALUES

3 Starch — Meat — Veg. — Fruit — Milk 2 Fat

Nutrition information for — 1/9 of the recipe, without frozen yogurt		Preparation Time — 15 min.	Oven Time — 35-40 min.
Calories 270	Fat .... 9.5 g Fiber .... 1 g	Sodium .... 210 mg	Total Carbohydrate .... 43 g
Calories from Fat 31%	Saturated Fat .... < 1 g Cholesterol .... < 1 mg	Protein .... 5.5 g	Sugars .... 22 g

Tips on sugar

My recipes contain somewhere around ¹/₂ the sugar of other dessert recipes. The nutrition information provided in this book includes grams of "sugar" (lower right, under carbohydrates). **Every 4 grams of sugar you see equals 1 teaspoon of sugar.** Up to 3 teaspoons (or 12 grams) of sugar is an acceptable amount for a dessert. You can easily flip through the recipes and see which recipes have the most and least amounts of sugar.

P.S. Understanding "grams of sugar" also helps you evaluate breakfast cereals, telling you which ones have a lot of sugar and which ones don't. Check it out!

Applesauce Dumplings

Hungry for something sweet and there's nothing in the house? Try this simple to whip up apple dessert that requires no apple peeling! My thanks to Grandma Minnie for this neat find.

3 cups	applesauce, unsweetened
1/2 cup	water
1 tsp	cinnamon

Place in a wide mouth non-stick pan and turn on medium heat.

1 cup	reduced-fat *Bisquick*®
1/4 c	sugar
1/2 cup	skim milk

In a medium bowl, combine just until moistened.

Applesauce should be boiling by now. Remove from heat and drop 6 even dumplings onto applesauce.

Cover and return to heat. Simmer 12 minutes. Serve warm.

| 6 scoops | (1/2 cup each) **vanilla fat-free ice cream *or* yogurt** |

Top each with a scoop.

EXCHANGE VALUES

2 Starch — Meat — Veg. 1 Fruit .5 Milk — Fat

Nutrition information for — 1 dumpling, 1/2 cup sauce, 1/2 cup frozen yogurt		Preparation Time — 10 min.	Cook time — 12 min.
Calories 260	Fat .... 1 g Fiber .... 1.5 g	Sodium .... 308 mg	Total Carbohydrate .... 56 g
Calories from Fat 4%	Saturated Fat .... < 1 g Cholesterol .... 0 mg	Protein .... 6 g	Sugars .... 10 g

Great ideas from people like you!

"For many years now I have loved the "Peanut Buster Parfait" at Dairy Queen. With my new commitment to healthy eating, I decided to substitute fat-free frozen yogurt for the ice cream and chocolate syrup for the hot fudge. I also order the small instead of the medium. The result: I am just as satisfied without feeling at all deprived."

—STACEY W, 26,
celebrating the
6th month of her
new healthy lifestyle.

Congratulations Stacey! You've successfully saved 200 calories and 25 grams of fat, while not feeling deprived. This is what it's all about!

Brownie Banana Split

This recipe utilizes the convenience of the new low-fat box mixes, and adds nutrition via wheat-germ and fresh fruit! This simple dessert ends up with nutritional value to go along with the sugar. Its heavenly appearance makes it a favorite for entertaining.

Preheat oven according to box directions.

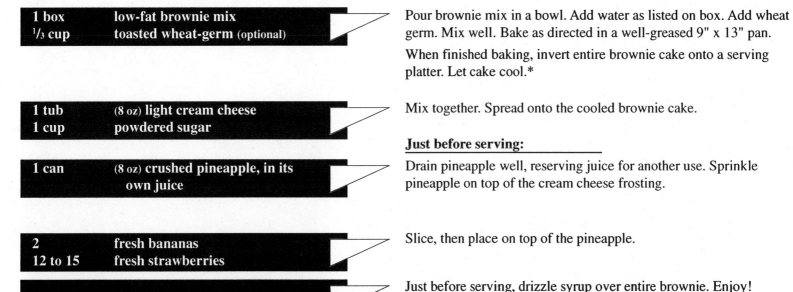

1 box	low-fat brownie mix
1/3 cup	toasted wheat-germ (optional)

Pour brownie mix in a bowl. Add water as listed on box. Add wheat germ. Mix well. Bake as directed in a well-greased 9" x 13" pan.

When finished baking, invert entire brownie cake onto a serving platter. Let cake cool.*

1 tub	(8 oz) light cream cheese
1 cup	powdered sugar

Mix together. Spread onto the cooled brownie cake.

Just before serving:

1 can	(8 oz) crushed pineapple, in its own juice

Drain pineapple well, reserving juice for another use. Sprinkle pineapple on top of the cream cheese frosting.

2	fresh bananas
12 to 15	fresh strawberries

Slice, then place on top of the pineapple.

1/4 cup	chocolate syrup (squeeze bottle kind)

Just before serving, drizzle syrup over entire brownie. Enjoy!

EXCHANGE VALUES

3 Starch	— Meat	— Veg.	1 Fruit	— Milk	1 Fat

* If you have 6 or less guests, cut cake in 1/2 and only top 1/2 now. Do the other 1/2 another day, since the fresh appearance does not keep overnight.

Nutrition information for — 1/2 square		Preparation Time — 30 min.		
Calories 275	Fat .... 6 g	Fiber .... 3 g	Sodium .... 200 mg	Total Carbohydrate .... 50 g
Calories from Fat 19%	Saturated Fat .... 2.7 g	Cholesterol .... 9 mg	Protein .... 5 g	Sugars .... 40 g

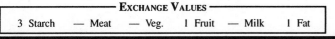

Index

INDEX Recipes Alphabetically

AUTHENTICALLY ORGANIC FOOD

EDEN®

Each EDEN® brand food is selected and prepared by Eden Foods as if it were for our own children.

The EDEN® brand means:
no irradiation, no preservatives,
no chemical additives,
no food colorings, no refined sugars,
no genetically engineered ingredients,
and the safest, most nutritious,
certified organically grown food
that could possibly be offered.

DOUBLE
ORGANICALLY GROWN
CERTIFIED®

Please support certified organic farmers, They are society's brightest hope for change.

Ⓚ parve
Most Eden products are kosher and parve

For more information about EDEN® products, call us at 800 248-0320.

Eden Foods, Inc.
701 Tecumseh Road
Clinton, Michigan 49236

Coupon 1 (Top Left)

Coupon 2 (Top Right)

Coupon 3 (Middle Left)

Coupon 4 (Middle Right)

Coupon 5 (Bottom Left)

Coupon 6 (Bottom Right)

CLIP & SAVE ON QUALITY EDEN® PRODUCTS

Absolutely Everything You Need for Healthy Living

With Great Prices  Farm Fresh Produce

Fast Check-out and Convenient Parking

...Why shop anyplace else?

A really fun little place to shop
for fruits & vegetables and a bunch of other cool stuff

2281 W. Liberty 662-6000
Mon-Sat: 9am-8pm
Sun: 9am-6pm (summer)
Sun: 10am-6pm (winter)

Save A Fast Food Junkie!

Do all your Holiday shopping in 5 minutes!

Give the gift of health that everyone needs.

HOW?

Give the gift of *Lickety-Split Meals!*

Pricing for *Lickety-Split Meals*

Buy in quantity and save!

Quantity	Price	Shipping		
1 book	$29.95 each	$ 3.00		
2 books	$29.95 each	$ 4.00		
3 books	$27.95 each	~~$ 5.00~~	FREE	SAVE $11
5 books	$25.95 each	~~$ 7.00~~	FREE	SAVE $27
10 books	$22.95 each	~~$10.00~~	FREE	SAVE $80

ORDER FORM

Qty. _____ x Price $ _____ = Total $ _____

6% Sales Tax (MI only) _____

Shipping _____

TOTAL DUE $ _____

Happy Lickety-Split cooking!

Thank you for your order!

Choose from 3 ways to order:

1 **Mail** your order to ➡ **Zonya Health International**
(Check or credit card orders) **PO Box 275**
Walled Lake, MI 48390-0275

2 **Call** anytime, **toll-free** ➡ **(888) 884-LEAN**
(Credit card orders)
If you get our voice mail, it's very trustworthy!

3 **Fax** your order, anytime ➡ **(248) 960-8157**
(Credit card orders)

Make checks payable to: Zonya Health International

Credit Cards: ☐ Visa   ☐ Mastercard   Exp. Date _____

Signature _____

Your phone number _____

Today's date _____

Ship to _____

_____

_____

_____

_____

Autograph books to: _____

_____

_____

What do you think of *Lickety-Split Meals?*

It would be just the best, if you could take a moment to share your opinions about this book. It is my life's work to update and improve it with every reprint. All responses will be acknowledged!

In advance, I Thank YOU!!!

Fax to: (248) 960-8157

or

Mail to: ZHI Publishing
P.O. Box 275
Walled Lake, MI 48390

Your name, address and phone:

_____

_____

_____

_____

	Poor				Great!

The recipe layout　　　　　　　　　1　2　3　4　5
Comments: _____
_____

The grocery list/guide　　　　　　　1　2　3　4　5
Comments: _____
_____

Page by page health and fitness tips　1　2　3　4　5
Comments: _____
_____

The flip-chart design, easel back & page numbering system　1　2　3　4　5
Comments: _____
_____

The graphic design & cartoon-like illustrations　1　2　3　4　5
Comments: _____
_____

Has this book helped you to lose weight? Lower your cholesterol? Save you time?
If so, please explain! _____
_____
_____
_____

Recipes I'd like to see added: (If you have a recipe you'd like to submit, please send it on!) _____
_____

Recipes I'd like to see changed: _____
_____